D0153720

The Hélène Cixous Reader

This is the first truly representative selection of texts by Hélène Cixous. The substantial pieces range broadly across her entire oeuvre, and include essays, works of fiction, lectures and drama. Arranged helpfully in chronological order, the extracts span twenty years of intellectual thought and demonstrate clearly the development of one of the most creative and brilliant minds of the twentieth century.

The editor's introductions to each piece will be especially helpful to readers new to the writings of Hélène Cixous.

With a foreword by Jacques Derrida, a preface by Cixous herself, and first-class editorial material by Susan Sellers, *The Hélène Cixous Reader* is destined to become a key text of feminist writing.

Susan Sellers studied at the Universities of London and the Sorbonne and has taught in the Ecole Normale Supérieure, near Paris, and the University of Paris VIII. She has written extensively on the subject of feminist thought.

The
Hélène Cixous
Reader

Edited by Susan Sellers

With a preface by Hélène Cixous and
foreword by Jacques Derrida

London and New York

First published 1994
by Routledge
11 New Fetter Lane, London EC4P 4EE

Simultaneously published in the USA and Canada
by Routledge
29 West 35th Street, New York, NY 10001

Reprinted 1996,1997, 1999, 2000

Routledge is an imprint of the Taylor & Francis Group

© 1994 Routledge, the collection as a whole
© 1994 Hélène Cixous, the translations
© 1994 Susan Sellers, editorial matter

Typeset by Florencetype Ltd, Kewstoke, Avon
Printed and bound in Great Britain by
T.J. International Ltd, Padstow, Cornwall

All rights reserved. No part of this book may be reprinted or
reproduced or utilised in any form or by any electronic,
mechanical, or other means, now known or hereafter
invented, including photocopying and recording, or in any
information storage or retrieval system, without permission in
writing from the publishers.

British Library Cataloguing in Publication Data

A catalogue record for this book is available from the British Library

Library of Congress Cataloguing in Publication Data

Cixous, Hélène
[Selections, English, 1994]
The Hélène Cixous reader/edited by Susan Sellers: with a
preface by Hélène Cixous and foreword by Jacques Derrida.
p.   cm.
Includes bibliographical references and index.
I. Sellers, Susan   II. Title
PQ2663.I9A6   1994   93 – 41292
848′.91409–dc20

ISBN 0–415–04929–6 (hbk)
ISBN 0–415–04930–X (pbk)

CONTENTS

FOREWORD[1]
—— ❧ ——

Jacques Derrida

In the chapter of Hélène Cixous' "FirstDays of the Year" entitled "Self-portraits of a blind woman", a certain *"Story of Contretemps"* begins with a *bench*.[2] It begins on a bench – and it's also a scene of reading, a reading of sexual difference: between separation and reparation, the in-between between Separation and Reparation.

Each one of the two words, *Reparation* and *Separation*, remains all alone. Each one all alone is a sentence, but that sentence is a question ("Reparation? Separation?"). Each one stands in its solitude – and, between the two, there is the between. But the between which opens in the instant someone enters, some "one," Onegin. I'll read a passage, it's better to read, always:

> Because this *Story of Contretemps* begins with a *bench* (. . .)
> What I love: the race, what Marina loves: the bench.
> Each one reads in her own book. The author: hesitates. In Marina's: a bench.
> A bench. On the bench Tatiana. Enter Onegin. He doesn't sit down. Everything is already broken off. It's she who gets up. Reparation? They remain standing, the two of them. Separation? All two of them.[3]

"All two of them": *"tous les deux"* is one of the most singular works of French grammar. Hélène has a genius for making the language speak, down to the most familiar idiom, the place where it seems to be crawling with secrets which give way to thought. She knows how to make it say what it keeps in reserve, which in the process also makes it come out of its reserve. Thus: *"tous les deux"* can always be heard as *all the "twos,"* all the couples, the duals, the duos, the differences, all the dyads in the world: each time there's two in the world. The singular name of this plural which nonetheless regroups couples and dual unities, *"tous les deux"* thus becomes the subject or the origin of a fable, history and morality included. The fable says everything that can happen *to* sexual difference or *from* sexual difference. Here, in the more narrowly delimited sequence of this *Story of Contretemps*, it remains impossible to decide if this *"tous les deux,"* which repeats the earlier *"tous les deux"* (I reread: "Reparation? They remain standing, the two of them. Separation? All two of them. But it's only he who speaks. He speaks for a long time. All the time. She, she doesn't say a word."), means *both of them*, him and her, in the most ordinary and obvious sense (when "*tous les deux*" means the one and the other, both together, in chorus, equally, indissociably, of common accord, all two of them as one, in this inseparable) or "*all the twos*," "reparation" and "separation," the one and the other, the reparation which doesn't separate itself from the separation, that is from the irreparable separation, the irreparable separation of the pair disparate in its very appearance. In this second hearing, what makes *tous les deux* inseparable includes also the separation which unites them, the experience of distancing or inaccessibility which conjoins them still.

But it's only he who speaks. He speaks for a long time. All the time. She, she does not say a word. Between them, speech does not give the word [*les paroles ne donnent pas le mot*].[4]

Not to give the word, for speech, is strange. This complicates the questions of what it means to *give the floor* [*donner la parole*], to *give* **one's** *word* [*donner* **sa** *parole*], which gives still something else, to give a thing and to give the word, to give in general, to give the given. So it happens now that wordless speech comes to us, in any case speech which, if it has the word, and maybe the closing word or the password, does not give it. Is speech which does not give the word the same thing as speech which does not give the floor? Not to give the floor to the other, to interdict the other or to deprive the other of the right to respond, and certain people who are also orators or rhetoricians know how, it is always in speaking that this operation takes place. But maybe we need to distinguish here between, *on the one hand*, "*donner le mot*" which can mean to unveil the password or the closing word, to turn over the secret or the key of a reading, for example of sexual difference and, *on the other hand*, something else entirely, "*se donner le mot*" [*to give oneself* or *one another the word*] (that is, just what we haven't done, Hélène and I, today: *se donner le mot* is to agree together as accomplices to stage an operation, to plot, to sketch the "plot" of an intrigue; unless absolute conspirators, those who haven't had to decide on their conspiracy with a contract, don't even need to give the word to find themselves at the appointment, with or without contretemps, my other hypothesis being that there are no appointments without the space of the contretemps, without the spacing of the contretemps, and there is no contretemps without sexual difference, as if sexual difference were contretemps itself, a *Story of Contretemps*.)

(. . .)

I'll resume my reading of *FirstDays of the Year* repeating a bit for memory:

Everything is already broken off. It's she who gets up. Reparation? They remain standing, the two of them. Separation? All two of them. But it's only he who speaks. He
speaks for a long time. All the time. She, she doesn't say a word. Between them, speech
does not give the word.

Has entered: Time, long time, distancing: with large strokes between the two of them
he digs and digs (. . .)[5]

How can time enter? How can we say of time that he arrives, that he enters
in a stroke, "with large strokes"? One must be two, in two, "all the twos"
for that, maybe, on the verge of giving each other the floor, if not the
word.

In the preceding paragraph, a sentence began with this inversion of the
subject: "Enter Onegin." Onegin speaks "a long time. All the time." Hélène
says "all" ["tout"]. After the singular "tous" of "tous les deux," we have
here the no less singular "tout" of "tout le temps." How can one "all the
time"? give, give oneself or take all the time? What then remains? This
gives all the more for meditation: from one totality to the other, is not the
most common trait precisely the impossibility of totalizing? The two
idiomatic occurrences of "tous" and "tout," have to do with fracture, with
infinite separation or interrupting distance: difference itself. So beautiful
and so mysterious an invention, so impossible, as beautiful and as impossible as "tous les deux," this "tout le temps" with no remains is clearly the
most enigmatic subject of that difference between him and her. We're
going back in time, we're recounting it backwards to precede it with its
fable. We hear "tout le temps" as for the first time from a poem and as if
the internal and intense versification of this "tout le temps" came down to
saying the time of time, the staggering origin of temporality itself, there
where time in a stroke enters on stage. One must be two, "all two of
them," for this anabasis of time to have a chance of happening, "between
the two of them."

Has entered Time, long time, distancing: with large strokes between the two of them
he digs and digs: "I was not born [born (né) is masculine in the reading: it's he who
speaks] for happiness, my soul is foreign to it. Marriage would kill us. Loving you from
too close very quickly I would grow accustomed, and the love would end. If I were to
love, it would be from afar, from time to time, separately."[6]

"Separately" comes all alone, this time. The word advances all alone,
separately. The word "separately" proceeds in solitude, separated after a
comma, at the end of the sentence and the end of the citation, his citation,
before the quotes. It is very powerful. He says that if he were to love, it
would be "separately." How can one love "separately"? But how else can
one love than "separately"? Each one the other, but each time each one for
him or herself, each one in secret, each one secretly, in the throes of love.

About this, the other in the end can know nothing, can never perceive anything, nor even ever anything called seeing. One can not love separately
and one can not love but separately, in the separation or the disparity of
the pair. At an infinite distance, because *incommensurable*: I will never be
at the same distance – from you, as you, as you from me. No common
measure, no symmetry. Infinite separation in the couple itself and in the
parity of the pair.

[. . .]

Now it happens that he, he says that *if he were to love* . . . What? It resem-
bles a hypothesis, a fiction, a mere possibility. But that possibility can only
take form, as a possibility, by announcing itself as an experience: is there a
difference between saying "I love" and "if I were to love," "I love you" and
"if I were to love you," "as if I were to love you," "as if I were
to love," the "as," a separation–reparation of love, disjoining–adjoining,
se-reparation, re-separation of love in what conjoins it, conjugates or conju-
galizes it to itself? The suspensive modality of the possible, which seems to
cause the "epochē" of a declaration of love, signifies maybe that love can
belong only to the order of faith or testimony, not at all to that of proof
or certainty. Neither knowledge nor assurance, only a "love, if there is such
a thing, if there were such a thing – I would love you, because I love you."

Now it happens that he, he who says that if he were to love "it would be
from afar, from time to time," he would also love, thus, "separately."

One can always read this scene as a paradigm of sexual difference, more
precisely a paradigm of sexual difference as it is in general recounted, nar-
rated, organized. It is a story, maybe a fable, and an interpretation. It is thus
also a reading, with an ear for the fabulous narrative which we have always
been told, that is, that *he*, unlike *she*, he the separate one, he loves in
fiction and discontinuity, distancing and transcendence.

[. . .]

He (Onegin) says: "If I were to love, it would be from afar, from time to
time, separately." Close quotes. It has to do here, we were saying, with a
scene of reading on the subject of a paradigm of sexual difference. It does
not have to do with sexual difference itself (which does not exist as such,
in the present, in the real, beyond all reading) but with a scene of *reading*
of sexual difference about which Hélène Cixous reminds us, in another
paradox, that if sexual difference is always *read*, it is also *reading*, which is
to say that it is read, as sexual difference, *in* and *by* sexual difference, across
it: it is always a *she* or a *he* who reads it. Double genitive of the expression
"reading of sexual difference." This signifies that there is no asexual, a-
sexed or meta-sexed reading of sexual difference because it is at once read
and reading. Elementary but indispensable precaution directed at hurried

readers or impatient philosophers who rush toward the most inane of conclusions: "Ah, thus you say that sexual difference is always an effect of reading! So you deny its reality or its truth, what a confession!" Is it necessary to specify that it is exactly the opposite, in any case something else entirely? Because we were just stressing the point, sexual difference reads, as much as it is read, there is no a-sexed or meta-sexual reading. And there is neither truth nor reality without trace, which is to say without some relationship or return to the other; and there is no experience of the trace which isn't going after the other's number and isn't engaged from the outset in this interpretative deciphering which *reading* here figures. ("What I love: the race, what Marina loves: the bench. Each one reads in her own book. The author: hesitates. In Marina's: a bench.")

And indeed, just after the line we cited a moment before and which was itself a citation in quotes ("(. . .) If I were to love, it would be from afar, from time to time, separately"), Hélène Cixous, unless it's the "author," starts a paragraph and writes:

Marina reads. Love, that's it, the story tells her, a bench, and between *she* who enters on the bench, and *he* who enters, *he* and *she* in the halo of the italics which isolate.
  . . . But before the bench, the race. And before the race: the letter. The letter of Tatiana. She writes: (. . .)[7]

It has indeed to do with a scene of reading and writing: with the eyes no less than with the voice, because the italics of "*he*" and of "*she*" are remarked. Marked in what Marina reads, they are remarked, of course, by Hélène Cixous, the "author," in what *we* read here, in one of these *FirstDays of the Year*. Visible in these "Self-portraits of a blind woman," italics make "he" and "she" into citations, indirect references, through the narrative, the fable or the speech, the reading or the interpretation, of another man or another women. These citations, these "he," "him" or "she" in italics remain effects of reading, they emerge as isolates, insularities, islands or archipelagos: "*he* and *she* in the halo [the halo, but you hear the telephone call: hello, it's me, hello, yes, without italics, without mention of "he" or "she", without a third party] of the italics which isolate."

And later, the letter (thus, read) of Tatiana said, or rather offered to the reader:

. . . But before the bench, the race. And before the race: the letter. The letter of Tatiana. She writes: "This was decreed from above: it is the will of heaven. I am *thine* . . ." She says *thou* [tu] to *him*, she says *thou* to the one who will come, who is going to come, who comes, to the stranger who is *him*, it is indeed *him*, and there she is who, hearing him come from the end of time, bends her bow, and says: *Thou. Thou*, the violent Thou, with which I thee and thou God, because I do not know him, with which I order him to exist, and *He* is *him*.[8]

The "*he*" or the "*him*" in italics exists only on her order. He comes to be; to ek-sist(er) out of the performative (jussive, as it's called) by which she orders him not this or that, but simply to be, and to be "he." Ordering it of him, she leaves him to be what he has to be, what in being he has. Between "be," "be who you are," and "I leave you to be who you are," "I love you," "I love who you are," the difference no longer appears. All of this *seems* to institute sexual difference in the most pragmatic, the most performative *act* of reading/writing, here the experience of an originary apostrophe recalling also the origin of apostrophe, the "thou" which, interrupting the silence of that which is silence [*tu*], brings to birth, engenders and provokes, convokes, calls but in truth *recalls* the "he" into being [*à l'être*]. Because this act is not only an appearance which *seems to give itself* sexual difference, it is not simply active or decisional, creative or productive. Reading as much as it writes, deciphering or citing as much as it inscribes, this act is also an act of memory (the other is already there, irreducibly), this act takes note. In recalling thou, it [*il*] recalls itself.

NOTES

1 Excerpts from "Fourmis" by Jacques Derrida, in Mara Negron (ed.), *Lectures de la dif-férence sexuelle*, Paris: des femmes Antoinette Fouque, 1994. Published with the author's permission. Translated by Eric Prenowitz. [Ed.]

2 Hélène Cixous, *Jours de l'an*, Paris: des femmes Antoinette Fouque, 1990. The passage in question concerns a section of *My Pushkin* by Marina Tsvetaeva in which Pushkin's novel *Eugene Onegin* figures. [Trans.]

3 Ibid., pp. 190–1. "The two of them," and "all two of them" both translate the French idiomatic expression *tous les deux*, rendered more literally by "all the twos." [Trans.]

4 Ibid., p. 191. [Ed.]

5 Ibid. [Ed.]

6 Ibid. [Ed.]

7 Ibid. [Ed.]

8 Ibid. [Ed.]

PREFACE

Hélène Cixous

Like all those whose vital substance is cut from the same fabric as writing, I am constantly impelled to ask myself the questions engendered by this structure which is at once single and double: questions of the ethical, politico-cultural, aesthetic, destinal value of this constitution; questions of the necessity of writing for myself and for others; of the usefulness, the strangeness of forever being here and elsewhere, ever here as elsewhere, elsewhere as here, I and the other, I as other, etc. . . . Stretching out existence, enlivening it, troubling it, surprising it. Questions cross my horizon like herds of wild geese, "omens" according to Stephen Dedalus, but of what?

I am thus of the species of travelers – (of where I am, the interior or the earth), of the *Wanderschaft* Hölderlin or Trakl spoke of as did Aeschylus or Homer . . .

Having never been without writing, having writing in my body, at my throat, on my lips (is it an illness, a supplement, a second blood?) to me my texts are elements of a whole which interweaves my own story, are the seasons, days in the Great Year of my life; our time is made up of a succession of simultaneously single and collective often brutal experiences, thus my life's path will have crossed through exile + a world war + a second exile – change of country + colonial – decolonial wars + children brought into the world or lost + joys + bereavements + joys acute as bereavements . . .

Sometimes we live the wars between nations as personal events. Sometimes a private drama appears like a war or natural catastrophe. Sometimes the two wars, the personal and the national, coincide. Sometimes there is peace on one side (in one's heart) and war on the other. I and the world are never separate. The one is the double or the metaphor of the other. I doubtless owe this I of two scenes to my genealogy. I was born at/from the intersection of migrations and memories from the Occident and Orient, from the North and South. I was born a foreigner in "France" in a said-to-be "French" Algeria. I was born in not-France calling itself "France." To tell the truth we have to trap the appearances with quotation marks. We are not what we are said to be. At the age of three I knew that we are destined to be the orphans of Paradise. We remember happiness we have never known. At the age of three I saw that Evil was in power and that resistance is clandestine. There are two camps, for the whole of time.

I go, we go. On the way we keep a log-book, the book of the abyss and its shores.[1] Everyone does. My books are thus like life and history, heterogeneous chapters in a single vast book whose ending I will never know. The difference indicated in the genres of the books I write reproduces the eventful aspect of a life in our century. A woman's life into the bargain.

People either know or don't know that I have four or five forms of written expression: poetic fiction, chamber theater or theater on a world scale, criticism, essays – without counting the notebooks I write only to myself and which no one will ever read, where I exercise a different style. No one fragment carries the totality of the message, but each text (which is in itself a whole) has a particular urgency, an individual force, a necessity, and yet each text also has a force which comes to it from all the other texts.

One cannot speak the same type of language or use the same literary form on every occasion or for every scene. I have several French languages. Amongst my languages there is one I prefer, though I shall not say which.

Sometimes I experience reading returning to "the author" I am in the following manner: according to the country of reading, according to the state of cultural dissemination in such a country, such a language, I am "known," defined or coded very differently and in a way that is to me unexpected. In France, I am mainly known through my seminars, and most especially through my theatrical works. (My plays have been performed at the *Théâtre du Soleil* before 150,000 spectators.) Now the theater public may be totally unaware that in other spheres I am the author of things which are not theatrical. Inversely, in the USA, Canada, Japan . . . people are unaware that I am an author for the theater, and I am often classed, sometimes even exclusively, in the category of theoreticians. This is how I appear on contemporary scenes as if I were a quarter of myself. Yet it is the whole that makes sense. That which cannot be met on one path, and which I cannot say in one of my languages, I seek to say through another form of expression.

To briefly indicate directions: in my fictional texts I work in a poetic form and in philosophical contents on the mysteries of subjectivity.

Let us talk about this, for the fin-de-siècle period invites such discussion. It seems – you have heard this as well as I – that there are fashionable proceedings, especially in the English-speaking world, on the theme of subjectivity. The trend, the code, the "canon," are in themselves trendy tools for thought (I do not mean "modern," for whatever is "code" is already outmoded and ready to fall into disuse). Now the fashionable code, these days, holds subjectivity, which is confused (unwittingly or not) with individualism, in suspicion: there is confusion – and this is a pity for everyone – between the infinite domain of the human subject, which is, of course, the primary territory of every artist and every creature blessed with the difficult happiness of being alive, and stupid, egotistic, restrictive, exclusive behavior which excludes the other. Whereas subjectivity is the wealth we have in common and, by definition, the subject is a non-closed mix of self/s and others; the human subject who, in the Bible for example, calls himself our like. No I without you ever or more precisely no I's without-you's. I is always our like. When I explore I – I take as object of observation a human sample. There is no true art which does not take as its source or root the universal regions of subjectivity. For those of us who write in French, we are the descendants of Montaigne. Our modern literature – *eternally modern* – was inaugurated by the man who announced four centuries ago:

You have, here, Reader, a book whose faith can be trusted (. . .)
  Here I want to be seen in my simple, natural, everyday fashion without striving or artifice: for it is my own self that I am painting. Here, drawn from life, you will read of my defects and my native form so far as respect for social convention allows: for had I found myself among those people who are said still to live under the sweet liberty of Nature's primal laws, I can assure you that I would most willingly have portrayed myself whole, and wholly naked
  And therefore, Reader, I myself am the subject of my book: it is not reasonable that you should employ your leisure on a topic so frivolous and so vain
  Therefore, farewell.
  From Montaigne; this March, One thousand five hundred and eighty[2]

And if Shakespeare is always the most modern of authors, century after century, it is because this subject full of others he was brought hundreds of individuals into the world, all exemplars of a powerful subjectivity. A subject always asks, not in a mean way: what am I? but: what is a human subject, what is it that makes us live so well and so badly, so that after millions of years we still do not know how to die nor what death is? . . . *A subject is at least a thousand people.*

This is why I never ask myself "who am I?" (*qui suis-je?*) I ask myself "who are I?" (*qui sont-je?*)[3] – an untranslatable phrase. Who can say who I are, how many I are, which I is the most I of my I's? Of course we each have a solid social identity, all the more solid and stable as all our other phases of identity are unstable, surprising. At the same time we are all the ages, those we have been, those we will be, those we will not be, we journey through ourselves (Joyce, Shakespeare remind us) as the child who goes snivelling to school and as the broken old man . . . We: are (untranslatable).[4] Without counting all the combinations with others, our exchanges between languages, between sexes – our exchanges which change us, tint us with others.

In French the phrase "who are I?" (*qui sont-je?*) also plays the music of the differance writing/voice; for our French ear hears, when I pronounce my question, the phrase "who muses?" i.e. who dreams. Who are I when I muse?[5] When I dream who dreams? In dreams am I not all the characters of my dreams? We are all this numerous and coalescent personality, who inspired Joyce's motley heroes, whether Bloom-Ulysses-Shakespeare Booloohoom or Here Comes Everybody. To rise above the interior chaosmos each one of us gives ourselves a spokesperson I, the social I who votes, who represents me. I have an I who teaches. I have an I who escapes me. I have an I who answers for me. I have an I who knows the law. The I who writes gives speech to all the other Is. In dreams I has not yet eaten the fruits of the forbidden tree. We dream while we are asleep and we dream while we are awake. We are dreams even without knowing it. We humans, in other words dreams by nature, we are almost wholly non-identifiable. It is what makes us surprising, diverse, unpredictable. Thus troubling. Thus frightening and conversely enchanting. In each one of us our own contrary slumbers. I ask myself, but I do not answer myself.

Pure I, identical to I-self, does not exist. I is always in difference. I is the open set of the trances of an I by definition changing, mobile, because living-speaking-thinking-dreaming. This truth should moreover make us prudent and modest in our judgements and our definitions. The difference is in us, in me, difference plays me (my play).[6] And it is numerous: since it plays with me in me between me and me or I and myself. A "myself" which is the most intimate first name of You. I will never say often enough that the difference is not one, that there is never one without the other, and that the charm of difference (beginning with sexual difference) is that it passes. It crosses through us, like a goddess. We cannot capture it. It makes us teeter with emotion. It is in this living agitation that there is always room for you in me, your presence and your place. I is never an individual. I is haunted. I is always, before knowing anything, an I-love-you.

Derridean deconstruction will have been the greatest ethical critical warning gesture of our time: careful! let us not be the dupe of logocentric authority. We are not "pure" I. A gesture dictated by humility, and which recalls us to humility.

On the one hand there is thus a textual region where I work immersed, in the depths, to explore the universe of what we commonly call the human soul. Soul! What a beautiful word! Like: god! What a word! We say: soul, as if we knew what it is and where it is. In the vicinity of this unknown-one, I proceed exploring with the help of my myopia: I scrutinize "the movements of the soul," from close up, I observe the passions at the moment they manifest themselves, such as they express themselves, translate themselves, first of all in our bodies.

Where does the tragedy first of all take place? In the body, in the stomach, in the legs, as we know since the Greek tragedies. Aeschylus' characters tell, first and foremost, a body state. Myself – I realized this afterwards – I began by carrying out a rehabilitation of these body states since they are so eloquent, since they concretely speak the troubles of our souls. In this area I work under the microscope, as a spiritual anatomist.

On the other hand, in the theater, the stage which opens before me has macroscopic dimensions: one thinks in terms of continents, peoples, armies, heavens. As in Shakespeare, the stage is the planet, the Globe; and the body is the famous real and symbolic Renaissance body, the body politic in which the organs are factions, nations, individuals in history.

And in the world-as-stage or the stage-as-world, there are also the gods. There has never been theater without "gods," in other words superior powers, who interfere in our affairs, at least, as in Shakespeare, while they mock us. At the theater today as always we are flies to the gods. But the gods themselves are part of us. What are they? They also have modern names: pulsions, "drives," the id, laws, order and disorder, the paradoxical instance, the double-bind, etc. ... personal "fate," in other words structure. Everything which is in me while being stronger than me, and which "overvaults" me and overvaults itself. As it was expressed by the spirit of the Renaissance: as above so below – and let us add: as below so above, no below without above etc.

And so what about fiction, are there no gods? Is there greater than us in fiction? Who is our other, the I stranger to I? What serves as Above for our Below? The answer is language, or rather Language, our unlimited territory which always precedes us.

Language englobes us and inspires us and launches us beyond ourselves, it is ours and we are its, it is our master and our mistress. And even if it seems to be native or national, it happily remains foreign to those who write. Writing consists first of all in hearing language speak itself to our ears, as if it were the first time.

To live language, inhabit language, what luck and what a venture. This ship, this ark is haunted by the passing of all the inhabitants and voyagers who have spent time or lives in languages, without ever remaining detained prisoner inside a language reduced to a single function, the phatic (as is the sad case of most people, who speak language as in the time before caves). But there is the language that is rich, full, vibrant with the echoes of the passengers who went from foreign language to foreign language on board their native language, tasting one and the other, writing in one, reading in others, embellishing one with the others, grafting and multiplying.

Our own subjective singularities are in truth composed, on the one hand, of many other near or distant humans, we are carriers of previous generations, we are, without knowing it, heirs, caretakers, witnesses of known or unknown ancestors; on the other hand we are full of others originating from the books we have read. We think we speak the English, or French, of today. But our English or French language of today is of yesterday and elsewhere. The miracle is that language has not been cut from its archaic roots – even if we do not remember, our language remembers, and what we say began to be said three thousand years ago. Inversely language has incorporated in our own times, before even we know, the most recent elements, linguistic and semantic particles blown by the present winds.

Here is an example, which I find magnificent and comic, magnificently comic and comically magnificent, that I have taken from an American magazine destined for the general public dated April 1993. It is the beginning of an illustrated fashion article:

Deconstructionism may be the darling of Europe but in the US it's a love–hate thing. Creases are ironed out, raw edges refined, grunge given a touch of polish.

In New York, memories are not only short, they are entirely selective. Grunge – the so-called fashion revolution which has launched a thousand headlines in the past six months – seemed, at the American collections last week, never to have happened.

Here, in these few lines, treasures snatched from the most noble, the most elaborate, the most complex thoughts and discourses of our century and the sixteenth century imperceptibly touch and are exchanged.

Here, "deconstruction" (though does the woman who goes to buy a dress know what this is?) has become a term that adds a "commercial" mark, a surplus value of "modernism" to domains totally unforeseen by the author of the thinking of deconstruction. Here is a word derived from philosophical thinking, that of Derrida, which no longer resides in philosophy, but "launches" fashion products, bathroom items, sports equipment, political attitudes. In brief a word which, having left its native shore, henceforth circulates in the world's blood.

And so this magical word made banal meets (does it know?) another formula equally magical and rendered banal, this one centuries ago, that reverberates under a made-up form in the phrase quoted: The revolution which has launched a thousand headlines. What makes a comeback here in fashionable dress is Marlowe's beautiful verse, as he looks on the face of the beautiful Helen: "Was this the face that launched a thousand ships?"

As we say in French *on ne croit jamais si bien dire* (we never think to speak so well). While we think we are talking about fashion, language like the Fausts of Marlowe and Goethe institutes extraordinary marriages in its secret alchemy.

We are the learned or ignorant caretakers of several memories. When I write, language remembers without my knowing or indeed with my knowing, remembers the Bible, Shakespeare, Milton, the whole of literature, each book.

Then, I who write, I inscribe an additional memory in language – a memory in progress – of what I have read personally, noticed, retained from a text or a language to the other. And the whole is poured back, sometimes consciously, sometimes unconsciously, into the river I sail.

So writing then? yes, it is, from this chorus of songs of the whole of time, making a new song stream forth. Sometimes this is called a style.

A new language? No. A virgin way of listening and making the always newold language speak.

Affair of the ear: it is enough to accord with language for it to deliver its secrets.

How does the fact that I have more than one scene of writing help me? At this precise moment, now, as I question myself as if I were another who knows, there is a form of reply. I see that in the poetic text, often or indeed always, I deal with love which is our fate, twisted thing, tortuous, delicate, eager, insatiable, the best and worst thing, the junction point between everything and nothing, the oxymoric knot of all existence, love which makes gods and cattle meat of us – but never with hate.

God knows that hate is a vast dimension of our existence; it is this which leads nations to the slaughter house and ourselves to the scene of crime.

Now hatred I can only admit and let it speak in the theater.

It is in the theater that I can take on our cruel daily enigmas, the presence amongst us of the fight for life, the existence of death drives, the irresistible movement to action, the sudden assassination, or the eternal assassination which misogyny is, etc.

– Why only in the theater?

– God knows: I do not.

If one can speak of a 'personal tradition', in my own tradition I have never conceived of poetic writing as separate from philosophy.

To me writing is the fastest and most efficient vehicle for thought: it may be winged, galloping, four-wheeled, jet-propelled etc. – according to the urgency.

The difference with philosophical discourse is that I never dream of mastering or ordering or inventing concepts. Moreover I am incapable of this. I am overtaken. All I want is to illustrate, depict fragments, events of human life and death, each unique and yet at the same time exchangeable. Not the law, the exception.

My kingdom is the instant, and of course I am not its queen, only its citizen.

I always work on the present passing . . .

Translated by Susan Sellers and revised by Hélène Cixous

NOTES

1 In French "log-book" – *cahier de bord* – also contains the word for "shores" – *les bords*. [Ed.]

2 Michel de Montaigne, "Au lecteur," in *Oeuvres Complètes*, Bibliothèque de la Pléiade, Paris: Gallimard, 1962, p. 9; *The Essays: A Selection*, translated by M.A. Screech, London: Penguin Classics, 1993, p. 3. [Ed.]

3 The French expression *qui sont-je?* (literally "who are I?") recalls the phrase *qui songe?*: "who muses/dreams/contemplates?" See also note 5 below. [Ed.]

4 *Sommes* – "are" – can also mean "sum up" or "summon." [Ed.]

5 *Qui sont-je quand je songe?* [Ed.]

6 There is a further "play" in the French on the aural similarity between *jeu* – translated here as "play" – and *je* – "I." [Ed.]

ACKNOWLEDGEMENTS

The editor would like to thank her translators, Deborah Cowell, Stephanie Flood, Ann Liddle, Catherine MacGillivray and Donald Watson, her editors, Talia Rodgers and Moira Taylor, at Routledge, and her copy-editor, Sara Beardsworth. Especial thanks are also given to Marguerite Sandré for her detailed and invaluable readings, to Sarah Cornell for her work in launching the project, and to Hélène Cixous for her constant encouragement and support.

The editor and publishers would gratefully like to acknowledge for the inclusion of material in this collection: Hélène Cixous for permission to translate an extract from *Neutre*, Grasset, 1972; Carol Barko (translator) and Schocken Books for an extract from *Inside*, New York, 1986; Editions du Seuil for permission to translate an extract from *Prénoms de personne*, © Editions du Seuil, Paris, 1974; Betsy Wing (translator) and University of Minnesota Press for English translation copyright © 1986 of an extract from "Sorties" in *The Newly Born Woman*, Minneapolis; Antoinette Fouque and the Editions des femmes for permission to translate extracts from *Souffles*, Paris, 1975, *La*, Paris, 1979, (*With*) *Ou l'art de l'innocence*, Paris, 1981, *Limonade tout était si infini*, Paris, 1982, *Jours de l'an*, Paris, 1990, and *Déluge*, Paris, 1992, and for permission to reprint an English extract from *Vivre l'orange/To Live the Orange*, Paris, 1979; Catherine MacGillivray (translator) and Antoinette Fouque and the Editions des femmes for extracts from *Manne aux Mandelstams aux Mandelas*, Paris, 1988; Jo Levy (translator) and John Calder Publishers Ltd for English translation copyright © Jo Levy 1985 and the Editions des femmes copyright © 1977 for an extract from *Angst* reproduced by permission of the copyright holders and the Calder Educational Trust, London; Betsy Wing (translator) and University of Nebraska Press for reprinting of an extract from *The Book of Promethea*, Betsy Wing's translation and introduction © 1991 by the University of Nebraska Press (originally published as *Le Livre de Promethea* © Editions Gallimard, Paris, 1983); The Open University Press for extract from "Extreme Fidelity," in *Writing Differences: Readings from the Seminar of Hélène Cixous*, Milton Keynes, 1988; Hélène Cixous and the Théâtre du Soleil for permission to translate extracts from *L'Histoire terrible mais inachevée de Norodom Sihanouk Roi du Cambodge*, Théâtre du Soleil, Paris, 1985 and

L'Indiade ou l'Inde de leurs rêves, Théâtre du Soleil, Paris, 1987; Catherine MacGillivray (translator) and *Qui Parle: A Journal of Literary Studies* for "The Place of Crime, The Place of Forgiveness"; and Columbia University Press for extracts from *Three Steps on the Ladder of Writing*, © Columbia University Press, New York, 1993.

INTRODUCTION

Hélène Cixous is the author of some forty books and over a hundred articles, including works of fiction, drama, philosophy, feminism,[1] literary theory and literary criticism. Of this vast oeuvre by far the majority are works of fiction, and so it is somewhat surprising that Cixous should be known, in the English-speaking world at least, as primarily a theoretician and critic. Of her books published to date, thirty-four are works of fiction or drama.[2]

The Hélène Cixous Reader comprises translated extracts from across the full range of Hélène Cixous' oeuvre, illustrating her work as a feminist and literary critic, and the concerns, scope and style of her fictional and dramatic writing. The extracts are presented chronologically in order to reveal the development of Cixous' thought, and each text is prefaced with a short introduction situating the passage in the context of the work from which it is taken and Cixous' oeuvre as a whole. All the text by Hélène Cixous, apart from preliminary pages, is in a serif typeface. Interpolated editorial comment and notes are in a sans serif typeface.

Biography

Hélène Cixous was born in Oran, Algeria, in 1937 of a Spanish/French/Jewish father and German/Jewish mother. She grew up speaking German and French, though she also heard Spanish and Arabic.[3] When she was eleven her father died of tuberculosis, an event Cixous has described as having a formative influence on her as a writer.[4] In an essay entitled "De la scène de l'Inconscient à la scène de l'Histoire: Chemin d'une écriture" – "From the Scene of the Unconscious to the Scene of History: Pathway of Writing" – Cixous outlines how loss and the need for reparation became key motivating forces in her writing:

I believe that one can only begin to advance along the path of discovery, the discovery of writing or anything else, from mourning and in the reparation of mourning. In the beginning the gesture of writing is linked to the experience of disappearance, to the feeling of having lost the key to the world, of having been thrown outside. Of having suddenly acquired the precious sense of the rare, of the mortal. Of having urgently to regain the entrance, the breath, to keep the trace.[5]

Writing as the reparation of loss is a major theme of Cixous' work.[6] Evoking psychoanalytic accounts of the human subject's formation, Cixous views language as compensation for and a means of living – and inscribing – loss:[7]

Everything is lost except words. This is a child's experience: words are our doors to all the other worlds. At a certain moment for the person who has lost everything, whether that is, moreover, a being or country, language becomes the country. One enters the country of languages.[8]

Cixous' mother, in widowhood forced to provide for the family, trained and then became a midwife. Cixous has described in a radio broadcast transmitted in 1987, "Au bon plaisir d'Hélène Cixous" – "At Hélène Cixous' Pleasure," the effect this early introduction to the world of women, birth and the body had.[9] In the first of two passages translated here from *Souffles* – "Breaths" – a feminine voice induces the labor of self-birth; in *La* (denoting the feminine article as well as the musical note) the mother's role is envisioned as the one the self must adopt. Cixous herself has two children.[10]

After a brilliant period as a student, during which she passed the *agrégation* in English,[11] Cixous began a doctoral thesis on the work of James Joyce with the English scholar Jean-Jacques Mayoux.[12] She was awarded a *Docteur ès lettres* in 1968 while teaching at the University of Nanterre. In the same year, Cixous was invited to found the experimental University of Paris VIII where she was appointed to a Chair in English Literature.

Gender, femininity and writing

Cixous has emphasized how this opportunity to create a new university enabled her to study and teach literature in ways she had previously felt were unacceptable. In "At Hélène Cixous' Pleasure" she explains that most of the texts she was required to read as a student and young teacher were by men:

It was always men. Each time I came up against a wall, except for two or three exceptional works which did not prohibit me. But I was always speaking in the place of someone else. Where was my place then? Where were the women?[13]

Cixous describes how the chance to initiate a new research program prompted her to begin working on "the presence of women in literature, on what sexuality signifies, what the body signifies in literature".[14] This led to the inauguration of a new doctorate and center for research, the Centre d'Etudes Féminines – Center for Feminine Studies – in 1974.

Cixous has remained Director of the Center since that date, conducting a regular fortnightly seminar throughout the academic year.[15]

Whilst Cixous' work is the subject of lively discussion among feminists, her relationship to the feminist movement is a complex one. She was involved in debates led by Antoinette Fouque – who founded the Des femmes (women's) publishing house – and the influential "Psych et Po" group,[16] yet has never directly allied herself to any single movement or cause.[17] In "At Hélène Cixous' Pleasure," Cixous explains her wariness of adopting what she describes as masculine procedures in the struggle for equality, arguing that women's liberation must be accompanied by the institution of a new socio-symbolic frame. In the extracts presented here from *The Newly Born Woman*, Cixous outlines how thinking has become dependent on a process of differentiation entailing opposition to and annihilation of whatever is thereby constituted as other. She argues that women's sexuality has been obliterated, excluded or neutered as part of this process,[18] creating a situation in which men apparently have everything to gain from maintaining the status quo. As an approximation of the ways men and women therefore tend to respond to the social, political and cultural order, Cixous employs the terms "masculine" and "feminine" to denote the possible poles of response to its law. However, as Cixous explains in the passage reprinted here from "Extreme Fidelity," although women are, at present, more likely to adopt an open, questioning, "feminine" attitude than men, we all continually fluctuate between gender roles, sometimes assuming defensive, "masculine" positions, at other times willing to risk prohibition, and at other times combining elements of each. The terms "masculine" and "feminine", therefore, can be viewed as markers which could be exchanged for others.

For Cixous, then, sexual difference is important in the role it plays in determining gender behavior, with its capacity to uphold or challenge the existing order, rather than as anatomical difference per se. Cixous nevertheless contends that sexuality is vital, seeing in the differences between the sexes the potential for alternative insights and ways of understanding the world.[19] She suggests that women's real or imagined experiences of pregnancy and childbirth, for example, entail the possibility of a radically different relation to the other:

It is not only a question of the feminine body's extra resource, this specific power to produce some thing living of which her flesh is the locus, not only a question of a transformation of rhythms, exchanges, of relationship to space, of the whole perceptive system (. . .) It is also the experience of a "bond" with the other, all that comes through in the metaphor of bringing into the world (. . .)

There is a bond between woman's libidinal economy – her *jouissance*, the feminine Imaginary – and her way of self-constituting a subjectivity that splits apart without regret.[20]

The Book of Promethea concerns this endeavor to create an alternative subject position, in which both self and other coexist in a mutually enabling love.[21]

For Cixous, language is endemic to the repressive structures of thinking and narration we use to organize our lives.[22] Since woman has figured within the socio-symbolic system only as the other of man, Cixous suggests that the inscription of women's sexuality and history could recast the prevailing order. She sees writing as the locus and means of this reformation.[23]

Ecriture féminine

Cixous' name is most often associated with that of *écriture féminine* – "feminine writing." For Cixous such a writing is feminine in two senses. First, while Cixous suggests that feminine writing is potentially the province of both sexes, she believes women are currently closer to a feminine economy than men. As a result she sees in women's writing the potential to circumvent and reformulate existing structures through the inclusion of other experience.[24] In particular, Cixous stresses that the inscription of the rhythms and articulations of the mother's body which continue to influence the adult self provides a link to the pre-symbolic union between self and m/other, and so affects the subject's relationship to language, the other, himself and the world.[25] Second, since a feminine subject position refuses to appropriate or annihilate the other's difference in order to construct the self in a (masculine) position of mastery, Cixous suggests that a feminine writing will bring into existence alternative forms of relation, perception and expression. It is in this sense that Cixous believes writing is revolutionary. Not only can writing exceed the binary logic that informs our present system and thus create the framework for a new "language" and culture, but, she stresses, through its transformations, feminine writing will initiate changes in the social and political sphere to challenge the very foundation of the patriarchal and capitalist state. Feminine writing is:

a place (. . .) which is not economically or politically indebted to all the vileness and compromise. That is not obliged to reproduce the system. That is writing. If there is a somewhere else that can escape the infernal repetition, it lies in that direction, where *it* writes itself, where *it* dreams, where *it* invents new worlds.[26]

The extracts collected in this *Reader* illustrate Cixous' vision of feminine writing. In the "Prédit" ("Prediction") to *Prénoms de personne* ("First Names of No One"), writing's capacity to propel the reader beyond the repressive, self-referential viewpoint of the masculine is explored. For Cixous the multiple and heterogeneous possibilities generated by the signifying function are intrinsic to this process, as the extract from *Neutre* –

"Neutral" – demonstrates. In *La* writing is portrayed as beyond censorship; in *Limonade tout était si infini* – "Lemonade Everything Was So Infinite" – it is a powerful ally against oppression. In *"(With) Ou l'art de l'innocence* – "(With) Or the Art of Innocence" – and *Three Steps on the Ladder of Writing*, feminine writing is depicted as preceding prohibition and the destructive patterns of thinking and relating "knowledge" creates. The feminine writer, Cixous stresses, must work to relinquish this socially constructed self, creating, in its place, a form of "exchange in which each one would keep the *other* alive and different."[27] This endeavor is the subject of *Vivre l'orange/To Live the Orange* and *Manne aux Mandelstams aux Mandelas* – "Manna to the Mandelstams to the Mandelas."

Influences

Living and working for most of her adult life in Paris, Cixous became acquainted with many of France's leading intellectuals, including Michel Foucault, Jacques Lacan, Gille Deleuze and Jacques Derrida. Her association with Derrida in particular has remained strong.[28] The works of Sigmund Freud[29] and Martin Heidegger[30] also have an important bearing on her writing. Among her literary influences, Cixous has counted Friedrich Hölderlin, Franz Kafka, Heinrich von Kleist, Rainer Maria Rilke and William Shakespeare.[31] In "First Names of No One" Cixous discusses texts by E. T. A. Hoffman, James Joyce and Edgar Allan Poe; in *Three Steps on the Ladder of Writing* she includes reference to Anna Akhmatova, Ingeborg Bachmann, Thomas Bernhard, Paul Celan, Fyodor Dostoevsky, Jean Genet, Osip Mandelstam and Marina Tsvetaeva.[32] Her most important literary influence nonetheless remains the Brazilian writer Clarice Lispector.[33]

Clarice Lispector

In "At Hélène Cixous' Pleasure," Cixous describes the work of Clarice Lispector as the most complete example to date of feminine writing. She suggests that whereas most women's writing remains caught "in the dualistic opposition that governs almost all human relations,"[34] Lispector's writing derives from "an economy of the passions, an economy of exchanges with the other that are not governed by appropriation, by ego capitalization." In Lispector's texts, Cixous stresses:

there is a return of the living, a dazzling revaluation of primary values. One is no longer in the economy of opposition, one is in the economy of the gift. And of love. Of how to give.[35]

Lispector's achievement, Cixous continues, is to portray opposition, and then to "carry the reader further," delineating alternative responses which do not depend on subjugation:

How can the gift be given without creating the other the prisoner of the gift? This is extremely hard to do in reality, even in the strongest and most generous relationships. It is the subject of Clarice Lispector's writing. She does not make a theory of it, she gives concrete examples. Her narratives contain the possibility of a practice. Perhaps this possibility can only exist in texts. But at least in her writing it is there, it makes itself felt, it appears.[36]

Cixous and the theater

During the early 1980s Cixous began a collaboration with Ariane Mnouchkine and the Théâtre du Soleil (Sun Theater) that was to have a profound impact on her work. Cixous has suggested that in writing for the theater she was finally able to circumvent the self-regarding mechanisms that had hampered her fiction, to produce a writing of the other.[37] Her engagement with historical others in the two plays she wrote for the Théâtre du Soleil – L'Histoire terrible mais inachevée de Norodom Sihanouk Roi du Cambodge ("The Terrible But Unfinished Story of Norodom Sihanouk King of Cambodia") and L'Indiade ou l'Inde de leurs rêves ("Indiada or the India of Their Dreams")[38] has added a new dimension to her work.

In the "Conversations" to Writing Differences: Readings from the Seminar of Hélène Cixous, Cixous highlights the reader's role in feminine writing.[39] For Cixous, a feminine Reader implies a collectivity of texts dealing with the fundamental issues of existence in ways that question our perception of ourselves and others, and so challenge us to create a better life.[40] It is to the feminine reader, then, that the Hélène Cixous Reader is addressed.

Susan Sellers
Paris, 1993

NOTES

1 I am using "feminism" in its broadest sense here to denote work on women and sex and gender issues. See below for a more precise account of Cixous' relationship to the feminist movement.

2 See the Bibliography for details of Cixous' book publications.

3 See, for Cixous' account of the impact this plurilingualism had, "De la scène de l'Inconscient à la scène de l'Histoire: Chemin d'une écriture," in *Hélène Cixous, chemins d'une écriture*, edited by Françoise van Rossum-Guyon and Myriam Diaz-Diocaretz, Presses Universitaires de Vincennes, Saint-Denis and Rodopi, Amsterdam, 1990, p. 16.

4 See, for Cixous' account of her father's death in relation to her writing, "De la scène de l'Inconscient à la scène de l'Histoire: Chemin d'une écriture," p. 18.

5 Ibid., p. 19. The translation is by Deborah Jenson with modifications by the editor.

6 See, for example, the extracts from Cixous' first published and most recent fictions – *Dedans* ("Inside") and *Déluge* ("Deluge") – below.

7 See, for a detailed discussion of this point, Susan Sellers, *Language and Sexual Difference: Feminist Writing in France*, Basingtoke: Macmillan, and New York: St Martin's Press, 1991, pp. 40–8.

8 "De la scène de l'Inconscient à la scène de l'Histoire: Chemin d'une écriture," p. 19. The translation is by Deborah Jenson with modifications by the editor.

9 Transcripted extracts from this broadcast are held in an archive on behalf of Hélène Cixous by Marguerite Sandré (address available on request).

10 Cixous divorced in 1964.

11 This highly competitive, if archaic, examination for the selection of teachers is still widely considered as a pinnacle of scholastic achievement in France.

12 Cixous' thesis is published as *L'Exil de James Joyce ou l'art du remplacement*, Grasset: Paris, 1969. The English translation by Sally Purcell, *The Exile of James Joyce*, is published by London: John Calder and New York: David Lewis, 1976; reprinted by Riverrun (New York) 1980.

13 Taken from a transcript of "Au bon plaisir d'Hélène Cixous" ("At Hélène Cixous' Pleasure"), broadcast in 1987. The translation is by Deborah Jenson with modifications by the editor.

14 Ibid.

15 Cixous' seminar, which is held on a Saturday, is open to visitors.

16 "Psych et Po" is an abbreviation of "Psychoanalyse et Politique" – "Psychoanalysis and Politics." The group had an influential role in shaping French feminist intellectual debate from the late 1960s on.

17

In 1975 Antoinette Fouque, who directs the des femmes publishing house and who was one of the founders of the women's movement in 1968, asked me for a book. This is how I came to the women's movement and began to discover this world (. . .) Terrific confrontations prevailed. On the one hand there were Antoinette Fouque's interests (. . .) which drew on psychoanalysis, and on the other social-reformist interests (. . .) I was in complete solidarity with the movement that was emerging under the influence of Antoinette Fouque and the Editions des femmes, I did what I could, published with them, was present at demonstrations, but I took no initiative (. . .) Women matter to me enormously, which does not mean I confine myself to this world. I think it must be unenclosed, as free and broad as possible.

From "At Hélène Cixous' Pleasure", 1987
The translation is by Deborah Jenson with modifications by the editor.

18 The second extract translated below from "Breaths" presents a graphic illustration of this point, as the mother is tortured for the secret of the origin.

19 See, for example, "Conversations," in Susan Sellers (ed.) *Writing Differences: Readings from the Seminar of Hélène Cixous*, Milton Keynes: Open University Press, and New York: St Martin's Press, 1988, p. 151:

> I could write a thesis on the theme of giving birth in texts by women, it would be fascinating. It's a metaphor which comes easily to women, dictated by their experience (. . .) During childbirth a discovery is made inside the body. We can transpose the discovery, using it to understand moments in life which are analogous. A man will understand different things differently. Their bodies are sources of totally different images, transformations, expressions.

20 *The Newly Born Woman*, translated by Betsy Wing, Minneapolis: University of Minnesota Press, 1986, p. 90.

21 See "The Book of Promethea," below.

22 The extract from *Angst*, below, illustrates the impact masculine language has on a feminine I; the passage from *Jours de l'an* – "FirstDays of the Year" – explores the negative constructions language carries in a portrayal of the ways death has been symbolically invested.

23 See, for example, the first extract from *Three Steps on the Ladder of Writing*, below.

24 See, for example, *The Newly Born Woman*, pp. 95–6.

25 Ibid., p. 88, pp. 90–100.

26 Ibid., p. 72.

27 Ibid., p. 79.

28 Derrida was Cixous' accompanying keynote speaker at the 1990 conference "Lectures de la différence sexuelle" – "Readings of Sexual Difference" – organized by the Centre d'Etudes Féminines in collaboration with the Collège International de Philosophie (International College of Philosophy). Derrida also introduced Cixous' 1991 Wellek lectures at the University of California, Irvine.

29 See, for example, *Prénoms de personne*, Paris: Seuil, 1974, pp. 13–111.

30 See "To Live the Orange," below.

31 "At Hélène Cixous' Pleasure".

32 See also "Difficult Joys," in Helen Wilcox, Keith McWatters, Ann Thompson and Linda R. Williams (eds), *The Body and the Text: Hélène Cixous, Reading and Teaching*, Hemel Hempstead: Harvester Wheatsheaf, 1990, pp. 5–30.

33 See "To Live the Orange," "Extreme Fidelity" and "Three Steps on the **Ladder of** Writing," below. For a more detailed introduction to Cixous' work on Lispector, see (for readers of French) *L'Heure de Clarice Lispector*, Paris: des femmes Antoinette Fouque, 1989; (for readers of English) *Reading with Clarice Lispector*, edited and translated by Verena Andermatt Conley, Minneapolis: Minnesota University Press, and Hemel Hempstead: Harvester Wheatsheaf, 1990.

34

> In the dualistic position that governs almost all human relations, it happens that the strong, high, active place is almost always occupied by men, and the other by women. This is a cultural trait. But it has become so traditional that one does not escape it (. . .) Women who have written have almost always written in this opposition, and through the act of writing have found themselves in a masculine position. In a strong, phallic position.
>
> From "At Hélène Cixous' Pleasure," 1987
>
> The translation is by Deborah Jenson with modifications by the editor.

35 Ibid.

36 Ibid.

37 See "The Terrible But Unfinished Story of Norodom Sihanouk King of Cambodia," below.
38 See below.
39 See "Conversations," pp. 146–8.
40 Ibid.

Neutral

Neutral: difficulties of translating Cixous into English

The difficulties of translating a writer like Hélène Cixous are immense. No translation is ever faithful, since the translating language will inevitably erase, add to or alter the meanings of the original, a process that becomes especially significant in the case of a writer like Cixous who actively incorporates the possibilities generated by language into her text. The translator is forced to obliterate, invent, distort, producing a version of the original which, except for the recourse of an occasional note, renders all such transactions invisible.

The following passage from Cixous' *Neutre* – "Neutral" – published in 1972, which delineates a writing where the signifying function – rather than an omnipotent masculine subject – directs the narrative, is presented here in the original French alongside an English translation. Some of the problems raised by the extract are common to all English translations from French. Line 12, for example, highlights differences of gender by italicizing the masculine, feminine and plural articles, an emphasis lost in English where gender is normally only attributed according to male or female sex. Thus a passage in which the subject is in the feminine gender in French will most usually be translated into English by the neutral "it," unless it is clear that the feminine is synonymous with female. This erasure also occurs, as in line 11, wherever the feminine subject – here *la peau* ("skin") – accords femininity to its accompanying adjectives. The loss is particularly consequential in terms of Cixous' work on gender.[1] A second problem common to English translations from French involves the use of the pronoun *on* – literally "one" – as in the phrase *on coule la lessive* (line 23). *On* has greater currency in French than it does in English, where "one" seems overly formal. Translating idioms is difficult in any language. Here, Cixous plays on the cliché *de fil en aiguille* – literally "from thread to needle" – which means "by association" (see lines 54–5: *de page en aiguille* – literally "from page to needle"); while the text ends with a reference to the French expression *faire f(eu) de tout bois* – literally "to make fire from every wood" – with its sense of using all the available means (line 112).

Cixous deliberately employs the suggestions produced by language itself in her writing. This is illustrated in line 32 which has *délire ou délier ou déliter*, the alliterative generation of which is lost in a literal translation. Lines 62–3 play on the aural resemblance of *s'aime* ("loves oneself") and *sème* ("sows"). *Tronc* ("trunk") begets *donc* ("therefore/thus") (lines 7–8, see also line 65); *hasard* (most usually "chance") spawns *bâtard* ("bastard") (lines 60, 64–5).

Much of this play disappears in translation. Line 24, for example, has *la mord* (literally "bites it/her") which is a homophone of *la mort* ("death"). The reiteration of *sans* ("without") in lines 33–6 similarly evokes its homophone *sens* ("sense"). Line 59 has *livré* ("delivered") which contains the French word for "book" *livre*.

Cixous is an inventive writer, constantly coining new words. Her neologisms here include *appalit* (line 42), which contains *pâlir* ("pale") as well as *appeler* ("call"), and *virtueux* (line 73), which has *vertueux* ("virtuous") with the Latin prefix *vir* meaning "man." *Estine* (line 50), created to form "Palestine," is as meaningless in French as it is in English.

The passage illustrates a further aspect of Cixous' writing style in its reference to other texts. The main allusion here, given by the author in a note, is to Edgar Allan Poe's "The Gold-Bug." Numerous elements of the text, such as the apparently bizarre depiction of "the light of teeth" in line 26, derive from Poe's tale.[2] Other references are to Shakespeare's *Hamlet* (lines 44–6), and Racine's *Les Plaideurs* in the author's deformation of lines 38–40.

The translators contributing to this volume have each found their own solutions to the problems that confronted them. Some have adopted a literal approach, while others have preferred a more approximate rendering of the effects of the original in English. It is my hope that through this diversity something of the complexity, playfulness and poetry of Hélène Cixous' writing will be conveyed.

The passage appears on pp. 19–23 of *Neutre*, Paris: Grasset, 1972, and is translated by the editor.

Holocaust . . .

        if, nameless, powerless, ageless and sightless,
        am, lacking air and resources,
        lacking light and space and
        also time, and yet not without desire and
        movement, but the limbs cut from
        the trunk,
        Neuter therefore,
        come to engender myself,
        who am I?

. . .

thick skin of smoke directed from bottom to
top *the* fire [m.], *the* smoke [f] . . . *the* ash(es) [f or pl],
no Wind
and from top to bottom, unrecognized, the mouth.

The one is not without the other
    "The one is not without the other"
. . .   delirium the ash or ashes in every
    sense therefore, : (a mixture of yellow saffron
    white grey black, and, strangely, carmine,
    ash) descend from top to bottom of the
    Desire

Holocauste ...

si, sans nom, sans force, sans âge et sans
voir, suis, manquant d'air et de ressource,
manquant de lumière et d'espace et de
temps aussi, pourtant non sans désir et
mouvement, mais les membres retranchés
du tronc,
Neutre donc,
en viens à engendrer moi-même,
qui suis-je ?   10

...

épaisse peau de fumée orientée de bas en
haut *le* feu, *la* fumée ... *la* ou *les* cendre(s),
pas de Vent
et de haut en bas, méconnue, la bouche.

L'un n'est pas sans l'autre
    "L'un n'est pas sans l'autre"
...   délire la cendre ou les cendres en tous les
sens alors, : (un mélange de jaune safran
blanc gris noir, et, bizarrement, carmin,
cendre) descendre du haut en bas du   20
Désir

the ashtray, a sheet full of ashes
when you pour the washing
bites it a sheet full of nothing and in
the night,
the light of teeth

Just as the one is not without the other,
the one cannot be *thought* without the other. Not I one
without I other
delirium: the one is Without-the-other, and what
is not here is hidden here – in this corner –

Delirium or unbind or split *the* ash [f]

No f . . . without f . . . therefore no without without
without and even, without doubt, no doubt without
doubt, no son without father, no physis without
engendering, no engendering without kind
etc. . . .
etc.: by automatism: no power without
money, without money no Swiss, and by
a slip of the tongue, no money no *cuisse* [thigh].

Impossible to think the one without the other and without
either the one or the other: the proper here pales, the
heart darkens.

le cendrier, un drap plein de cendres
quand on coule la lessive
la mord un drap plein de sans et dans
la nuit,
la lumière des dents

De même que l'un n'est pas sans l'autre,
l'un ne peut être *pensé* sans l'autre. Ni J'un
sans J'autre
délire : l'un est un Sans-l'autre, et ce qui   30
n'est pas ici est caché ici – dans ce coin –

Délire ou délier ou déliter *la* cendre

Pas de f . . . sans f . . . donc pas de sans sans
sans et même, sans doute, pas de doute sans
doute, pas de fils sans père, pas de physis sans
engendrement, pas d'engendrement sans espèce
etc. . . .
etc. : par automatisme : pas de pouvoir sans
argent, sans argent pas de Suisses, et par
lapsus, pas d'argent pas de cuisse.   40

Impossible de penser l'un sans l'autre et sans
ni l'un ni l'autre : le propre ici appalit, le
cœur sombre.

If: "I am but mad when the wind is north-north-west., (by) the
southern wind I can tell a twin from its twin . . .[3]
where am I from?
from which region, or corner, of land or culture?
from which pale estine?

No son without fear and worse still no
twin without terror; and no terror without
satisfaction.

Rather than creation, What follows threads the pages of a secret
narrative, delving deep, all the harder to hunt because sown with a
great number of metaphors badly joined the one to the other, and
from the moment this is displayed here, in this., delivered to
Semantic hazard, and to this hazard bastard of the Letter for the
Letter, in as much as the Letter loves (sows) itself, as we have seen
it and heard it pleasure itself from the first words in certain
narcissistic effects (thus it is not by hazard that *hazard* is accompanied by *bastard* and *trunk* by *thus*). The aim of this narrative – in so
far as Narrative of the narrative – is precisely to reconnect the
greatest number of possible parts to hazard, or to retrieve them, to
make them parts of its own body, to give them sometimes human
form, rarely tropic form, to draw new and still uncalculated riches
from this virtuous marriage,

Si : "Je ne suis fou que par vent nord-
nord-ouest., (par) vent du sud je puis
distinguer un jumeau de son jumeau . . ."
 d'où suis-je ?
 de quelle région, ou coin, de terre ou
 culture ?
 de quelle pâle estine ?   50

Pas de fils sans peur et pire encore pas de
jumeau sans terreur ; et pas de terreur sans
satisfaction.

Plutôt que de création, Il s'agit ensuite de page
en aiguille d'un récit secret, creusant en
profondeur, d'autant plus difficile à chasser que
semé d'un grand nombre de métaphores mal
jointes l'une à l'autre, et dès l'affichement ici-
même, en ce., livré au hasard de la Sémantique,
et à ce hasard bâtard de la Lettre pour   60
la Lettre, dans la mesure où la Lettre s'aime
(sème), comme on l'a vue et entendue se plaire
dès les premiers mots à certains effets narcissiques
(ainsi ce n'est pas par hasard que *hasard*
s'accompagne de *bâtard* et *tronc* de *donc*). Le
but de ce récit – en tant que Récit du récit –
est justement de rebrancher au hasard le plus
grand nombre de parts possibles, ou d'en
racheter, d'en faire des parties de son corps
propre, de leur donner parfois figure humaine,   70
rarement figure tropique, de tirer des richesses
nouvelles et encore incalculées de ce mariage

– to make of absurdity the proof of its vitality, in the manner of
the dream-work, supposing that this Narrative is a normal subject,
even if it is secret, that it keeps its head on its shoulders
– proving its power by joining together unreconcilable terms,
even if it means appearing in the first place monstrous or mad
or farcical: Now it is *here* that the adventure, begun under the
sacrificial exergue (and this is not without importance), would
seem to fail (the book, a vulgar cenotaph then) (the
disappointing conclusion as in the quest of the Gold-Bug[4]
released from the top of the 7th east branch of a Liriodendron
Tulipiferum through the left eye of a skull fixed to the branch, in
the rays of the setting sun, following the cryptogrammatical
indications given by a piece of parchment covered in signs penned
by the renowned Kidd with the help of a regulus of cobalt solution
dissolved in spirit of nitre while warm, which fades on cooling –
dead Ash therefore – but revived by heat, red signs, skull and bug
recording the exact spot where the treasure is hidden) that it
should take *The* Risk [m], or *the* Risk [f], of pursuing it, desiring it,
bringing it to bay, with the professional relentlessness of hunting
dogs and birds,

virtueux, – de faire de l'absurdité la preuve
de sa vitalité, à la façon du travail du rêve,
étant posé que ce Récit est un sujet normal,
même s'il est secret, qu'il garde la tête sur
les épaules
– de prouver sa puissance en attachant ensemble
des termes inconciliables, quitte à paraître
d'abord monstrueux ou fou ou bouffon : Or   80
c'est *là* où l'aventure, commencée sous l'exergue
sacrificiel (et ce n'est pas sans importance),
semblerait échouer (le livre, un vulgaire cénotaphe
alors) (l'issue décevante comme de la
quête du Scarabée d'Or
lâché du haut de la 7e branche est d'un Liriodendron
Tulipiferum à travers l'œil gauche d'une
tête de mort fixée à la branche, aux rayons du
soleil couchant, suivant les indications
cryptogrammatiques données par un morceau de   90
parchemin couvert de signes tracés par le fameux
Kidd à l'aide d'une solution de régule de cobalt
dissous dans l'esprit de nitre encore chaud,
laquelle s'efface en refroidissant – Cendre
morte alors – mais ravivé par la chaleur,
signes rouges, crâne et scarabée consignant le
point exact où le trésor est enfoui) qu'il faudra
prendre *Le* Risque, ou *la* Risque, de le
poursuivre, le désirer, l'acculer, avec l'acharnement
professionnel des chiens et oiseaux de   100

that Deviation does not deviate, for they have been given the taste
of Flesh; the treasure is hidden, the Bug released, the burrower is
human: let him excavate and search. However the Narrative,
haggard, wonderfully wild, still flees, he never settles or scarcely
(the comparison with the treasure stops at the earth's surface)
primitive, even brutal in his behavior, while his work shows him to
be very subtle, capable of the newest and most delicate deviations
and advances, brilliantly elusive but gripping; making f . . . from
any wood. Leader.

chasse, que Détour ne détourne pas, car on leur
a donné le goût de la Chair ; le trésor est enfoui,
le Scarabée lâché, le fouisseur est humain :
qu'il creuse et fouille. Cependant le Récit,
hagard, merveilleusement farouche, fuit encore,
il ne se pose pas ou guère (la comparaison
avec le trésor s'arrête à la surface de la terre)
primitif, brutal même dans son comportement,
alors que son travail le montre très subtil, capable
de détours et avancées les plus neufs et   110
délicats, génial insaisissable mais saisissant ;
faisant f . . . de tout bois. Meneur.

NOTES

1 See "Extreme Fidelity," below. [Ed.]
2 "Teeth" is among the first words to emerge in Legrand's account of his deciphering of the cryptogram in Poe's "The Gold-Bug." The word sheds "light" on the remaining characters and thus enables the parchment to be read. [Ed.]
3 The quotation, translated literally here from the French, is from *Hamlet*, II. ii. 385–6: "I am but mad north-north-west. When the wind is southerly, I know a hawk from a handsaw." [Ed.]
4 Edgar Allan Poe. [Cixous]

Inside

Dedans – translated into English as *Inside* – is Hélène Cixous' first full-length work of fiction. Published in 1969, the same year as her doctoral thesis *L'Exil de James Joyce ou l'art du remplacement* – *The Exile of James Joyce or the Art of Replacement*, and preceded only by the collection of short stories *Le Prénom de Dieu* – "The First Name of God," it won the French literary Médicis prize for that year.

Cixous has cited her father's premature death from tuberculosis when she was eleven years old as a formative influence on her as a writer. *Inside*, like much of her early fiction, centers on the relationship to loss and death. In an article entitled "De la scène de l'Inconscient à la scène de l'Histoire: Chemin d'une écriture"[1] – "From the Scene of the Unconscious to the Scene of History: Pathway of Writing" – Cixous writes:

> *Inside* necessarily wrote itself inside the father, in looking for him even into death and in *returning*. There is something simple and mysterious in the origin of a writing: "I" am in the father whom I carry, he haunts me, I live him. There is a relationship between father and language, father and "symbolic."[2]

The notion of "inside" has numerous manifestations and meanings within the narrative. It is the tomb of human mortality figured by the father's death,[3] as well as the paradise of childhood before expulsion and knowledge of the world. As is suggested by Cixous' reference to the symbolic, psychoanalytic descriptions of the human subject's formation offer a useful point of entry to the text. Part One of *Inside*, from which the first of the two extracts presented here is taken, can be read as an account of the state prior to separation in which the distinction between self and other still has to be imaged. The disembodied mouth in this passage, with its physical resemblance to the female sex, acts as the birthplace of this transition, its feminine status and function underscored in a reiteration of the feminine (mouth and lip are both feminine in French) unfortunately lost in the English translation and in its assumption of a role similar to that played by the mother in the individuation process. The mouth is also the father's, its masculinity indicative of the symbolic/linguistic order within which the "I" must take up a place. As the words animate the self the mouth disappears, and the "I" is propelled through this absence "inside" a recognition of difference. The "I" is "inside" a body demarcated by physical limitations.

The following passage is taken from pp. 63–5 of Carol Barko's translation *Inside*, New York: Schocken Books, 1986. The French passage is on pp. 97–101 of *Dedans*, Paris: Grasset, 1969.

A mouth with a firm line is speaking to the bowl of undelineated night. The mouth is speaking to me, inside me however, I see its firm lips forming speech. I see a mouth speaking inside me, I do not see myself, I am black, filled with a soft pliable substance, an unlimited mass, silent, vibrant. The lips in profile articulate vigorously: their color? a young man's lips, full, carmine perhaps, though shaded, warm, a living man, young, eloquent: they persuade me. He's right, thinks my black pasty mass kneaded to attention. Fibers stretch me taut, pulling on invisible ends of myself – am I contractile? I must have an end.

He wants to persuade me: his lips are near, so near they appear immense though not disturbing. I know they are bigger than I, about whom I know nothing. Still, seeing the full lips in profile, I discover how infinitely small I am. The firmness of the speech rubbing, rubbing kneads my pasty mass, firing me up, I hollow myself out, going round faster and faster, turning round, I pick myself up and make for the corners of the mouth, it sucks me in, I swell up in reply, I'm burning, ah! I'm being torn apart, I'm opening up, ah! I'm freezing in the middle there, let's close up, tighten up, I'd rather have the heat, the path made by the hole in the center is a little steep, but I'm using it to resist the cold: on the outside someone is knocking at me with quick short strokes, I let the echo of the noise come in, no more, out with the cold! I concentrate myself around the lips, I am convinced, closed, dark, warm. The mouth is testing, the upper lip curves me a slight question which throws me back ever so slightly to the left beneath it, and not to the right or in front. This is where I am at the moment I pull myself together; it's all done, I make a sign, the mouth says not one word more, we understand each other, but that makes my grief explode: I'm left so alone and black when it vanishes. I am there, no doubt about it, but I miss it. Later on I miss the mouth and remember, I still miss it, I stay on reaching out toward the space that embraced it, maybe it will speak to me again, I start waiting for it, facing its absence, my smooth bearing, my taut substance, mesmerizing my fibers over to the left, I stay on, so I'm the one who stays and it's the mouth that comes and goes. I'm coming into myself, at least I have some direction, even if I'm not moving. He was strong, the lips I knew were his did not frighten me, I was penetrated by his words without seeing them: it was enough to see the mouth speaking to me inside me. He's not getting smaller, he's just not there anymore.

A blue hand stretches out palm down, on the left, below. The fingers appear, the outer edges spread out and vanish between the dark blue and my blackness. The five fingers barely apart point toward the place where the mouth was. The blue hand hesitates or rather floats, resting on the moving surface that is me, or rather slides over my congealed surface, but where is it going? how far? fine hand long blue fingers sliding up to where I am and then am no more, and suppose it were to go all the way to the edges? my substance hopes it will float, slide, nothing being impossible in the time they inhabit. The thickness of my hope turns to metal, riveted to the hole's wound knocked over and over again tick tock knock by lit-tle/knocks cold/knock, knock, and hop, my thickness clings to the hollow of the palm, and off we go in one leap toward the edges. In its narrowness it is female, smaller too than the mouth, yet sufficient, less commanding, but self-assured. It's true, there's no connection between speech and movement; for the moment, I'm comfortable in the hand because I'm not ashamed at all to be indefinite, and ignorant. When the mouth spoke to me, the sharpness of its lines blurred every attempt I made to know: two concave curves, two convex curves, connecting at a fixed point, and I a soft amorphous shape without even a center before there was a wound, I trembled, you could have said I barely existed. So there has been progress: I remember, I am extensible, and no doubt prehensible, I can distinguish between large and small, black and blue, form and myself. If there were some light maybe I would even see myself; I must have seen myself, before the time of the fingers, otherwise I wouldn't have recognized the mouth. Things fall into place, there is progress. At the same time, there is contradiction: the mouth was bigger than I, admittedly, since I felt it. But the hand, smaller than the mouth it's true, has not yet reached the edges. What can we make of this? a problem involving surface, or territory, or matter, my surface, my extent. I am made of a small organic being, living, continuous, surrounded by matter without will without force, without end, or, if it has an end, with no awareness of its end. I feel enormous and soiled. Who knows what I'm doing, nor do I know from where? O the cleanliness of the mouth, so detached, but all the same magnanimous.

Colors, the other side is coming to life – Skin I am inside that skin, stretched out between its lips and fingers.

In Part Two of *Inside*, the childhood scenario alters to that of the adult. In Part One, the "I" lives "inside" a fantasy of continuous union that necessarily entails her "death," since her negation of loss prevents her access to the symbolic and removes her from engagement with the world. In this next extract, the "I" confronts the reality of the human condition figured here in an encounter with the specter of her own death. The ambiguity of the last lines – which are also the last lines of the text – highlights the paradoxical nature of the human situation. Separation brings loss, yet the language this produces offers the possibility of inscribing and vanquishing loss. The "I" can say "kiss off" to death. "New tales" can be created. As the echo of Shakespeare's *King Lear* suggests, to be "inside" the human condition is to be both imprisoned and free.[4]

The passage is from pp. 134–6 of Carol Barko's translation of *Inside*. The French version appears on pp. 206–9 of *Dedans*.

Later I went back into the house. It was our house.

Then I opened the closet where I'd forgotten all the dresses I'd gone through in my life, from the pink crepe de Chine with a bees' nest pattern which had never smelled like honey, and which I slipped on, my nostrils flaring as the skirt slipped over my head, to the dress I'm wearing today for my death. My dress is blue like the sea where my body has grown, slept, aged; it's a young girl's dress. Inside I'm laughing. I lie down on the bed, under the becalmed and peaceful ceiling. My dress floats and balloons about my thighs, bursts out laughing, turns dark, goes green at the edges, froths just above my knees, I am wearing sea and I gently seaweed my green hair. A bride, I am young and I wait for the night. The night is at the other end of the city, camped out on the terrace of the last house where my father is waiting for me. I hurry. I am dressed in my royal king-blue queen-blue dress, the most beautiful of all, the one that holds me tightly like his arms. Because there wasn't enough material, my mother cut a bodice that flattens my breasts, but my skirt is full enough for running. I run through the scalding city toward the sweet waters of my father-spouse. The city is long, and the night short, I run, I am a raving morning glory, the streets climb, I straddle them, the trees whip their steaming flanks, the sun wraps itself in a tallith and rolls out the carpets of the sky. When the streets are exhausted, I have reached the walls. The white door opens, the blue door fades away, through the white one goes my flesh on fire, my soul streams through the blue. But in my impatience I have forgotten forms and limits, I have forgotten the shores, the walls, the steps, the porches, the others. Someone goes past and goes through the white door at the same time I do; I didn't see her, this woman with the long dark neck wearing a dress of faded blue, too tight and too big for her. She bumps into me, hangs on to my waist with an enormous arm which goes twice around me, and she takes advantage of the horror that paralyzes me by tearing off a piece of my royal king-blue queen-blue dress with her powerful hand.

I lower my eyes drowned in tears of fear, and I see feebly quivering through the rent in the blue space of my betrothal an old, white, misshapen thigh floating in skin too big for it. It is me tomorrow and I'm already thirty and could be sixty in my young girl's dress, and I sit down on the granite terrace of the last house. We form the eternal couple, me in my blue dress from the old days, he in his granite suit. Now I'm sick and tired of standing at the shores of death and I'm sick of substitutes. And though I am the princess of anterior time and the daughter of a dead god, and the mistress of tombstone inscriptions, of books of stone, of seawater gowns, I am not happy. I want him to come, I deplore loneliness, boredom, deception, I, too, am betrayed, like his mother, I hate beauty, dust, patience, passion, the stubborn wish for death, silence, the nobility of the soul, the deprivation of the body, and I rejoice in my power to speak, in the fact that I am ten years old, thirty years old or sixty, and that I can say kiss off kiss off to death.

Come, says he, let's away to prison, we two alone, without her without them, alone I will make you alone, alone you will make the night with your lips on my eyes and I shall see you beyond walls and time. If you will have me I will hold you in my arms and we shall create new tales. If you won't I shall ask your forgiveness. You will be up above and down below and I shall be inside. Outside, the mystery of things will dry up, under the sun the generations will wash up worlds over words, but inside we shall have stopped dying.

NOTES

1 "De la scène de l'Inconscient à la scène de l'Histoire: Chemin d'une écriture," in *Hélène Cixous, chemins d'une écriture*, edited by Françoise van Rossum-Guyon and Myriam Diaz-Diocaretz, Paris: Presses Universitaires de Vincennes, and Amsterdam: Rodopi, 1990, pp. 15–34. An English translation of an early version of this article exists as "From the Scene of the Unconscious to the Scene of History," translated by Deborah Carpenter, in *The Future of Literary History*, 1989, edited by Ralph Cohen, New York and London: Routledge, pp. 1–18. [Ed.]
2 "De la scène de l'Inconscient à la scène de l'Histoire: Chemin d'une écriture," p. 19. Editor's translation. [Ed.]
3 This is the explicit subject of *Tombe* ("Tomb"), published in 1973. [Ed.]
4 See *King Lear*, V. iii. 8–19. [Ed.]

First Names of No One

Prénoms de personne – "First Names of No One" – published in 1974, is a collection of readings of works by Freud, Hoffman, Kleist, Poe and Joyce. The "Prédit" – translated as "Prediction" – published here in its entirety, offers an introduction not only to the readings that follow but also to Cixous' view of literature and practice as a literary critic. Writing is equated here with the desire that can propel *personne* beyond the rule of "opposition, aggression (and) enslavement" currently in force, beyond lack, castration, the Law and death. Texts are valued according to their ability to bring the subject into play and give "life without limits"; it is in literature, Cixous stresses, that the logic of "repression" and "negativity" may be circumvented, leaving the subject free to "evolve." Above all, writing proffers an "elsewhere" with the potential to reinvent the "homogenising, reductive, unifying reason" that has led to the socio-political and intellectual impasse in the West. The reader's role – as distinct from the critic's application of theory to a text – is viewed as intrinsic to this invention process.

Cixous' text plays on a number of meanings that are regrettably lost in an English translation. The *personne* – "no one" – of the title can also mean person, individual, and its feminine gender contrasts with the mastery and unicity attributed to the masculine subject. Thus, in the last lines of the text, the French carries the possibility that the name given by the textual voice will be that of a feminine person. *Propre* – translated here as "proper" – also contains the sense of ownership as in the English word "property," and hence underscores Cixous' insistence that the "proper" entails the desire for possession.

The "Prédit" is on pp. 5–10 of *Prénoms de personne*. Paris: Seuil, 1974. The translation is by Deborah Cowell.

Prediction

I ask of writing what I ask of desire: that it have no relation to the logic which puts desire on the side of possession, of acquisition, or even of that consumption–consummation which, when pushed to its limits with such exultation, links (false) consciousness with death. I do not believe that writing – insofar as it is a production of desire – or the desire which can do anything, cannot be defined, nor that it is to be defined in accordance with death's border. Death is nothing. It is not something. It is a hole. I can fill it with fantasies, and give it a name, freely. I can also think castration. But nothing human, nothing real, obliges me to. Nothing can stop me from thinking otherwise, without accounting for death.

Life without limit, the whole of life: this is what will be in question in these texts. I say *question* because all of them have this question in common, which they answer differently, about the possibility of limit-lessness.

What happens in this non-place where the word "fiction" only names in order to inscribe the blurred and shifting lines of that adventure, beyond genres and oppositions, where the real is not definable by an opposite, where the literary is not an emanation of something else, wait-ing to be printed, where fantasy is not merely a stop-gap, where desire is not a dream, where, in the plureal, the other place to come announces itself?

What do the adventures of the plureal have to say to me? All of the reflections, readings and analyses which set forth from the non-place of fiction are stirred by so many questions, between literature and philoso-phy. I wanted to read as, when and where I understood that my reading would relate me to the real that I wanted to transform: for me, fiction, which is a kind of action, is effective. The desire which produces it will make possible what desires it. This is what will be in question here: the effectiveness of fiction, its upward soar; and a certain desire, the partici-pation of the subject, its evolutions, and its possibilities in life. So I have set free some texts here, texts which I love for what they have to say about desire and the plureality which it entails.

These apparently unconnected texts are in fact related; they share the same hearth; the source of their motives, and of their desires, is the same. All of them speak of the search for the limit, the regret of the limit (a limit to be defined doubly, as:
– the limits imposed in the real on life, on freedom, on individual pos-sibilities, by the institutions and their go-betweens: laws, etc.;
– the limits imposed on writing by the literary establishment).

This limit has several "sites" and names: on the near side of its limit-ing face, its name would be death, and all the figures of death which are given to death by psychoanalysis or projected by fantasies. Hunters of death, these texts pursue it and drive it out in the same impulse.

But the limit is also a vertiginous peak, from which elsewhere, the other, and what is to come, can be seen.

There, fiction is emblematized: it is that combination of the threshold and the unknown, which enlivens.

These texts say it, or speak of it, "in the name" of "No one": the extremity, the peak, will set us trembling if we venture there. Subjectivity vacillates, between no one and all of its possible individualities.

It is no one, always more than one, who is the diverse "hero" of all the works whose story is told here, a subject capable of being all those which it will be, desiring infinity, put at risk far from a central ego, and irrepressible. In every place that it passes through, structures burst open, the affective or social economy changes form, unknown possibilities for desire and life surge out; exchange loses its privileged position, and the *gift* takes it away.

No one is not attached to a name, no name links it to someone. Every other is always all those who precede him and which he traverses in his advance. It is not an accident if No one was Ulysses' name at a crucial moment, nor if Ulysses springs forth again as the *Ulysses* of James Joyce, with all its thousands of singularities.

The struggle on two fronts

All of them say the struggle must be led on two fronts; legitimacy must be doubly assaulted:

– the front of subjectivity, insofar as it harbors and secures the lure of unicity, of totalization, and, by this means, of conservatism and totalitarianism. It is not a question of making the subject disappear, but of giving it back its divisibility: attacking the 'chez-soi" (self-presence) and the "pour soi" (for itself), attacking income; to show the fragility of the center and of the ego's barriers is to prevent the complicity of the ego as master with authority (and the notion of authorship), with repression and its pretenses, with property in all its forms.

All of them have dismantled the great Proper, the someone denominated, but they have done so in order to allow the infinite No one to speak – which means:

– the artist of subjectivity will also have to struggle on the front of intersubjectivity: the critique of logocentrism cannot be separated from a putting in question of phallocentrism. Poe's texts, like those of Joyce, in a different form, denounce the playacting which is constituted around the threat of castration, and whose real "author" is the little anti-life calculation. These artists of deconstruction know about debts and about gifts: on the stages where they put them into play, repression and negativity run the road to real ruin. The logic of the gift-that-takes tips over; another logic predicts an eroticism without injury. The conjugal grammar is dislocated. The new desire soars out.

I have always loved desire. Certainly not the desire which believes itself to be determined according to a lack which it raises up and upon which it depends, so much so that it cannot get over it. That desire, conniving with the forces of death, whose company it keeps, and which it fears, is confused with its limit. It is afraid of itself; it fears being satisfied. It has to use ruses to maintain itself, at a distance from actualization: because it does not venture as far as the real, it has scarcely any chance of changing it. It desires itself more than it desires its object; it is very familiar, this desire to desire, which so often passes for desire itself, when it is only desire's remorse and prudence. It moves slantwise, in paradoxes, sustaining itself on contradictions, assuring itself of its own impossibility. It is animated by a calculating spirit which manages its investments and its counterinvestments, so that lack is never lacking. It preserves itself, surrounding itself with prohibitions, threatening itself with, and living off, danger, enveloped in lures and veiled with absences. It is very familiar: it is responsible for making the law and authorizing the laying down of the social order which it pretends to abhor. It is upon its weakness that power counts, upon its detours that reformism is constituted, upon its petrifying fear of castration that the Church is built. It is through its duplicity that eroticism is marked with lack, and disfigured. It goes hand in glove with the ideology of mastery, even when it speaks of sovereignty.

It is beneath the sign of an uncertain desire for liberation, a desire–fear, that some of the texts I read here align themselves: Edgar Poe is one of the great prowlers of the limit zone, but he nevertheless ends up confining (himself) to its near side. But still the limit of the limit appears, in the text which it incites and which it blocks off at the same time. Of Joyce, I say that he keeps as close as possible to that unheard-of place until suddenly the marvelous openings appear, in *Ulysses*, from which *Finnegans Wake* is catapulted forth; this is the text of texts, the readable-untranslatable. Here an extremity is invented. This non-place which undoes and reconstructs itself is given to behold to the mass of singularities, the multiple mutating figures which constitute Stephen Bloom, in one of the most funnily, and pitilessly, deconstructive parts of *Ulysses*: the place called "Ithaca," point of no-return home, so that those returning there are carried off by the text which traverses them, and with which their bodies form a dazzling diaspora. It is written in a crushing anticatechismal style, and all the lessons expressed there affirm the power of a place beyond personal identities. They are left to ferment, for another genesis.

Nevertheless, it could only be after the Circean moment in Joyce's work that a shattering schizophrenization could come to finish off and disperse the remainders of theological logocentrism with which a great number of texts before the "Wake" are still burdened: it is this irresistible rise towards the moment of breaking with what went before that I will describe in the readings that follow. Joyce's critical deconstructive passage is, like all enterprises of its kind, two-faced: one face is turned towards the institutions which are to be dismantled, the other towards what might be. The critical part of Joyce's text is still saturated with theological milk – a milk which has gone sour and which makes the subject vomit. Poison and potion still form an ambiguous mixture in *Ulysses*, which is a book of liquidations, of expulsions, and irresistible departures. But these bitter crossings had to be made: passages through the mother, over the sea, and through the signified, for in this universe, where the paternal-mother is too powerful, the subject will have great difficulty in disengaging itself from the deteriorating effects of this desire (the debasing of women; the ideology of mastery, of the forbidden, etc.), a whole trafficking of sexuality which is close to superstition (the valorization of loss, and of virginity; a self-parodying Hegelianism which works the dialectic of recognition from the point of view of a master jealous of the slave). This "discipline" must crack, and perhaps it is the thinking which remains within the phallocentric order that will be discharged, as a result of what happens so urgently on the side of the signifier under pressure from the formal forces. In Joyce, writing has resources which will produce something uncontrollable. My reading tells the story of these little calculations, at the moment when the threat of the Incalculable surges forth, when the cracks break open.

Then, there will be elsewhere. Here I speak only of those who have desired it, too early in history to succeed in getting there, for there are only two possible paths which lead to it: the one which can neither be taken nor invented, the one which carried Artaud away; and then the one which remains to be invented on the basis of a change of the mental structures of the whole of Western society. This change is not definable now, within our discourse. But it announces itself, outside everything: opposition, aggression, enslavement; how desire says it will be, absolutely unsubdued.

For the signified

Insofar as the literary text speaks about something, when literature is a means of crossing over towards the signified, where fiction is a way of inventing new meanings, the text is thinkable in accordance with an operation whose activity is double: I read it by means of a critical-philosophical reflection, and push it to the threshold where its newness seduces me and yet undoes me. I want to read at the summit, where hope and necessity change the world, life, the subject, and point the text-peaks upwards: those of Hoffmann, Kleist, Poe and Joyce – texts of the edge, texts of the outside.

A literary-philosophical practice is to be defined.

On the basis of a conception of "modernity" which has been elaborated with the help of several "scientific" discourses, or discourses which are ordered upon the text, in the last few years, a theorization of reading is being produced on the critical scene. Practice, it has been noticed, is somewhat rarer: the reader seems to be fascinated, to the point of alienation, by the study of the instruments rather than by the operations they are supposed to be used for.

So little has been read. What is more, the texts which are being read tend to be of the same kind: they are said to belong to "modernity," which they sustain with tokens of the originality of their meaningfulness: these texts are close to us in time (and can be reappropriated by our discourses).

This is merely, it must be said, an effect of culture: the choice of texts is determined partly by the language used by the critics, that is, French; and partly by their fascination with major-marginal works – which is often justified, but which has almost exhausted their resources; and lastly by the excessive attention which is given to the workings of the signifier, upon the signified. Excessive, because sometimes it goes as far as the scotomization of the signified, and, at the limit, its foreclosure.

In fact, literature has been working at this subversive activity on which it is now congratulated for a long time. In the days before Marx and Freud, before the conjoined efforts of psychoanalysis and linguistics, and of anti-idealism, had radicalized deconstruction – which is now being actively pursued, and is massively widespread – what was happening in literature? The same struggle existed, in other forms, and was led in other ways; perhaps more violently, because more desperately, with the bare text, less subversive, and more offensive. The same bastions were to be destroyed, for the German Romantics as for the French: logocentrism, idealism, theologism, everything that supports society, the scaffold of the political economy and the subjective economy, the pillars of property. The repressive machine has always had the same accomplices: homogenizing, reductive, unifying reason has always been an ally of the Master, of the one Subject, stable and socializable; and it is here, at the base of it all, that literature had already been striking its blows, where the theses and concepts of Order imposed themselves, by denouncing them on the level of the signified. Well before Bataille, Hoffmann and Kleist had begun the putting to trial of Hegelian idealism, and the confining "dialectic" of Recognition, with such ferocity. Celebrating expenditure in their song, the poets of protest shake up conservative narcissism, and break the yokes and the ties. They tear the subject from its enslavement, cleave the proper, take the puppet to pieces, cut its strings, disturb and blur the mirrors. Already Hoffmann had set free the difficult and intoxicating knowledge that "I" is multiple. Before Kierkegaard, his characters are stirred by an intense pseudonymic activity, a dance of individualities which traces the open group that is No one. Already, Kleist's ironic blows had been unleashed on the Law. That the Proper goes hand in glove with death is said better by Poe than by anybody else: death administers the conjugal home, and Poe describes its perverse and troubling work, while Joyce mocks its trifling economy.

These great destroyers are also great givers of strength, and of forms: through this shaking of the literary ground, those who crack it open pull off amazing effects, glimpses of ways out. How can we hold on to them? It is by moving onwards, beyond the known, that No one and you, other reader, will hear the textual voice, which still remains to be heard, and which gives to each of us, after all, No one's name.

The Newly Born Woman

La Jeune Née – The Newly Born Woman, coauthored with Catherine Clément and published in 1975, is perhaps the text by Cixous most widely known in the English-speaking world. It contains Cixous' ground-breaking essay "Sorties" – translated into English as "Sorties: Out and Out: Attacks/Ways Out/Forays" – in which she examines the phallocentric enterprise and sketches an alternative possibility for self/other relations.

In the first of the two passages from "Sorties" reprinted here, Cixous explores the ways in which thinking has become dependent on a differentiating process that entails opposition to and appropriation of whatever is thereby designated as other. She argues that this oppositional practice has become endemic to the extent that it appears "eternal-natural." Cixous suggests that woman has figured within this system only as the construct of man, with the result that "she" has become non-existent, "unthinkable." Cixous sees in a reclamation of the feminine the potential to challenge, undermine and replace the masculine order.

The following passage is from "Sorties" in *The Newly Born Woman*, Minnesota: University of Minnesota Press, and Manchester: Manchester University Press, 1986, pp. 63–5, and is translated by Betsy Wing. The French text appears on pp. 115–19 of *La Jeune Née*, Paris: Union Générale d'Editions, 1975.

Where is she?
Activity/passivity
Sun/Moon
Culture/Nature
Day/Night

Father/Mother
Head/Heart
Intelligible/Palpable
Logos/Pathos.
Form, convex, step, advance, semen, progress.
Matter, concave, ground – where steps are taken, holding- and dumping-ground.
Man
Woman

Always the same metaphor: we follow it, it carries us, beneath all its figures, wherever discourse is organized. If we read or speak, the same thread or double braid is leading us throughout literature, philosophy, criticism, centuries of representation and reflection.

Thought has always worked through opposition,
Speaking/Writing
Parole/Écriture
High/Low

Through dual, hierarchical oppositions. Superior/Inferior. Myths, legends, books. Philosophical systems. Everywhere (where) ordering intervenes, where a law organizes what is thinkable by oppositions (dual, irreconcilable; or sublatable, dialectical). And all these pairs of oppositions are *couples*. Does that mean something? Is the fact that Logocentrism subjects thought – all concepts, codes and values – to a binary system, related to "the" couple, man/woman?

Nature/History
Nature/Art
Nature/Mind
Passion/Action

Theory of culture, theory of society, symbolic systems in general – art, religion, family, language – it is all developed while bringing the same schemes to light. And the movement whereby each opposition is set up to make sense is the movement through which the couple is destroyed. A universal battlefield. Each time, a war is let loose. Death is always at work.
Father/Son   Relations of authority, privilege, force.
The Word/Writing   Relations: opposition, conflict, sublation, return.
Master/Slave   Violence. Repression.
We see that "victory" always comes down to the same thing: things get hierarchical. Organization by hierarchy makes all conceptual organizations subject to man. Male privilege, shown in the opposition between *activity* and *passivity*, which he uses to sustain himself. Traditionally, the question of sexual difference is treated by coupling it with the opposition: activity/passivity.
There are repercussions. Consulting the history of philosophy – since philosophical discourse both orders and reproduces all thought – one notices[1] that it is marked by an absolute *constant* which orders values and which is precisely this opposition, activity/passivity.
Moreover, woman is always associated with passivity in philosophy. Whenever it is a question of woman, when one examines kinship structures, when a family model is brought into play. In fact, as soon as the question of ontology raises its head, as soon as one asks oneself "what is

it?," as soon as there is intended meaning. Intention: desire, authority –
examine them and you are led right back . . . to the father. It is even
possible not to notice that there is no place whatsoever for woman in
the calculations. Ultimately the world of "being" can function while
precluding the mother. No need for a mother, as long as there is some
motherliness: and it is the father, then, who acts the part, who is the
mother. Either woman is passive or she does not exist. What is left of her
is unthinkable, unthought. Which certainly means that she is not
thought, that she does not enter into the oppositions, that she does
not make a couple with the father (who makes a couple with the son).

There is Mallarmé's tragic dream,[2] that father's lamentation on
the mystery of paternity, that wrenches from the poet *the* mourning, the
mourning of mournings, the death of the cherished son: this dream
of marriage between father and son. – And there's no mother then.
A man's dream when faced with death. Which always threatens him
differently than it threatens a woman.

"a union
a marriage, splendid   And dreams of filiation
– and with life   that is masculine, dreams
still in me   of God the father
I shall use it   issuing from himself
for . . .   in his son – and
so not mother then?"   no mother then

She does not exist, she can not-be; but there has to be something of
her. He keeps, then, of the woman on whom he is no longer dependent,
only this space, always virginal, as matter to be subjected to the desire he
wishes to impart.

And if we consult literary history, it is the same story. It all comes back
to man – to *his* torment, his desire to be (at) the origin. Back to the
father. There is an intrinsic connection between the philosophical and
the literary (to the extent that it conveys meaning, literature is under the
command of the philosophical) and the phallocentric. Philosophy is
constructed on the premise of woman's abasement. Subordination of the
feminine to the masculine order, which gives the appearance of being
the condition for the machinery's functioning.

Now it has become rather urgent to question this solidarity between
logocentrism and phallocentrism – bringing to light the fate dealt to
woman, her burial – to threaten the stability of the masculine structure
that passed itself off as eternal-natural, by conjuring up from femininity

the reflections and hypotheses that are necessarily ruinous for the strong-hold still in possession of authority. What would happen to logocentrism, to the great philosophical systems, to the order of the world in general if the rock upon which they founded this church should crumble?

If some fine day it suddenly came out that the logocentric plan had always, inadmissibly, been to create a foundation for (to found and fund) phallocentrism, to guarantee the masculine order a rationale equal to history itself.

So all the history, all the stories would be there to retell differently; the future would be incalculable; the historic forces would and will change hands and change body – another thought which is yet unthinkable – will transform the functioning of all society. We are living in an age where the conceptual foundation of an ancient culture is in the process of being undermined by millions of a species of mole (Topoi, ground mines) never known before.

In the second passage from "Sorties," Cixous posits a form of bisexuality as an alternative to the destructive masculine hegemony. She sees the admit-tance of difference as the foundation of this bisexuality, a position she sug-gests women necessarily already adopt. Drawing on psychoanalytic accounts of the self's formation, Cixous stresses that women have retained a closer relationship to the m/other, the body and hence to love. She argues that writing offers a "passageway" to a new relation between self and other in which both coexist, and she outlines her vision of a feminine writing.

Cixous describes the differences between what she terms a masculine and feminine "economy" in terms of attitudes to giving. Developing the thesis expounded in Marcel Mauss' "Essai sur le don. Forme et raison de l'échange dans les sociétés archaïques"[3] – "Essay on the Gift. Form and Reason of the Exchange in Archaic Societies" – she argues that the masculine is concerned with property, and that any gift functions to reinforce his (*sic*) position. The feminine gift, in contrast, is given without calculation and for the other's pleasure.

This passage appears on pp. 84–8 of *The Newly Born Woman* translated by Betsy Wing. The French reference is pp. 155–63 of *La Jeune Née*.

What I propose here leads directly to a reconsideration of *bisexuality*. To reassert the value of bisexuality;[4] hence to snatch it from the fate classically reserved for it in which it is conceptualized as "neuter"

because, as such, it would aim at warding off castration. Therefore, I shall distinguish between two bisexualities, two opposite ways of imagining the possibility and practice of bisexuality.

1. Bisexuality as a fantasy of a complete being, which replaces the fear of castration and veils sexual difference insofar as this is perceived as the mark of a mythical separation – the trace, therefore, of a dangerous and painful ability to be cut. Ovid's Hermaphrodite, less bisexual than asexual, not made up of two genders but of two halves. Hence, a fantasy of unity. Two within one, and not even two wholes.

2. To this bisexuality that melts together and effaces, wishing to avert castration, I oppose the *other bisexuality*, the one with which every subject, who is not shut up inside the spurious Phallocentric Performing Theater, sets up his or her erotic universe. Bisexuality – that is to say the location within oneself of the presence of both sexes, evident and insistent in different ways according to the individual, the non-exclusion of difference or of a sex, and starting with this "permission" one gives oneself, the multiplication of the effects of desire's inscription on every part of the body and the other body.

For historical reasons, at the present time it is woman who benefits from and opens up within this bisexuality beside itself, which does not annihilate differences but cheers them on, pursues them, adds more: in a certain way *woman is bisexual* – man having been trained to aim for glorious phallic monosexuality. By insisting on the primacy of the phallus and implementing it, phallocratic ideology has produced more than one victim. As a woman, I could be obsessed by the scepter's great shadow, and they told me: adore it, that thing you don't wield.

But at the same time, man has been given the grotesque and unenviable fate of being reduced to a single idol with clay balls. And terrified of homosexuality, as Freud and his followers remark. Why does man fear *being* a woman? Why this refusal (*Ablehnung*) of femininity? The question that stumps Freud. The "bare rock" of castration. For Freud, the repressed is not the other sex defeated by the dominant sex, as his friend Fliess (to whom Freud owes the theory of bisexuality) believed; what is repressed is leaning toward one's own sex.

Psychoanalysis is formed on the basis of woman and has repressed (not all that successfully) the femininity of masculine sexuality, and now the account it gives is hard to disprove.

We women, the derangers, know it only too well. But nothing compels us to deposit our lives in these lack-banks; to think that the subject is constituted as the last stage in a drama of bruising rehearsals; to endlessly bail out the father's religion. Because we don't desire it. We don't go round and round the supreme hole. We have no *woman's* reason to pay allegiance to the negative. What is feminine (the poets suspected it) affirms: ... and yes I said yes I will Yes, says Molly (in her rapture), carrying *Ulysses* with her in the direction of a new writing; I said yes, I will Yes.

To say that woman is somehow bisexual is an apparently paradoxical way of displacing and reviving the question of difference. And therefore of writing as "feminine" or "masculine."

I will say: today, writing is woman's. That is not a provocation, it means that woman admits there is an other. In her becoming-woman, she has not erased the bisexuality latent in the girl as in the boy. Femininity and bisexuality go together, in a combination that varies according to the individual, spreading the intensity of its force differently and (depending on the moments of their history) privileging one component or another. It is much harder for man to let the other come through him. Writing is the passageway, the entrance, the exit, the dwelling place of the other in me – the other that I am and am not, that I don't know how to be, but that I feel passing, that makes me live – that tears me apart, disturbs me, changes me, who? – a feminine one, a masculine one, some? – several, some unknown, which is indeed what gives me the desire to know and from which all life soars. This peopling gives neither rest nor security, always disturbs the relationship to "reality," produces an uncertainty that gets in the way of the subject's socialization. It is distressing, it wears you out; and for men this permeability, this non-exclusion is a threat, something intolerable.

In the past, when carried to a rather spectacular degree, it was called "possession." Being possessed is not desirable for a masculine Imaginary, which would interpret it as passivity – a dangerous feminine position. It is true that a certain receptivity is "feminine." One can, of course, as History has always done, exploit feminine reception through alienation. A woman, by her opening up, is open to being "possessed," which is to say, dispossessed of herself.

But I am speaking here of femininity as keeping alive the other that is confided to her, that visits her, that she can love as other. The loving to be other, another, without its necessarily going the rout of abasing what is same, herself.

As for passivity, in excess, it is partly bound up with death. But there is a non-closure that is not submission but confidence and comprehension; that is not an opportunity for destruction but for wonderful expansion.

Through the same opening that is her danger, she comes out of herself to go to the other, a traveler in unexplored places; she does not refuse, she approaches, not to do away with the space between, but to see it, to experience what she is not, what she is, what she can be.

Writing is working; being worked; questioning (in) the between (letting oneself be questioned) of same *and of* other without which nothing lives; undoing death's work by willing the togetherness of one-another, infinitely charged with a ceaseless exchange of one with another – not knowing one another and beginning again only from what is most distant, from self, from other, from the other within. A course that multiplies transformations by the thousands.

And that is not done without danger, without pain, without loss – of moments of self, of consciousness, of persons one has been, goes beyond, leaves. It doesn't happen without expense – of sense, time, direction.

But is that specifically feminine? It is men who have inscribed, described, theorized the paradoxical logic of an economy without reserve. This is not contradictory; it brings us back to asking about their femininity. Rare are the men able to venture onto the brink where writing, freed from law, unencumbered by moderation, exceeds phallic authority, and where the subjectivity inscribing its effects becomes feminine.

Where does difference come through in writing? If there is difference it is in the manner of spending, of valorizing the appropriated, of thinking what is not-the-same. In general, it is in the manner of thinking any "return," the relationship of capitalization, if this word "return" (*rapport*) is understood in its sense of "revenue."

Today, still, the masculine return to the Selfsame is narrower and more restricted than femininity's. It all happens as if man were more directly threatened in his being by the non-selfsame than woman. Ordinarily, this is exactly the cultural product described by psychoanalysis: someone who still has something to lose. And in the development of desire, of exchange, he is the en-grossing party: loss and expense are stuck in the commercial deal that always turns the gift into a gift-that-takes. The gift brings in a return. Loss, at the end of a curved line, is turned into its opposite and comes back to him as profit.

But does woman escape this law of return? Can one speak of another spending? Really, there is no "free" gift. You never give something for nothing. But all the difference lies in the why and how of the gift, in the values that the gesture of giving affirms, causes to circulate; in the type of profit the giver draws from the gift and the use to which he or she puts it. Why, how, is there this difference?

When one gives, what does one give oneself?

What does he want in return – the traditional man? And she? At first what *he* wants, whether on the level of cultural or of personal exchanges, whether it is a question of capital or of affectivity (or of love, of *jouissance*) – is that he gain more masculinity: plus-value of virility, authority, power, money, or pleasure, all of which reenforce his phallocentric narcissism at the same time. Moreover, that is what society is made for – how it is made; and men can hardly get out of it. An unenviable fate they've made for themselves. A man is always proving something; he has to "show off," show up the others. Masculine profit is almost always mixed up with a success that is socially defined.

How does she give? What are her dealings with saving or squandering, reserve, life, death? She too gives *for*. She too, with open hands, gives herself – pleasure, happiness, increased value, enhanced self-image. But she doesn't try to "recover her expenses." She is able not to return to herself, never settling down, pouring out, going everywhere to the other. She does not flee extremes; she is not the being-of-the-end (the goal), but she is how-far-being-reaches.

If there is a self proper to woman, paradoxically it is her capacity to depropriate herself without self-interest: endless body, without "end," without principal "parts"; if she is a whole, it is a whole made up of parts that are wholes, not simple, partial objects but varied entirety, moving and boundless change, a cosmos where eros never stops traveling, vast astral space. She doesn't revolve around a sun that is more star than the stars.

That doesn't mean that she is undifferentiated magma; it means that she doesn't create a monarchy of her body or her desire. Let masculine sexuality gravitate around the penis, engendering this centralized body (political anatomy) under the party dictatorship. Woman does not perform on herself this regionalization that profits the couple head-sex, that only inscribes itself within frontiers. Her libido is cosmic, just as her unconsciousness is worldwide: her writing also can only go on and on, without ever inscribing or distinguishing contours, daring these dizzying passages in other, fleeting and passionate dwellings within him, within the hims and hers whom she inhabits just long enough to watch them, as close as possible to the unconscious from the moment they arise; to love them, as close as possible to instinctual drives, and then, further, all filled with these brief identifying hugs and kisses, she goes and goes on infinitely. She alone dares and wants to know from within where she, the one excluded, has never ceased to hear what-comes-before-language reverberating. She lets the other tongue of a thousand tongues speak – the tongue, sound without barrier or death. She refuses life nothing. Her tongue doesn't hold back but holds forth, doesn't keep in but keeps on enabling. Where the wonder of being several and turmoil is expressed, she does not protect herself against these unknown feminines; she surprises herself at seeing, being, pleasuring in her gift of changeability. I am spacious singing Flesh: onto which is grafted no one knows which I – which masculine or feminine, more or less human but above all living, because changing I.

NOTES

1 All Derrida's work traversing-detecting the history of philosophy is devoted to bring-ing this to light. In Plato, Hegel, and Nietzsche, the same process continues: repres-sion, repudiation, distancing of woman; a murder that is mixed up with history as the manifestation and representation of masculine power. [Cixous]

2 "For Anatole's Tomb". This is the tomb in which Mallarmé keeps his son from death and watches over him as his mother. [Cixous]

3 Marcel Mauss, "Essai sur le don. Forme et raison de l'échange dans les sociétés archaïques," in *Sociologie et Anthropologie*, Paris: Presses Universitaires de France, 1950. [Ed.]

4 See *Nouvelle Revue de Psychanalyse 7, Bisexualité et différence des sexes* (Spring 1973). [Cixous]

Breaths

Souffles – "Breaths" – published in 1975, the same year as *La Jeune Née* (*The Newly Born Woman*), is the first of a series of fictional texts that deal with loss in relation to the mother and the attendant (re)birth of a self that is both female and feminine.

In the first of two passages from "Breaths," a feminine voice, linked to the body and the pre-symbolic union between mother and child prior to the Law's intervention, incites the "I" to a new relation with herself, others and the symbolic order. The voice – also figured here as an eagle – belongs to "the time when the soul still speaks flesh" and has not "been subjected to the injury of censorship." Its pulsion "escapes," "destroys," "touches," "produces," inducing the self to labor. Her (re)birth is her own – "destroys and recommences me" – and that of others – "I am laboured (. . .) for your ascensions."

The passage illustrates the difficulties of rendering the play of genders in French in an English translation. "Voice," for example, is feminine in French, and thus naturally entails the adoption of a feminine pronoun and agreement endings. In English "voice" has no intrinsic gender, yet employing the pronoun "it" obliterates the strong insistence on the feminine in the French. Transposing the text into the feminine is also a falsification of the French, and undercuts Cixous' view of bisexuality as this is expressed in the second of the two passages presented above from *The Newly Born Woman*. In the sentence beginning "Dances: the rhythm of her body at each second," for example, whilst the feminine "voice" is the subject and can thus accurately be translated into English as such – "body" (*corps*), and hence its accompanying possessive adjective (*son*), are masculine and, given the convention, therefore also to some extent genderless. A more gender-precise translation of the French line, *Danse: le rythme de son corps à chaque seconde, l'élan, inscrit jusqu'en l'immobile suspens, le réveil dans le sommeil, et celui de sa vie entière*, might therefore read: "Dances: the rhythm of its/his body at each second, the lift, inscribed even in motionless suspense, the wakefulness of sleep, and of its/her whole life." Even this contortion, however, would not convey the full impact of gender which marks almost every word.

The passage is pp. 9–12 of *Souffles*, Paris: des femmes, 1975, and is translated by the editor.

This is the enigma: softness is born from strength.

And now, who is to be born?

The voice says: "I am there." And everything is there. If I had such a voice, I would not write, I would laugh. And no need of quills so more body. I would not fear being out of breath. I would not come to my aid enlarging myself with a text. *Fort!*[1]

Voice! A jet, – such a voice, and off I would go, I would live. I write. I am the echo of her voice her shadow-child, her lover.

"You!" The voice says: "you." And I am born! – "Look," she says, and I see everything! – "Touch!" And I am touched.

There! the voice opens my eyes, her light opens my mouth, makes me cry out. And I am born from this.

I do not know.

Who? *Selbst jetzo, welche denn ich sei, ich weiss es nicht*[2]

Which?

This is the enigma:

. . . "it opens the rock . . ."

I am, even now . . .

Her body makes me speak: there is a link between my breath and her brilliance. A bound! Before me! In a gust of wind. Surprise! Beauty tears a cry from me, yes! There is a link between this type of star and my soul's irruption! thus she fills the air it stirs, and through the mingling of its rays with my breath a field composed of star's blood and my gasping is born. Her beauty strikes me. Produces streaming. Makes me flow. She seduces my forces. Gentleness. Gives me the desire to complete her. Emptying me. Destroys and recommences me. *Da!*[3]

Recasts me. Projects new traits. Now at last I resemble her! How beautiful I am! Aspiration is what I am. Summons the most brutish powers of my being for the hymn that the voice makes resound in me: my forgotten tongues, my piercing sounds, my liquids, the guttural music with which I formerly masturbated my ear drums, vibrate again, the brasses, the tumbas[4] again cadence the pit of my stomach, again my cymbals, my German tongues.

The supports of the years fly away like straws at the shock of a single beat. Sings the most carnal of my flesh. From the time when the soul still speaks flesh, and the flesh understands itself in every tongue, we hear ourselves internally to our nerves' end. Gives herself! And again reopens me – the depths are recovered – still strikes again – Thunder of the gift. The voice there![5] Gives! Eagle! But first of all the tongue, violence of the adoration. I want. I listen. Flies! J'e't'

Eagle!

I see her fall upon me with the certainty of the master of the air who never misses its mark, a fall of stone, the elegance of a bird about its royal business. Praise it with resounding cymbols![6] Sure to the finest sinews of her perfection and taking pleasure in herself, her harmony, intact from the effort that pinches or twists. Naturally above those impure, supervised sounds that ill-trained voices ill produce. Such a voice can only pour forth from a place apart, she can only breathe from a proud body. Had she once been subjected to the injury of censorship, she would not have these precise, delicate, sustained tones. Black notes. The voice. Speaks. Not quickly, but sharp and full, without the help of inflection, supporting herself on the firm air. She knows its subtlest details. Cuts. Dances: the rhythm of her body at each second, the lift, inscribed even in motionless suspense, the wakefulness of sleep, and of her whole life. (We see that it has not belonged, administered, composed, rounded its angles, not adhered. That it shakes, escapes, cuts, wings, crosses. Scales. Refuses.)

Rises from the greatest dilation of her breast, without listening to herself. Does not assume airs. She gushes, shocks, we are caught. Attacks. We are moved. If I had such a voice, I would not write, I would fight. Strike.

". . . and the water gushes!"

I do not swallow her like your saliva; I do not suckle her I do not kiss her with the tenderness that swells the lips of my cunt when it embraces your penis; nothing of our approximations, of our penetrations our capturings. Not our oracles. She does not dissolve. Host, cake, seeds, sperm, poppy-seed cake, man's milk, my delights, she is not that. Does not introduce herself into my body. She strikes, and I am populated. Her violence touches in me all the ignored points where my breaths explode, pounds them, destroys them. I am labored. Ravages. She roars. And from the unheard ruin of my night unimaginable landscapes emerge in colossal irruptions, created for your ascensions. The mountains I am incapable of rise for you, there where I would have hollowed my seas. I was not ready for these heights! I must now prepare myself for these summits. Jungfrau. To work! Overwhelmed with pleasure at the enormity of the effort I must make. Her voice. Tears down the blinds, unmasks the depths, denudes me, gives the face of this surmounting in which I will be us or nothing. There is nothing without her voice. Necessary – her violent demand, happily. Without her no genesis, no catastrophe. Nothing written: she suppresses the time of signs, lets the metaphors fall and without losing a second

Annuls the zones, membranes, divisions, splits open and returns my debris, forces me . . .

The second of the two passages from "Breaths" focuses on the mother from a very different perspective. Echoing Cixous' suggestions in the first of the

two extracts reprinted above from *The Newly Born Woman* that man's fear and desire to appropriate the origin for himself has led to woman's annihilation, the mother is tortured for her "secret."

Cixous' vision of feminine writing is one of non-exclusivity, and her insistence that the feminine writer convey not only those incidents that will present the author in a flattering light but also incorporate the darker, more destructive side to the human psyche, is borne out in this horrific exposition of the desire for the mother's abasement and possession.

The passage is on pp. 58–62 of *Souffles* and is translated by the editor.

"Here is the enigma. And if you find the answer before this party is over then I will give you thirty sheets . . ."

. . . Tempest.

I am not indifferent to her lack of beauty: I want her less beautiful still, coarser, heavier, less kept. Thus all the more adorable, riper for the gutting. O ancient formless mother, nameless non-body, my mystery, frame, coffer, at your sight the harsh joys the brutal visions my malicious artists offer my divinity rise to my eyes in the stream of tears from my furthermost flesh. No need to open my mouth: my executioners (drawn all of a piece from the all-powerful decision of my first desires, huge, ready to serve) are trained to hear beyond sound the fine waves my will emits, my robots with abundant muscle, know to prepare the elected body with appropriate swiftness. Let this operation be a pure one: let it be stripped bare, without the ornament of gesture or expression, in a strict economy. Without preliminary pathos. My torment will be fitting. Let my helpers be handsome, dull, stupid. Let them hover with a bestial majesty above my schemes the coldness of which they must preserve.

The victim will be gagged: before the appointed hour no cry must reach my ears without exception. Let their virginity remain intact until my signal. I order that she has been chosen heavy and fat from among all women. White. That she be not endowed with youthful attractions, with adornments, with these weaknesses that endeavor to win looks and engulf them. I want her powerful with thick, strong flesh; let her be well fed beforehand so she is full.

". . . to lose breath?"

Let everything assure us of her maturity. Her solidity should overwhelm me. Preferably she would be over forty; I want her relieved of ignorance. Separated from the uncertainties of the vague; let no past come to worry her, slow her down; let her advance filled only with the present; without anyone pushing or pulling her. Let her have maternal respect in respect of herself. I ask that she has taken pleasure in herself and that the calm of those who own themselves emanates from her person. Let her breathe strength in rest: that on seeing her we know it would have been sweet to have been dominated by her in the shadow of her triumphant mass and that she had not once looked at us, that she had subdued us by the enormous power of her appearance, yes that she had forced us to our knees by her very bulk. Mistress she could have raised us everything against her. For her our boiling emotion, our bestial tenderness. My executioners designed for her: their collective force exceeds hers. Thus they seized her without violence but by deploying a vast quantity of energy. Perfect brutes: we will dispense with their faces, their muscles are enough for me. Sufficiently human but not too human, in order that the sufferings may be conveyed by their bodies without reverberation. They have nothing, I want it this way, to express: if they were even minutely affected everything would be ruined. Their strength is there to raise and lower hers. Let them be non-existent.

I alone have the key . . .

I have planned a harmonious portico: the extreme precision of our instruments is essential: I must neither hear nor see her, although we perform between her arms. Let it proceed without attracting attention, each part of a more troubling elegance. Oiled. Its joints. The polished hinge-pins in their sockets. Everything glides and turns with grace. Except for the pincers and cuffs, which will shine with a calculated brilliance, let the apparatus veil itself and become part of the air. We will all only have eyes for the unique object.

Of this parade.

I command. In the wink of an eye I will have solved all the technical details: now, we are ready, we are alone, let no one disturb me from now on.

Everything obeys me – Not yet! Let us delay for a moment, so that I may feel my stomach churn with anticipated pleasure until I whimper for joy. You will bring her to me in a while: stop! I want to see you offer her to me in anticipation several times. Wait! The primitiveness of my joy frightens me. A moment, my man servants, stay without moving, almost non-existent. Go!

The moment before, she suspected nothing. Fear never brushed her. Extreme power slept on its resources. She adds herself to her completion. A simple coffer with framed sides, but in her breast the enclosed might of a nation at arms. I want her full to bursting. A swarm of bees in a lion's carcass. She was sleeping when we took her. On this chest which is a body to her I wanted a ridiculous spread of hair: so long, so black, so alarming, so garrison, covering her to her feet with faithful troops. The camp is on the watch round the tent where the leader forgets. I like her blinding herself without our having touched her. We will wake her with the promptest brutality. Let no one wake her, let us suddenly hurl her into the horror of the torment. Leave out the moments of weakness, chain the times of stress, let everything be of an unyielding violence. Let her be brought!

"Fetch the key. And if before the end of the seven days . . ."

At the sight of her, I stifle a shriek that would have split the arch. Armed guards in front of and behind her, archers, catalingpelts,[7] police helmeted with visors, would not displease me. But, no one. Steady my executioners, stand aside, keep to your vicious grip and let nothing prevent me from imprisoning her with my eyes. Ah! I am obeyed!

There she is! My blood ebbs away, I am emptied out. In my veins another, colder, harsher blood rises. I horrify myself. I would be congealed in such extasy if I were visible! I said: gagged! It is done. A cloth as thin as a bit crushes her tongue; how strong you are! already fury and humiliation cloud her eyes. But above all:

I wanted her pregnant: I need her full up. And slowed down. No interest in the contents: girl, honey or gold, it makes no difference. Pregnant, with a pregnancy which possesses and divides her. I want the pebble she carries to worry and betray her from inside as it weighs her down[8] (Perhaps I decided myself that one of mine would get her pregnant; I need her in the right condition, when towards the seventh month her swollen belly becomes difficult to control and the occupant turns against her.) Overtaken, inhabited, I have twice herself at my mercy: more than herself so less than herself. More vulnerable. She will take more. Our silences too are pregnant with the cries we will, if I want, soon have shrieked. How good I already feel!

The world is far behind us . . .

"O bound mother, how your belly moves me! Do you sense how the invisible desires you? How beautiful you are like this! I adore you in this disgrace! You will be nobly treated: I have given orders that your secret be torn from your body alive."

NOTES

1 The reference is to the *fort* ("here") and *da* ("gone") in Freud's study of children's attempts to compensate for and control loss through language. [Ed.]
2 What Hélène says, even after several lives (see *Faust* Part 2). [Cixous]
3 See note 1 above. [Ed.]
4 The French has *toumbas* which is a neologism playing on "tuba." [Ed.]
5 There is a play here on *Voix-Là* – literally "Voice-There", and *voilà* – "there is, are." [Ed.]
6 The French has *cymbles*. [Ed.]
7 The French has *cataphractes* a neologism in which "*cata*pult," "*phra*se" ("phrase") and *cataracte* ("cataract"/"waterfall"/"downpour") can all be heard. [Ed.]
8 The French has *en l'apesantissant*. [Ed.]

La – The (Feminine)

The first of three passages from *La* – "The (Feminine)" – published in 1976, offers a portrait of the feminine writer. Depicted as beyond censorship, feminine writing[1] is described as having the capacity to circumvent "reason" labeled here as an "enemy" of life." Drawing on the resources of the unconscious, in tune with the body's needs and pleasures, feminine writing is rooted in a liberating love. Humor is its keynote; its time the present including the acceptance, rather than refusal, of our inevitable death. Its purpose is transmission leading to growth, and a celebration of life in the face of death. As Cixous puts it, feminine writing is the art of "singing the abyss."

The following passage is on pp. 207–10 of *La* (1976), Paris: des femmes, 1979, and is translated by the editor.

Her affirmations
Her scene of wild writings forever escapes vigilance armed reason, force, jealousy, death wish,[2] Schadenfreude,[3] the traps and bites of life's enemies.

"I do not attend before the tribunals: of *Heliopolice* – of *Busiris* – of *Mêmefils*[4] – of *Pé and Dep* – of *Recti* – of *Seuil*[5] – of *Djétoudi*[6] – of *Nairef* – of *Re-stau* – of the region of shadows – of the kingdom of hatreds.

I do not defend myself before these tribunals.

I sign at my pleasure the forms of all my letters."

"This chapter to be written from dawn to dawn, without recommencement, before the waking of the SuperFathers High Surveillance. This will assure the victory of its humor over the Word of Death. This text is of an unfailing efficacy" (*Book of the Dead*, ch. XIX).

Show

Her art of living her abysses, of loving them, of making them sing, change, resounding their air with the rhythms of her earth tongues, regardless of the littoral and acoustic delimitations of their syllabysses.

Her art of crossing the whole of history and its little histories and the contests of the sexes, and of crossing unscathed the foul economies, in a spirited stroke,

from her inexhaustible source of humor

To vanquish the impossible each day and have always a yes in advance on chance

To liberate love and affirm it

Her forces directly connected without the least censorship to a battery of unconsciouses with inexhaustible resources,

She will thus never be encircled with no way out by the evil tongues
She will not be held prisoner for eternity.

(By the poor in spirit, the extirpators, the castrating castrated, the
assassins of the passions, the body-undertakers, the word-mummifiers,
the innumerable types of slaves of reason in language, the descendants
of the lovers of God with his grammar.)

The list of life haters is found almost in its entirety between the *Book
of the Dead* (ch. XVIII, 10 sections) and the *Book of the Yes* (chs "Twilight
of the Idols," "There where she finds to lose herself," etc.).

As dreamer and fantastic with double libido, voyager of several existences, she renounces none of her primitive liberties or those to come,
all her sources of pleasure and all her means of acquiring pleasure
persist in all forms which put them out of reach of the rivalry Principle

As linguist the freedom with which she crosses several unconsciouses
to transmit the secrets and powers of a soul in another tongue and of a
body in another in which to grow and transform without restraint.

And as artist of love, her knowing-pleasure overflows her individual
activities (psychical, cultural, historical) in the direction of the other: she
has an unconquerable propensity to unite, join, connect together
desires, languages, unconsciouses which the exigencies of Truthverility,
communications and indwarfstry threaten to transform into sicknesses,
and shelter them at the height of life.

She knows not no, name, negativity. She excels at marrying oppositions
and taking pleasure in this as a single pleasure with several hearths. Her
real happinesses are no less intense than her imaginary happinesses so
much more complete, so much more luxurious than Truthverility claims
all the more to command of modesty and reduction, and dancingly inde-
pendent with regard to the censor's consent. The pliancy of her libido,
accomplishing her comings and goings between the diverse parts of her
letters and her types and her forms, has the grace of nocturnal liberty and
the vigor of the conscious and unconscious woken dream.

She is simultaneously her animals of joy, her artists, her reasoning
beings, her animals of prey, her aggressive souls, her love persons.
Recite this chapter between heaven and the abyss
Wo Hass und Blitzstrahl eins ward, ein Fluch,[7]
There where hatred and the lightning flash are only a single maledic-
tion, consumed in a second
Where I would be able to see my death without dying, at the bounding
edge of my chasms, my roguish friends from the heights, where one day I

will see myself watching myself living a last day, in the illuminating joy of not having been followed by any of the race of the dead and any of the race of the censors and judges of life, of being surrounded only by my gay eagles, my birds of joy and my loves alone capable of our dangers, our distances, our red cages, the intoxicating splendor of our anguishes, our art of seeing always further always greater than the end of an end,

She who will have read this chapter between two nothingnesses will be able to come and go in time as she likes. She will become so robust during her lives that it will be easy for her to make sicknesses sick, to find in injuries the healing virtue that resides there, to thwart the threat of death of which the mask covers nothing.

She will heartily laugh

In this second passage from *La*, Cixous gives a humorous depiction of woman's role in instituting man as god. She demonstrates how women's fear – of separation, solitude, "death" – is culturally produced through such *hi*stories as the biblical account of Genesis, conspiring to prevent woman giving birth to *her*self.

The passage is on pp. 258–62 of *La* and is translated by the editor.

Decisive moment: the one when you will be really alone. And it is perhaps this that makes her hesitate: not the void, but the vastness of the solitude. It's as well if you are frightened of solitude. It's a sign that you have come to the moment of your birth.

Come on! I am finally where I have spent the first part of my existence frightened of getting to. All through this time you told yourself: "Woman cannot live without anchoring herself, gaining support, help from someone she could trust, someone stronger and more resistant than she." You even told yourself more specifically: "Woman is a being who cannot live cut off from the source. And this source is a person. Am I not proof that this definition is true?"

Yes, for half your life's path, you proved each day that there was truth in the conception. Not without hardship. What difficulties you had rendering at least personally this "truth" true! The panics, the anguishes, each time a source dried up; each time a god disclosed to you that, tired of nurturing, he was obliged to reveal to what extent he was mortal.

What terrors ensued! Quick a new source! Race to connect your life to a more inextinguishable source! this is what you were tied to, in defiance of reason, in order not to let yourself die, betray your belief, your "essence"; abandon yourself to anyone but yourself.

Seeing yourself condemned to the intolerable alternative: either running from the site of one exhausted source to another site, where there is no source as yet, and thus from hope to hope, running, running, believing, believing, hoping, invent by ploughing the space of traces of belief, hope, source, that in going back you take yourself for the sign that there is, was, will be one, that the error is yours, and that truth himself is waiting for you with an inextinguishable patience somewhere.

And on these trembling, endless journeys, you met up with groups of women and children, tribes, families, individuals, whose tense faces, eyes turned towards another space and feverish step indicated that these women too cannot live without the support of nurturing beings.

Would you have been able to stop yourself? One day? One moment? The time a question caught up with you? Which question? The question of the source? But this could only have come from the source. And there is no source. Or once make a halt: not make the link, let the "truth" of the source expose its death force, out of loyalty; as you were the proof of its life force, now be the proof of its negativity. But what proof? Thinking of this evidence is not giving it. You would only have given it by renouncing being it.

It was to become serpent.

(If the serpents had written History they would have proudly related how their ancestor had belonged to woman. And it was during a love dispute between woman and her companion, a dispute god had every interest in no one ever knowing he had been the adulterous cause, as for any oriental god, that the jealous companion violently seized her serpent. But serpents are a people with no writing and it is god who has the word.)

To have believed that there was a path. That there was only one path. That there was only one of them! To have believed that the thread which crossed through him was destined for her, that she was made for him, the natural prolongation of his original thread. And that she would thereby be the path from thread to line going from line to thread and back.

To the point of having detested the idea of a no-return, in imagining that the beings without a thread would disappear beyond a certain point into nothingness. To the point of having taken infinity for death.

It has to be said that there was always one god or other, lying in ambush at the right place, with his reassuring look of an enigma personified. Nothing more effective than a sphinx to keep you between two extremes, while life goes by. Or the day declines.

– The only enigmatic enigma: that our need for belief makes such long detours toward us, taking us so far, sometimes irretrievably too far, yes, so devilishly far, from ourselves. A chance in how many million for one of these germs of life to one day draw near – not refrain from drawing near – when no one had ever thought of it, even less believed, or at least dared to begin to think of it – when one is not sure one has not rather more than one god in one's bag, always ready to serve once again, a last hope of help, supplementary mother – to attain a woman and inseminate her

(– when a chain of (family, professional, love, literary) circumstances makes what she thoughtlessly calls her "life" "advance," in other words precipitate her so violently that she stumbles several times under the pressure, having rapidly to master from necessity the art of falling and picking herself up again, and when this external violence confuses its effects with those of her inner space: always feeling inexplicably confined in her small estate, having always been obliged for lack of air, expanse, to seek at all costs, on pain of an agony long as life, to connect her being to a greater being, and for more security to a being with no limits, when the need for an extension is so great that no passivity, inertia, anguish, resists its pressure, it happens that a young woman is borne so suddenly that the borders do not have time to raise themselves, the flood-gates to close up again, to an exceptional height – without even having had the feeling of climbing, on the contrary having had the unhappy sensation of crashing down, losing her way running dreadfully far from the path of salvation – from whence, as soon as she has caught her breath – which for some months has been seized by emotion, the abruptness of the change – and as soon as she has taken a few steps ahead by herself, she will not fail to discover that she is not dead, that she is not destroyed, that she is not mad, that blood runs through her body, and in her head thoughts which – then, surely – that she is alone up there,

yes, then, in such cases, there is always one of these gods, in whom all of us women claim to no longer believe, who comes by a miracle, to this desolate place, where no one human would ever dare to appear, it is thus definitely a god, and definitely a miracle, precisely at this moment, she was about to get up, she had even outlined a step – she believed, the unfortunate woman, that she had come to the lowest point of her existence, the next step she must have made the dizzy discovery that it is to the highest, most dangerous point that she had been carried, if a god had not at that moment come to her aid,

for the characteristic of our gods, those in whom for centuries we can no longer believe, is to prove that they exist precisely in these moments of trouble in which belief, in general, is about to die and in which we will be compelled to choose between madness and belief in ourself, "I am going to encounter myself," our soul petrified with fear cries out, "Quick, a god!"

– A god? But of course, right away!

At this moment, she is so tired, also so dazed by the extreme rapidity of events, she forgets that a god by definition never presents himself. And he who presents himself as god, she still knew this the day before, can only be one of these diabolical left-over mothers, always there to protect you from seeing ... from life!

Nevertheless this no-god is a bit god: he procures for her at that precise moment all the indispensable things, which are not to be found in that desert, from love, to a table, books, paper, and even a giant bed, so large and majestic that real authority emanates from it.

In an essay entitled "La Venue à l'écriture" – "Coming to Writing"[8] – published the year after *La*, Cixous describes writing as:

a way of leaving no space for death, of pushing back forgetfulness, of never letting one-self be surprised by the abyss. Of never becoming resigned, consoled; never turning over in bed to face the wall and drift asleep again as if nothing had happened; as if nothing could happen.[9]

Writing offers the means to overcome separation and death, to "give yourself what you would want God-if-he-existed to give you."[10]

In this final passage from *La*, the feminine "I" – and the god who would have prevented her – are cast "outside" in a reversal of the ultimately deadly "inside" portrayed in Cixous' first novel. Challenging the biblical account of the Fall as an excuse for inaction and inertia, the text imagines an alternative scenario in which there is encouragement to "raise our-selves" and "invent." Writing is the key to this (re)birth, for which the self must take on the role of mother. As Cixous stresses in "Coming to Writing":

It's all there: where separation doesn't separate; where absence is animated, taken back from silence and stillness. In the assault of love on nothingness. My voice repels death; my death; your death; my voice is my other. I write and you are not dead. The other is safe if I write."[11]

The passage is on pp. 267–70 of *La* and is translated by the editor.

Refuse to be one of these sickly women who drag along with their illness, from bed to bed, during a painfully prenatal life; one of these tenants of the hotel of lost Time, dispositions created around the worst of sufferings, jealousy of the already, of the past to which one cannot resign oneself to not having one's share, of death, mother, decay. Hermit of the shells mentality, of the grottoes, of rooms clad with ivy, of moss, of faded curtains, crab of the deep. Backwards before time. Not to be one of the race of the homesick, those who crawl with their birth-place on their back, necrophiliac sons: "When I return dead, mother, I will marry you. Wait for me on the other side!" Or: "I will marry you when you are dead." Those who would like to discover America returning home from a walk in the Tuileries, the unconsoled of birth, for whom all paths lead back to the port of departure.

Are you looking for lost Time? But who has had it? who has lost it? As if there were lost time, as if time was only lost, the disappeared! Not even the disappearance.

There is only time to lose. Whoever believes there is lost time does not count themselves among the living. Nor amongst the dead: for the dead have only one longing, to come back alive, afterwards, after, not yesterday, that, they lived, certainly not life from which they have after all detached themselves and of which they know the end in advance, not a life that bites its own tail, this, is no life, it is a serpent, but departs without the benefit of any reference, any security, nor memory, nor experience, nor maternal love, beginning life from zero, each day from zero, a life of beginnings.

"Outside!" I say addressing him as well as myself. What need have I of a bathrobe? I, therefore, big, burning with hatred, anger, impatience, I make good fun of the considerations of another epoch. When one wants to leave, it is not to come back, to go and conceal oneself differently. As for him, he too will go naked. And there we are, side by side in the moist force of our nudity – and each with all our ribs,[12] walking, through the rooms without hesitation, without lowering our head, we are not leaving paradise, no angel behind us with a brandished sword – all that only man's prehistory –

Without shame, without confusion, without provocation, without repetition. We will not return. No exhibition, nor inhibition.

The invited look solemn and stiff. All strangers. If you are an analyst, this makes you think: there is an interesting contrast between our indifference and the spectators' shame. In your dreams it is the opposite contrast we encounter. If to look and to show yourself awakens shame and anguish, it is because you are of these men who imagine that they have been chased out of paradise – or who pretend to believe it – for whom birth is a punishment. Moreover you are not born. You let yourself fall, you reveal your hate in allowing yourself to fall, on the pretext that you are obeying the law of gravity. In this you are in perfect agreement with death.

Your whole approach rests on the existence of the first Judgement. And what if you were not condemned? What a catastrophe for the lazy! All would not be lost! You would have to raise yourself! Invent! No more excuses! Who could well say: "I fear we cannot rid ourselves of God, because we still believe in grammar ..." A believer, still a friend of men!

But if you still believe in grammar, it is because the idea of being able to rid yourself of god fills you with terror. Fear of no-life, fear of life.

Put him outside! "And quickly!" I say. By my side, nudity of rage, he advances, naked, powerful, somber, full total presence, near, is it possible to be more present, nearer, more naked, more somber; more accessible, more hideously inaccessible? The true path of birth does not simply pass through the mother. Leaving our birth-place, moving away from the port, from the bay, this is not enough. Above all we must rid ourselves of the dead, gods and men who play the mother. Alone? With the cruelty, courage, wickedness, of the one who having begun to write against death, holds their work close against them – against death – with the cruelty, the courage, the solitude that is a part.

Alone? With solitude.

With such a need, such a fear, such a demand for solitude. Alone, at this angle of time, and from my solitary point of view, of course, I imagine that at this moment, tens, thousands of female animals of joy are in the process of hoisting themselves up with an ease perhaps greater than mine, of pulling themselves, of escaping, with the sky, the sun,[13] the earth for witnesses, from rooves, from windows, from corners, from terraces, from forests, from tunnels, from castles, from memories of which I know nothing, and by means which are still unknown to me.

NOTES

1　"Writing" is feminine in French. [Ed.]
2　In English in the original. [Ed.]
3　To gloat over others' misfortune. [Ed.]
4　Literally "Sameson." [Ed.]
5　Literally "Threshold." [Ed.]
6　A play on *j'ai tout dit* – "I have said it all." [Ed.]
7　This phrase is translated in the following line. [Ed.]
8　"La Venue à l'écriture," in *La Venue à l'écriture*, with Madeleine Gagnon and Annie Leclerc, Paris: Union Générale d'Editions, 1977, collected in *Entre l'Ecriture*, Paris: des femmes, 1986. The English translation by Deborah Jenson is "Coming to Writing," in *"Coming to Writing" and Other Essays*, Cambridge, Mass.: Harvard University Press, 1991. [Ed.]
9　"Coming to Writing," p. 3. [Ed.]
10　Ibid., p. 4. [Ed.]
11　Ibid. [Ed.]
12　The word for "side" and "rib" is the same here – *côte* – the play being on the biblical insistence that woman grew out of man's rib.
13　Both "sky" and "sun" are neologistically transposed into the feminine – *la cielle* ("sky"), *la soleille* ("sun") – emphasizing the feminine here in conjunction with *la* (f) *terre* ("the earth"). [Ed.]

Angst

Angst, published in 1977, continues a number of the themes explored in La. In Angst, the newly born woman must negotiate a place for herself within a symbolic order designed to protect the masculine. In the following passage, language, as the representative of this order, is depicted as a "web of metaphors" spun by the masculine il ("he") to entrap her. "He" talks "without hesitation in his own language," spinning "fictions" that annihilate her reality. The extract shows how the masculine desire to subjugate the other also ensnares him: he too is a fly struggling in the web of his making.

The passage is taken from Jo Levy's translation of Angst, London: John Calder, 1985, pp. 119–31. The French text is on pp. 154–68 of Angst, Paris: des femmes, 1977.

I had not been expecting anyone. I found myself in front of him. The Unexpected in person. He was standing before my bed, as if I had willed his presence. The stranger, instantly recognized as the-one-you-were-not-expecting. With the unquestionable self-possession of the unthinkable.

It is only today that the thought occurs to me: "at this precise moment the whole story of my death has been decided." What was happening in the room did not leave me the time nor the inclination to think. Things were going so fast that I was always falling behind. Directions were taken, paths pointed out, my movements suggested; a dialogue was going on, an oracle was overturned; the questions he asked me answered the questions I would only ever have dared ask myself; or god if he had existed. They were dangerous. Had he seen through me?

Things escaped from me and were taken up by the other. What I had never had was coming back to me. I had to admit that I had, doubtless, always known what I had just learnt – I had to acknowledge it. I believed he was reading my thoughts. There was a will in that room way ahead of me. As if my business was his; as if he had not only taken charge of my desires but of my destiny.

Perhaps he wasn't reading my thoughts. I thought he was. No time to check. I was falling behind at every sentence. I listened. Suspicious. Startled. I couldn't grasp the meaning; couldn't catch up. I was totally bewildered. I didn't understand anything. Though I didn't realize it at the time. Trying to grasp ten things at once, like chasing ten hares at a time. Even if I'd been ten dogs I would have been outrun; because the hares were continually turning into something else. A hunter was amusing himself.

He talked to me without hesitation in his own language. As if he were sure that I would understand it; that I had to hear it. It wasn't mine. It was a strange language whose pronouns came straight for me at every turn, pitilessly. A positive language. I couldn't say no. And he left no place in his voice for doubt. It was a voice that checked me, frightened me; made me want to run away, kept me willingly riveted to the bed which I couldn't leave, where I had gone to ground; buried myself; shrunk, felt myself getting younger and forgetting.

His tone was weary, yet deep and disturbingly calm. The voice of a survivor. God knows what languages it had gone through, what silences it had conquered amidst prayers and sobs, what corpses it had had to wrench itself free from in order to reach that low, serious pitch. That soothing tone that was crushing me. I was lying under his words, Jonah in the bottom of the boat. Escaping in my pretend-sleep: eternity broke loose; I was in my night-gown, ashamed, sick. He was addressing doubt personified: me: "I woke you up." It was not a question; he was announcing what had occurred. "I woke you up." "Yes." His peaceful voice, torn from so many battles, weighed on my chest heavier than death. To wake up done in, in the ship's hold. The boat thought it would be dashed to pieces. Instead of going to Nineveh, you had tried to escape to Tarshish.

"Get up." I was awake. I suspected it was the last awakening. The first or the last. The one that put paid to my longing for sleep. The one that pulls you out of the hold forever, pulls you from your soul's abysmal depths. To cast you forth into the sea. And you stay in its fish belly. You will sleep no more. Sleep won't come again. At that time I stopped sleeping. In the calm of his voice was the tremor of storms that had died down. I weathered the echo of torments that I couldn't imagine. His voice came from another time. All the waves and all the tears of several lifetimes washed over me. He wasn't yet thirty.

Is it by chance that in order to talk about the Trial I have finally been forced to return to the first bed? When I wanted to go back into the back room the door opened onto the first room. As if I couldn't get to the final scene. I have to go back through the three rooms, because truth wants me to. Perhaps it was because of what happened in the room where he was not expected. At times, because of my anguish, I think that the three rooms where we were struggling for our lives were only the same room lived in differently. This isn't completely untrue. If there had been ten rooms, ten lives to threaten, to save, ten deaths to die, I think things would have been arranged by the same secret authority for similar scenarios to be played out. There must have been one basic scene; unknown to me; but I can't have realized it, everything was arranged between the door and the bed. A battle was going on. I didn't notice the similarity until after the last replay. Sometimes I wonder whether the outcome hadn't been decided by our respective positions when the door opened: wasn't I still lying in bed? having already gone down among my dead? I didn't dare get up. "Come! Let's go to Nineveh for a coffee." His eyes on me, without the slightest embarrassment. My head almost burst. He was the one who *looks*. I asked him to turn round while I dressed quickly. I hid myself, clothed myself, didn't show myself to anyone, not to him, not to myself, mirrors made me look away.

It is very possible that the crucial scene had been set up for me in a previous story, outside me, outside the room. And so what I took for the beginning was nothing but the final revelation. All those who have watched themselves dying come to that conclusion. Ten years later you make the dubious discovery that when you were *not* waiting for anyone, you were, deep down, expecting someone; Else. The door opens. The person who comes in is so calm that your story halts. It can only be life or death. It can only be life – nothing – but – life.

When you were slipping on your dress he told you his name. He had his back to you. His three names hurt your ears. They were your son's names. Chance was on his side. Or a will more impressive than chance. Hadn't you heard the echo of another voice in his, reproaching you? What are you doing here, sleepy-head? Get up! Can't you hear the voice of voices? What is attracting death's frightening attention to you? Can't you hear death announcing itself? Reminding you of its three names? No room to think about it. You were already taken over – in case you thought of running away.

Nothing that happened between the first and the last room can be wiped out. Somewhere everything goes on, the torment continues in the past eternal. Every moment was lost, mourned, saved, as it was happening. I wasn't living, each gesture was a repetition, from way back in the past, after the separation, life was returning to life, nostalgic; I was looking at myself from the point of view of the eternal, once all was lost, and I wept in anguish.

In the city of Nineveh you went through what you can never live over again; every move over forever – the stranger was guiding me. I hadn't expected anyone. The night before I only had one desire: to lie under a ricinus and ask for the end. I was tired of life, far from the world. "I've had enough, oh time, let me go to sleep." Now, despite myself, I was up and dressed – (get up and eat). I was in the streets and the Present was by my side.

I didn't like the Present: his way of being calmly by himself, beside me, as if no one could disturb him, disturbed me. My nearness didn't change him at all. He could have been alone. He was stopping me from being alone and at the same time recalling me to my greater inner loneliness. And besides, something about his appearance stopped me from really seeing him, as if he were too much himself. Uniquely himself. And as if there was no one in Nineveh, no one round us at the bar, and no one beside him. And yet he turned to me, addressed me, as if he had been open to me from the very start. He allowed himself to be looked at without drawing back, without hiding a thought, he presented all his faces, not withholding a single one, unblinking, as if he wasn't being looked at, but bathed in a mysterious light. He irritated me. I was hardly out of my dazed, mindless state. His self-assurance paralyzed me. His way of being there, as if he had been rushed to Nineveh because of me. He hadn't sought it. Nature had decided it. He was obeying strange laws. As if he were willingly submitting to the will of a god. With a strength in submission equal to that will. While we were having coffee. His name at that time was Mensch. He assured me that was his real name. He was smiling, looking steadily at me, smiling.

Perhaps you had understood that morning who S was. But it wasn't the right moment. That would come later. In the bar you were still in the position of the prophet dazed with fear, so worn out by his vigils, that he doesn't distinguish between "knowing" and "knowing that he knows." He doesn't dare understand what he has understood. His smile was stopping you from looking at him. From thinking. His huge, brutal presence: nothing could have checked that presence, put it off, as if he were the Voice. He was weighing me down: a sly, even pressure which made me bristle. The weight of a colossal calm penetrating me. The force of a colossal silence weighing me down. I didn't dare block my ears.

I was sure he was doing it on purpose. That was a crazy thought. His way of being near without coming nearer, his keeping me away, repulsed me. I was flung out at a hopeless distance from him: when I touched bottom, in my innermost self, I still did not escape him, whereas he never ceased to be unapproachable. Daunting. He brushed against me on all sides, I was caught, imprisoned, restricted, but I never got to him. Continually drawing back, I was forestalled, anticipated and had the alarming feeling that I could not escape from his territory.

In the bar at Nineveh his familiarity shocked me. The glass pane that divided him from me did not protect me from him. He could stretch out his hand and put it on my arm. I should have pushed it away. But it was a strange, kind hand, which was trying to convey to my skin the secret of its light touch. It was trembling: "My strength is in my weakness."

He talked to me as if he were talking to himself, unpretentiously, as if no one was listening to him, in a low disturbing voice. As if all I was was a moment of himself. I felt I was hearing what should never have been heard. In the street his voice was too serious. He was laughing. His trembling arm slipped round my waist. How did I allow it? I didn't push it away. Because I was weak; a calm weakness that alarmed me. His fragility weighed on me unbearably. This being was too light. He made me think of death and I took the blame on myself, to avoid blaming him. He seemed about to fall over any moment. I was humiliated. I felt cheated. I was to blame.

I wanted to run away at every step; to wake up; I wanted it to be just a dream. His words forbade me. The clairvoyant, mysterious phrases, their shadowy texture, their fabric of threats. A day-spider, a night-spider, which was going to gobble me up?

His transparent sentences staggered me. You would have thought he was speaking for me. That was my fear. His fear. "Wasn't the story fraught enough? Confused enough?" His leap over anguish, my very anguish. "You can prevent what I was expecting from happening. Your Youth." As if my youth wasn't young, but ancient and definitive, because it was formed in an ageless time. "That proves your strength. It doesn't prove how strong my trust is. It proves my immense weakness." Things I might have said to him. That your strength frightens me. If I hadn't been cut off from myself. By each one of his phrases. "I had just fallen asleep. And here you are coming to frighten me." His regrets. My mute reproaches. How to describe the gaiety in his dread? When all was settled. The weariness in his flights of enthusiasm? And now I mustn't sleep any more. The flaunting of his weakness, as if he wanted to dazzle me. His way of glorifying it. With a gloomy admiration. How to understand his audacious diffidence? His morbid sentences too charged with sadness to be anything but oppressive. Like children they were calling me to come and help them. Their heads under the black sheets. As if they were afraid of not being heard. By me. Afraid of dying. Choked with suppressed tears. I was filled with mistrust. They fed on a mystery. Perhaps a poison. A hint of fear. Pleasure in terror. Perhaps nothing but a lie. The effect of a prophetic dream. I was filled with dread. Perhaps there was a danger. Why not name it? As if he were afraid of reprisals. If it were a question of dying, why not bring it out into the open? I wouldn't have listened to him anyway. It was a question of having lost the way. They boasted of being lost. I was lost too. "Yesterday I was so alone." The glass pane. "I couldn't even love any more. Every impulse came up against a pane of glass. I couldn't touch anything any more. I was without a single living contact. Yesterday I ... Everything came back to me, obliterated.

And now here I am wanting to touch you. When I can hardly get up. When you have come too late. When I had just made my peace. It proves you can never be sure of anything. What a state I'm in. And I can't lie down any more. My peace was so short-lived! I was so alone, so calm, fully prepared not to get up again."

But the anguish was different. The contorted black phrases were strained to breaking point, shattering and wounding me.

"I would have liked to be able to live." But I didn't want to. "I was like someone dying of thirst who hasn't the strength left to drink. That's how thirsty I was for love." Perhaps I wanted "to want," I would have been afraid of being punished. I abhorred what I longed for. I could only long for the worst. And any way, I didn't want to.

The whole difference was there: *he* spoke of himself with pity. As if he were talking of a god-like friend who had taken his last farewell. He was distancing himself to avoid seeing himself disappear. And now I was calling him back to the cruel bed. And *I* felt a pitiless hatred for myself. It wasn't the same glass pane.

The black words were avoiding something that must have been foul. He didn't "say" them. He "put them forward." They didn't wind their way towards me. They hedged. "You came at the right time for another!" Their power, craftiness – I was stung. Taken in. Their spidery legs. Their web of metaphors, smothered innuendos. I was summoned, pressed, beseeched. Accused of being slow, cautious. Recruited for a war. Without knowing the enemy. I didn't come looking for you. No one was holding me back. He was expecting me to join him in a quarrel whose origin I didn't know. A battle was beginning all over again. It was my fault. When I meet you on the day before the last. Complaints had been lodged. I was struggling in the web.

I suspected him of wanting to fabricate a story for himself. To trap me in. I felt I was turning into his fly. His food. A story to slow things down, so that he could enjoy it without reservation. But he himself was buzzing, writhing in the web.

He was playing chess with himself. He didn't place a word until he had measured his chances of protecting it. On the defensive. All the sentences calculated with an enemy in mind. Frenzied negotiations taking place, round the inevitable. Keep your distance. Keep quiet. Send out thoughts to reconnoitre. To test out the battle field. Instead of doves. Moles. Night butterflies. Seductive messages. They came back saying:

"fear, helplessness, hesitation." With an incredible force that roused my disbelief. But the body didn't lie. "I long to be able to love." His light-hearted laughter. "I really must have managed to shift ... Good for me!" Joy despite the heavy note in his voice. He had shifted silence. But it didn't last. He was serious again. Flight, cowardice, deadly weariness. Given what was to come: "Whereas every day this month I have been pushed to the brink."

It was a question of a journey: "What if I came back?" A temptation: "It is not getting there that I am afraid of now." And the anguish that wasn't mine, that was trying to gain my favour, my patience; to cling on to my unconscious. With the obstinacy of a child clinging to the skirts of life. This blackmail disgusted me. "I am afraid you'll get me wrong. My weakness is not blackmail. My fear is not weakness." Found out! Entangled more and more deeply in a mysterious connection to the Present. Since he was asking me: "Don't hate me, please," at the very moment I was beginning to hate him without knowing why. And so, driven from my cover, forestalled, more and more uncertain, and not daring to detest him: like the unbeliever obsessed with god who is wondering whether he will have to confess himself a believer, just to get god out of the way. But he was saying to me: "Today I have nothing to say in my favor. Once I come back, I will show you the best."

His lamentations moved me, put me off. Do those in league with death have a language to sing death's praises in? My hostility welled up, over-flowed. Who told you the name of the enemy? Perhaps it's someone else sheltering inside him? Who has come back to die? A battle was going on inside his body. His arm round my waist, too intimate, an error crept in, his voice was too naked, a feeling of obscenity. "I dreamt that I was living. I was surprised. I said to myself I only hope it isn't a dream."

His dreams of death. He was laughing. I had trouble laughing. The way his deaths lived inside him. This fairytale, or else it was a secret belief held by his people: they say that if someone who is dying manages to attract to him a human being who has never heard of death, and who has never pronounced death's name, he would be saved. His voice had the power to re-call the dead. Mine came back too. To Nineveh. To help him. The obscure, the insignificant, the lost, despite my protest. They hurled themselves upon me through him. They were in collusion: there was a link between their bodies and his – a particular kind of suffering. Something that went straight to my heart. They climbed over his chest. They were aiming for mine. My point of absolute vulnerability. This was the mystery: in the lungs, between the breasts; I felt it ploughing up my breast, thumping: another heart come to attack mine. I knew them by their cough. Their voices hoarse with blood. Their lungs pierced with bullets. Their mouldy, blackened bronchi, their chests caved in. Their death-rattle, like the howling of wolves. Their filthy bleeding. Their deadly silence. Their secret spittle. The way they slipped off like thieves. Their loneliness.

And so it was them! The ones I hadn't seen disappearing, the shameful dead. The illicitly buried. Another blow from one of my fathers! Their craving for vengeance. Their jealousy. (They should have made the effort before.) Their craving to be mourned. To make me pay for their defeat. To put their sickness, their mortality on me. To make the most of my body until I go mad. Until they die.

An ominous joke: your father's letter in 1935: "My love, I don't think I am deluding myself when I say to you that I foresee a brilliant future." Return it to the "presumed dead." With your sincere illusions. Never be sure of the morrow.

What are you doing here, sleepy-head! Quick, get up, can't you feel your life's on fire? Perhaps you knew who M was this morning, but you let yourself forget. And now, how can you wake up?

According to one of his stories he was once a young man from Mord. At that time he was called Man. Or perhaps that's his real name now? He has changed his name several times and begun life again in different countries. In my opinion he was a wandering Jew. He didn't deny it. He had devoted himself to writing. If you had been at their marriage you would probably have caught a glimpse of the truth, just an outline: seeing the couple sitting at the table of the law, and despite the light bridal veil you would have seen that M was a young woman with a prodigiously strong intellect and she was marrying a woman then called Schreiber. That didn't fail to cause a stir in the world since there had never been such a marriage before. But M had always had an iron will. A steady clear gaze. The thought of his strangeness was always with you, you began to get used to it. Even if he were no one, at least he was a living proof of Presence. Proof of a radiant reality. I was stunned by his strangeness. What the hell were you doing there?

Instead of dragging round Nineveh, run off to Tarshish, get back to your senses; go back to the books that have been written, printed, arranged on shelves – their covers are dull, their pages filled with honeyed words and all their lies are true. But I didn't know where I was any more.

You have been trying since this morning to get back to your right mind and you don't know yourself. And yet you did leave your reason somewhere close by. The only thing you are sure of is that you took leave of your senses this morning just before you got up, that's logical. No use searching your memory, no trace of an image. But your reason is around. And you remember the last thought, just a word, more like a movement: Run away! You don't know Nineveh and besides, it is confusing, unsettling; even if you have the feeling you have tramped through all its streets, you must have got them mixed up, or they've changed in your absence. Haven't you yourself changed? Didn't you end up that evening doing what you never should have done?

Didn't you find Your-self in the room alone with S, despite yourself. It was my room, but darker, the interior decor had been upset during the day, by chance. I was crouching on the divan, in the corner with no shield, with no reason, my wings folded; there was a whole network of threads in the air. I saw him cheerfully moving to and fro weaving, making knots, his proposals getting madder and madder, nearer and nearer. It was a question of my whole life. He was pulling it to pieces, I wasn't living it. He separated, unwound, killed, cut, picked through, eliminated, re-made me other distant and solitary lives. As if he were making love to my life, in his way, his head and neck moving, crossing out, rewriting, pages, extracts. And all in praise of his fictions he was annihilating my reality. After all that, how could you hope to come to your senses in Nineveh? Your reason certainly is in Nineveh, but it's beyond you.

To Live the Orange

Vivre l'orange/To Live the Orange, published in 1979, is an interesting text from the viewpoint of the English-speaking reader as it is presented in English as well as in French. The English translation was revised by Cixous and rewritten in places by her. This is particularly noteworthy in those passages where the play on the signifier in French could not be rendered in English and which Cixous consequently reworked.[1]

To Live the Orange is an important text on two counts. It gives an extended insight into Cixous' vision of feminine writing. In the 1977 essay "Coming to Writing," Cixous described the purpose of feminine writing in terms of an image of the m/other's face:

The moment I came into life (. . .) I trembled: from the fear of separation, the dread of death. I saw death at work (. . .) I watched it wound, disfigure, paralyze, and massacre from the moment my eyes opened to seeing. I discovered that the face was mortal, and that I would have to snatch it back at every moment from Nothingness (. . .) Because of my fear I reinforced love, I alerted all the forces of life, I armed love, with soul and words, to keep death from winning. Loving: keeping alive: naming.[2]

In *To Live the Orange*, this function of feminine writing is outlined in detail. Cixous compares those voices that obliterate what they express with those that "watch over and save (. . .) reflect and protect the things that are ever as delicate as the newly born." This (feminine) writing entails a going beyond the borders of the self, despite the innumerable difficulties, listed here as blindness, falsity, injustice, error, murder, hypocrisy, distraction, death – and "holding words out" in the other's direction. It is an inscription deriving from a level of being that precedes the automatic confines of thinking, "where each being evolves according to its own necessity, following the order of its intimate elements."

Cixous' account of feminine writing can be fruitfully compared with the work of Martin Heidegger. In an essay entitled "The Thing,"[3] Heidegger describes how thought has laid claim to things with the result that "the thing as thing remains prescribed, nil, and in that sense annihilated."[4] The alternative, that "the thing's thingness would have become manifest and would have laid claim to thought"[5] has, consequently, become unthinkable [*sic*]. Heidegger concludes that progress involves a "step back from the thinking that merely represents – that is, explains – to the thinking that responds and recalls."[6]

Loving, saving, naming what would otherwise be annihilated is political in a more immediate sense. Cixous humorously recounts how her contemplation of an orange is interrupted by a telephone call reminding her of the plight of women in Iran. This reminder, and its incitement to action, are also part of "the work of un-forgetting, of un-silencing, of unearthing, of un-blinding oneself, and of un-deafening oneself."[7]

To Live the Orange is Cixous' first tribute to the Brazilian writer Clarice Lispector. Cixous' discovery of Lispector's work in 1978 has had a profound and lasting influence on her as a writer and literary critic. Here she describes the joy of encountering a writer who is both feminine *and female* in a "ten year (...) desert of books" authored by men.[8]

The passage is taken from pp. 8–30 (even numbers only) of *Vivre l'orange/To Live the Orange*, Paris: des femmes, 1979. The translation is by Sarah Cornell and Ann Liddle and revised by Hélène Cixous. *Vivre l'orange/To Live the Orange* is reprinted in Cixous' *L'Heure de Clarice Lispector*, Paris: des femmes Antoinette Fouque, 1989, pp. 8–113. The passage reprinted here is on pp. 8–30 of this edition (even numbers only).

And there are women whom I don't wish to speak of, don't wish to withdraw from in speaking, don't wish to speak of with words that retreat from things, and the noise of their steps covers the throbbing of things, and with words that fall upon things and fix their quaverings and make them discordant and deafen them; I fear the fall of words on their voices. I can adore a voice: I am a woman: the love of the voice: nothing is more powerful than the intimate touch of a veiled voice, profound but reserved coming to awaken my blood; the first ray of a voice that comes to meet the newly-born heart. My heart is in the belongingness with a voice fashioned out of shining darkness, a nearness infinitely tender and reserved.

There are those of whom I cannot speak outside with words that come out making noise. Out of love for the infinite delicateness of their voices. Out of respect for the delicateness of the nearness. Those whose speaking is so profound, so intense, whose voices pass gently behind things and lift them and gently bathe them, and take the words in their hands and lay them with infinite delicateness close by things, to call them and lull them without pulling them and rushing them. There are women who speak to watch over and save, not to catch, with voices almost invisible, attentive and precise like virtuoso fingers, and swift as birds' beaks, but not to seize and mean, voices to remain near by things, as their luminous shadow, to reflect and protect the things that are ever as delicate as the newly-born.

There are those whose voice that like a flame lowers, scarcely speaks, but moves still nearer, still nearer to the secrets of things, lowers all the way to the earth, lies down, touches the imperceptibly trembling soil, listens to the music of the earth, the concert of the earth with all things, there are those women whose voice notes the signs of life in its minute beginnings. If they write, it is to surround the birth of life with the most delicate care. They have taught me that tenderness is a science. And their writings are voices changed into hands to come very gently to meet our souls, when we are searching, we have needed to leave a search for what in our being is most secret. Because a woman's voice has awakened our heart.

A woman's voice came to me from far away, like a voice from a birth-town, it brought me insights that I once had, intimate insights, naïve and knowing, ancient and fresh like the yellow and violet color of freesias rediscovered, this voice was unknown to me, it reached me on the twelfth of October 1978, this voice was not searching for me, it was writing to no one, to all women, to writing, in a foreign tongue. I do not speak it, but my heart understands it, and its silent words in all the veins of my life have translated themselves into mad blood, into joy-blood.

A writing came with an angel's footsteps, – when I was so far from myself, alone at the extremity of my finite being, my writing-being was grieving for being so lonely, sending sadder and sadder unaddressed letters: "*I've wandered ten years in the desert of books – without encountering an answer,*" its letters shorter and shorter "*but where are the amies?*" more and more forbidden, "*where the poetry,*" "*the truth?*" almost unreadable, messages of fear with no subject: "*doubt, cold, blindness?,*" I was afraid that it might become mad, I no longer dared to listen to myself, I was afraid that it might accuse itself of being the echo of my madness, myself discovering it so absolutely un-modern, unsuitable, unrecycled, so madly bent on demanding the impossible, on desiring, in our charnel-days, the coming of young songs as disinterested, rich and open, as vast and defenseless as in hymnal times, but such come no more to our lands, where all tongues have shriveled, there are no more habitable souls for their grandeur, I felt guilty that my writing was aside from reality, – busy searching for writings of the same age, of human origin, with which to learn how to call forth the tongues in which words still live, near by things, and listen to them breathe: guilty of naïvety, of pride, my writing, guilty of innocence, I alone responsible for all of its ills: and sometimes I judged it, sometimes I condemned myself, I acquitted it, I justified it. And thus: attacking myself, defending myself, attacking it. And sometimes reproaching myself for having religious writing, –

A writing came, with gleaming hands in the darkness, when I no longer dared to help myself, my writing so far away in pure solitude, so near the dried up torrent of Kerit, neither rain, nor dew, forever asking me forgiveness, I forgave it, I asked its forgiveness, neither food, nor ravens. I spoke no more, I feared my voice, I feared the birds' voices, and all of the calls that look outside, and there is no outside except nothingness, and are extinguished – a writing found me when I was unfindable to myself. More than a writing, the great writing, the writing of other days, the terrestrial, vegetal writing of the time when the earth was the sovereign mother, the good mistress, and we went to the school of growth in her countries. She gave me the desire not to flee the question that filled my throat with dry silence, with inert and deaf silence, when I was lost even from me, and my soul was so far away in such a sincerely hopeless retreat that even the music did not reach it, the lieder were failing, there was scarcely any more air, the music was perishing, the motets were yellowing, the music had passed, wasn't returning, the music was dead, even Mozart was mute and Mozart's name no longer drew tears from the stones, for music is a belief. And there was no belief in an exile of such an undeniable fatality, where there was scarcely anything left to breathe for a soul sans expanse, sans memory, sans impatience, no bigger than a tear.

What remained of a woman that I had loved being, was the last tear: and this tear I had given in answer to the question of grace, the one whose point I had turned against my writing: "*What have you in common with women? When your hand no longer even knows anymore how to find a near and patient and realizable orange, at rest in the bowl?*" Mute I fled the orange, my writing fled the secret voice of the orange, I withdrew from the shame of being unable to receive the benediction of the fruit giving itself peacefully, for my hand was too lonely, and in such loneliness, my hand no longer had the strength to believe in the orange, I had in common with myself only the shame and discouragement, my hand had no more the goodness of knowing the orange's goodness, the fruit's fullness, my writing was separated from the orange, didn't write the orange, didn't go to it, didn't call it, didn't carry the juice to my lips.

From far away, from outside of my history, a voice came to collect the last tear. To save the orange. She put the word in my ear. And it was nearly the nymph of the orange that awakened in my breast and surged forth streaming from the heart's basin. Certain voices have this power, I had always been sure of it. She put the orange back into the deserted hands of my writing, and with her orange-colored accents she rubbed the eyes of my writing which were arid and covered with white films. And it was a childhood that came running back to pick up the live orange and immediately celebrate it. For our childhoods have the natural science of the orange. There was originally an intimacy between the orange and the little girl, almost a kinship, the exchange of essential confidences. The orange is ever young. The influx of orange propagated itself to the ends of my bodies. The orange is the nearest star. With all of my life I thought it, with all of my thought I went toward it, I had the peace in my hands. I saw that the world that held the answer to the questions of my being was gold-red, a globe of light present here and tomorrow, red day descended from green night.

I asked: "*What have I in common with women?*" From Brazil a voice came to return the lost orange to me. "*The need to go to the sources. The easiness of forgetting the source. The possibility of being saved by a humid voice that has gone to the sources. The need to go further into the birth-voice.*"

And to all of the women whose voices are like hands that come to meet our souls when we are searching for the secret, we have needed, vitally, to leave to search for what is most secret in our being, I dedicate the gift of the orange. And to all of the women whose hands are like voices that go to meet the things in the dark, and that hold words out in the direction of things like infinitely attentive fingers, that don't catch, that attract and let come, I dedicate the orange's existence, as it has been given to me by a woman, according to the entire and infinite bringing-together of the thing, including all that is kin of the air and the earth, including all of the sense relations that every orange keeps alive and circulates, with life, death, women, forms, volumes, movement, matter, the ways of metamorphoses, the invisible links between fruits and bodies, the destiny of perfumes, the theory of catastrophes, all of the thoughts that a woman can nourish, starting out from a given orange; including all of its names, the silent name, laid upon my almost white leaf, the name as proper to it as god's name to god; its family name; and its maiden name; and the singular name, unique, detached from the dark-green air in which the voice of Clarice went to gather an orange among all of the oranges to lay it young and sound on the toile of a text prepared for it: she called this one "Laranja."

It was almost a young girl. It was an orange regained. Through the fine skin of the word, I sensed that it was a blood-orange. By a fine vibration in the toile, I sensed that Clarice closed her eyes to touch the orange better, to hold it more lightly, let it weigh more freely upon her text, she noted eyes closed to hear more internally the secret song of the orange. Every orange is original. And to all of the women for whom the need of fruit reflexion is a task of life, I dedicate the juice-filled fruits of meditation. To all women then. My ears of meditation.

My speleologist's ears. That listen to the growing of poetry when it is still subterranean, but struggling slowly in the breast to bring itself forth to the incantation of the outside, rejuicing and suffering from being only the breathing of matter. To all of my amies for whom loving the moment is a necessity, saving the moment is such a difficult thing, and we never have the necessary time, the slow, sanguineous time, that is the condition of this love, the pensive, tranquil time that has the courage to let last, I dedicate the three gifts: slowness which is the essence of tenderness; a cup of passion-fruits whose flesh presents in its heart filaments comparable to the styles that poetry bears; and the word *spelaïon*, as it is in itself a gourd full of voices, an enchanted ear, the instrument of a continuous music, an open, bottomless species of orange.

The orange is a moment. Not forgetting the orange is one thing. Recalling the orange is another thing. Rejoining it is another. At least three times are needed in order to begin to understand the infinite immensity of the moment. I have been living around an orange for three days.

I am scarcely beginning to measure its importance. Its bearings. During the three days three thin nights flow, three winks of a day, a blink after each flash of red lightning. Its radiance. The beginning of the moment lasts seventy-two hours which don't take place near the orange, seventy-two pages of the daily news of mortals, that I have not read, not received. The instant breathes, deepens, comes and goes, approaches, waits, continually. Does not divide itself. A month is a year long for a voyager of nine years. Three looks around an orange, from here to Brazil go to the sources in Lalgeria. The fruit shines in the hourless time. The juice of time flows according to the needs. I live submerged under the hour, sans souci, sans presentiment, sans peur. I work. I learn to swim underground. I do languages. I take orange courses. The telephone rings. – At that moment I was sojourning in inner Orient. Quite far from the peel of the world, in truth, but close to the center, just next to a nest of poems, with which my ears had already gone wild.

The orange is a beginning. Starting out from the orange all voyages are possible. All voices that go their way via her are good.

When the telephone rang, I was alive in the moment, I had orange all over, the peaceful light running orange before my windows was my philosophical joy, I was humid, my skin young, sweet, under the ever first rays of the fruit, the hour stayed still, I held it back in perpetual and tender excitation, breath fixed, bass sustained around the nest, when was I living, far from the cars, the lorries, the cannons, nearby the origin, under high yellow shadows, where was I living, in the first garden, surrounded by tender woods of voices – when the telephone pounced? When I didn't fear not being frightened, mistrustful, enraged? Far from the castles, the tanks, the battlements, armed only with tenderness. The telephone stamped, in my blessed myopia I saw it as it is in reality, when it spurs on, covered with white armor, shield, helmet, hauberk all of one grey, loud as Alerion.

Coming out of the light of the moment to go into the color gray is a violent, strange, artless exercise, an obligation without directions. It takes nerve. It's a matter of slipping between two oblivions, or of leaping from one memory to another memory, and the edges are hazy. I was changing milieux: one has to change from feet to blood.

The telephone shrieked. With one hand I grabbed it: I put my hand out of the window, I place it on its neck, I have not forgotten, I recognize that the telephone is also a living being, and I change eras. In the other hand I still held the orange a bit, just by the word. Out of its element, every orange alters, shrivels, loses its own virtues, its force of attraction, of assembling. I leave the orange to herself, in her climate. Word in hand, the descent begins. It is then that I discover how far the love of the origin has led me. Into what region of uncontrolled airs. The word is a mont-golfier: the descent obeys its paradoxical nature, and all the weight of the telephone, all the ironclad gravity can do nothing against the strength of its lightness. We float. The storm of the world rang. I had to let go of the orange to come back. From the moment to the sortie I counted 72 hours. In the evening I brought the telephone back to the height of my ordinary right ear. In the same moment the orange and the window vanish. There is only a disoriented voyager left in the office.

We lovers of origins, we're not afraid to return. There is a memory in our forgetfulness. The telephone was crying. It was Renata's anxiety:

"And Iran?"

One thing is not to forget the orange. Another to save oneself in the orange. But it's another thing to not forget Iran.

"And Iran? What were you doing?'

"I was learning the thing."

"While the orient was decaying, millions of veiled oranges trampled upon, precipitated into entirely modern prisons?"

"I was at the school of sources, in inner Brazil, a woman was teaching me slowness."

"And Iran? You were forgetting?"

There is a time for listening to the vibrations that things produce in detaching themselves from the nothing-being to which our blindness relegates them, there is a time for letting things struggling with indifference give themselves to be heard. There is a time for the heart-rending call of an Iran. One doesn't resound without the other.

"You were singing?"

"Guilty. Not guilty. Acquitted." I went along. Freely I toiled joyfully. In the tracks of a woman with athletic regards, a woman capable of letting the truth of beings surge forth in freedom, each truth singular in its own way, according to its measure and its rhythm, a woman whose eyes are strong enough, spiritual enough to not extinguish the other, a woman whose writing is courageous enough to dare to advance in a frightening movement of tearing away from all her being, to the truth of writing it, which is true madness, the madness of truth, the passion of approaching the origin of beings, at the risk of retreating from history.

I was following a woman in danger, freely, a dangerous woman. In danger of writing, in the fullness of writing, in the process of writing it, unto the dangers.

All of the dangers that we encounter on each journey toward the sources. Dangers of error, of falseness, of death, of nullity, of complicity in murder, of blindness, of injustice, of distraction, of hypocrisy. That we fear and that we seek. For we fear the greatest danger which is forgetting to fear.

(Under what conditions, could a woman say, without dying of shame, – what I am able to write this Monday only after three days of a suffocating terror – : "*the love of the orange is political too*" – at what cost?

And this sentence, if I end up by expressing it, on this Iranian day, my soul mingled with the syllables, if I let it be discovered, when I am so afraid of it, I who have not paid the price, first of all it is because it came to me from this woman with an heroic writing, close at hand and awesome as an angel: brilliant and detached.)

She went beyond borders, where the self is self only as a thought of the world and the world is world only with the shining exception of the self. She paid: she had the possibility of paying the price of light, of love. And this very possibility requires also that one begin by knowing its price and discharging it.

"Possibility" is a reserved word, – that doesn't judge. For I do not exactly know the nature of this force of paying: the force of being innocent.

I am not innocent. Innocence is a science of the sublime. And I am only at the very beginning of the apprenticeship. But in front of innocence I am like a young girl in front of the innumerable twinklings of a forest into which she longs to plunge but that she would wish to have caressed leaf by leaf. And as the poet before a mountain as before the promised poetry, driven mad by it but humbly confident in its force of presence.

There is the innocence. There is the radiance of Clarice so close at hand and difficult to approach, to touch. I am not in ignorance or innocence. Its murmuring nearness awakens me at five o'clock in the morning, the echo of its outburst in my night. Bonheur malheur. I am sure of innocence.

But undoubtedly I am still too sure of my insufficiency. I am innocent only at given, fragile moments, that I do not know how to keep, to save, to maintain. A stroke of innocence, coming from an exterior force, carries me off, I am saved, I am no one, detached from me by surprise, the energy has been given to me by the tension of a foreign arc, I have not labored, I have not paid for this voyage, at the very most I have begun to do a few exercises of the imagination. I know the goal but I haven't the knowledge of the ways. Undoubtedly I am not really innocent enough to not accuse myself of being so as soon as I feel myself borne up there. At the most innocent of innocence, at the most joyous, the joy is effaced and I am returned to the pain, to the ground, to mistrust. And I am the one who extinguishes the joy in breathing upon it. I am not humble enough to forgive myself the innocence. Not courageous enough; to stand the terrible gaiety of innocence. My memory is heavy and somber and intimidating.

She had the two courages: that of going to the sources, – to the foreign parts of the self. That of returning, to herself, almost without self, without denying the going. She slipped out of the self, she had that severity, that violent patience, she went out by décollage, by radiance, by laying bare the senses, it requires unclothing sight all the way down to naked sight, it requires removing from sight the looks that surround, shedding the looks that demand, like tears, dis-regarding to arrive at sight without a project, contemplation.

She had the double courage that women alone have when they have followed the course of fear and have descended it down to the desert, and have recognized it unto death, and there have tasted it to return from it, not without fear, but henceforth capable of living fear. Greater than it. The courage to disbelieve, and then the courage to begin to marvelously want to live *before*, before all exploration, before all reason, before god, before all hope. Or after.

They (only women) have gone moving away, until down in the depths of the self, the confinement of the being ceases, there where things remain free, all are equal in vitality, there is no insignificance, at the deepest level, where each being evolves according to its own necessity, following the order of its intimate elements, the level is full of peace of all colors, and they let themselves go in peace, after having undressed in the vestibule, and having paid the price of peace, and they bathe, in the middle of the world, according to the order of the breathing which is the difference of human things. Senses flow, circulate, messages as divinely complicated as the strange microphonetic signals, conveyed to the ears from the blood, tumults, calls, inaudible answers vibrate, mysterious connections are established. It is not impossible in the unrestrained conversing that among disjunct, remote, disproportionate ensembles, at moments, harmonies of incalculable resonance occur.

NOTES

1 The passage on p. 34 lines 7–8 in which she plays on the phonetic similarity in English between "Jew" and "joy" is a good example. [Ed.]
2 "Coming to Writing", translated by Deborah Jenson, in *"Coming to Writing" and Other Essays*, Cambridge, Mass.: Harvard University Press, 1991, p. 2. [Ed.]
3 "The Thing," in *Poetry, Language, Thought*, translated by Albert Hofstadter, New York: Harper & Row, 1975, pp. 165–82. [Ed.]
4 Ibid., p. 170. [Ed.]
5 Ibid. [Ed.]
6 Ibid., p. 181. [Ed.]
7 *Vivre l'Orange/To Live the Orange* (1976), Paris: des femmes, 1979, p. 78. [Ed.]
8 In her published writings and her seminar, Cixous' work prior to 1978 mostly concerned male authors. [Ed.]

(With) Or the Art of Innocence

In (*With*) *Ou l'art de l'innocence* – "(With) Or the Art of Innocence" – published in 1981, Cixous develops a number of the themes expounded in *To Live the Orange*. As in the earlier text, Cixous distinguishes in "(With) Or the Art of Innocence" between those who "chase after" words in order to "crucify" their meaning and those whose language "creates."[1] In the passage translated here, writing, in this creating sense, is deemed vital to living. The author describes her project as "writing you," an endeavor that is beset with difficulties. Language, arising from absence, is a chain of endless substitutions that remove us from the truth. There is the danger that the pre-existent language system will speak (for) us, and that its distortions will annihilate the complex reality of what we express.[2] Although the author cannot fulfil her aim of writing "the book of You," there is insistence in "(With) Or the Art of Innocence" on the positive benefits of the attempt: it is "the most beautiful of all failures." Through writing, the author may circumvent "the torture of the cut" and transgress "the law of silence": writing "approaches," "loves," "reads," "listens," "celebrates," "keeps." It can propel the subject beyond the self-interests of the ego, towards others. As in *To Live the Orange*, the other is heralded as crucial in effecting this self-transformation. The (re)acquisition of "innocence" – recalling the supposedly lost innocence of the biblical paradise prior to prohibition – portrayed here as deriving from an interior knowing "way below the surface of knowledge," and hence preceding self-promoting patterns of thinking and relating, is viewed as intrinsic to the process.

The passage appears on pp. 256–71 of (*With*) *Ou l'art de l'innocence*, Paris: des femmes, 1981, and is translated by Stephanie Flood.

I need writing; I need to surprise myself living: I need to feel myself quiver with living: I need to call myself into living and to answer myself by living: I need to be living in the present of the present: I need double-living: I need to come into life: I am afraid that writing will take the place of living: I need writing thinking of living; I write celebrating living: I need to accompany living with music: I need writing to celebrate living: this morning, I perfumed myself with essence of orange flower water: on the phial of essential oil there is the original label covered with Arabic signs that spirit me away on their sweeping curls to an unknown but imaginable neighborhood in Baghdad: I adore scripts: and the two most beautiful scripts in the world are Hebrew and Arabic, languages I can neither read nor speak, but which speak to my eyes as the voice in your voice, Antouylia, speaks to the ears of my heart: I need to trace the portrait of lives with letters, which do not represent, which are not unfaithful, which are neither faithful nor non-faithful, which conjure up its marvelous and transparent way of reminding us of the source, simply, just as light conjures up the sun: I write clumsy, insufficient, I write French, and I am sad because when I write, I really feel that I only-write, I accompany, but from so far away, I only write with the greatest possible love, but it is only shadow and allusion, not even only of my hand, but already spoken by French, not even of my composition.

All I am trying to say, Antouylia, is perhaps but this:

All the books that I could write revolve around the book that I shall never write, which allows all the others to be written, and this book of books is the book of You.

And in telling you this I am trembling in pain in joy and I am crying in terror, as if I had dared to want to tell god his real name, which is not simply god: for "god" is the word that enables us to avoid speaking to god directly. For ever since the beginning we have guessed that if we ever managed to pronounce just once the true name of God, all the truth dispersed in all languages and all the truth of lives that is concentrated in the body and reserved for love, would shatter in a single breath, just as if god, who ever since the beginning has not spoken to anyone had always made our name resound in His language, and once the true name rang out, all words in all languages would become unusable, so weak, false, bare, impotent, unforgettably merely words, the straw of thought, that we would no longer wish to speak. Yes, I also have guessed that, I myself, and you too, you remember no doubt, but I have never stopped ignoring it. And when I recall having thought it, it is by flash-memories that are so dazzling that I close my eyes and I forget.

Listen Antouylia: I am writing you. I am not writing you, You, I am writing to you. I write only in drifting towards you, in To. I, who cannot even describe the flowers you brought me, and which between them-selves act together with the transparence of the crystal vase, the seven lights visible this morning, the space being shifted by dozens of lines in a sumptuous geometry, I, who cannot even start to describe to you the action of your flowers that make rembrandt together, on the whole of my life. I shall simply say to you: twelve tulips, ten roses, I cannot even say: red, pink, all the reds and all the pinks in the world forbid me. I am shameful and delighted like a painter but I am less unfortunate than a painter as I do not paint. If I were a painter I would go mad on com-pleting each canvas. Does writing make a difference? Hypocritical, but effective. I can never see the end of a book. There is something in the never-endingness of writing it, in the unfurling of paper that spares me the torture of the cut: once suspended in appearance, writing continues. To be present at the framing would cut into my soul. Indeed, I can hardly ever look at a painting without suffering a feeling of mutilation. Am I projecting? I am protecting. I say to myself: writing is painting overboard. You can paint deep too. But the frame hurts my vision.

On all fronts I am cheating and I catch myself cheating.

Telling you is the most minor attempt at loyalty, it is the most elementary form of candor. But can I not suspect in confession a hope for absolution. And that is disloyal. Yet I cannot not tell you. I must methodically disavow what I have said, confession after confession ... whatever I say.

I wonder: when writing, am I transgressing? At first: no answer. Then: why am I asking myself if I am transgressing? If I were transgressing I would know, wouldn't I? I do not know. If I believed that it is a transgression, I would not dare, or would I? I am in uncertain incertitude. Sometimes I think that I believe I am transgressing without knowing it, non-transgressively. And sometimes I think: everything is transgression. And also; nothing is transgression.

Thinking a little to one side, it seems to me that I have just thought in the mirageful region of bad faith. And it also seems to me: my only chance of getting closer to the truth is to take the risk of the forest of falsities. But I will only find that out later.

This morning, I set myself the following problem: suppose there is transgression. What am I transgressing, when writing?

Am I transgressing by writing what I am writing? Or by not writing what I am not writing? Or both?

What law(s) am I transgressing?

At first I answered: yes, to everything, yes, I think so.

I think that one transgresses (1) the law of silence that must be observed in the face of everything that is bigger, more real, more living, more complex etc., in the face of almost everything. In the face of you. In the face of god-things and god-beings. But precisely, I say to myself, there is also the other law, the law of the echo, according to which one should know when it is allowed and when it is necessary to not demand the law of silence. Unfortunately no one can boast of knowing how to demand this law advisedly, neither too often, nor too rarely.

And what I also do not know is from what stage onwards silence must be kept; for one may think there must be writing until the beginning of silence; and also that elsewhere silence keeps itself in any case. For writing will never reveal the secret; and so writing, unless one were to make a mistake, would never transgress? Is it only if the sound of the words distracts us and if we fail to listen to the silence that there is wrong-doing?

So I would not be transgressing in writing what I am writing; but in failing to remember or to insist, in so doing, that writing is a writing only. I write – yet I am not unaware of it: everything that is written runs out of silence and everything is written running out of breath. But silence is not lost; it is kept to one side. But I am not unaware: writing is not an end. I think: I do not write to write, I write to read better: I write a more subtle body than my busy body, the tympan body, I write – I think – ears that are more refined than my ears, that only hear what makes noise, but do not hear what moves, works, speaks, exists incessantly without being noticed, without boasting. I write, have written, to slow down, to approach immersed in writing where everything can listen to everything else infinitely more slowly. But I am not unaware: there are approaches that draw away. Delaying can bring life, death.

I am not unaware but I do not know: here, where I circulate in the dis-orientations of this letter, on non-paths that are not voiceless paths but are almost-without-silences, I am living in non-ignorance, in its mother-of-pearl light of the early day. I am neither in a state of ignorance nor outside, here. I butignore.

But my only really cruel question is that to which I am often tempted to answer candidly yes, but I have never had the courage to do so, thank god. For I have been convinced until now that I would not survive it. And this question is: "should I be silent about you?"

If I have said so little, almost nothing, it is out of desperate caution: I distrust every word and every ear.

I need to tell your true which is infinitely complex, mobile, contradic-tory, taut, unprecedented. I am always a little frightened of not saying this, on account of what remains of my childhood faith: once I thought that the truth must be told. I believed that truth existed, and that it was what-is-said; and I thought that not telling hides a liar. I was always opening my mouth, and I uttered the words that came, but between lips and world all sorts of misfortunes occurred. In truth, I spoke carelessly, credulously, lightly, without calculating the distances to be crossed, nor the deafness, nor the element of mistaken translation, and by telling "the truth" not to the person who had inspired it in me, but to the first ears I encountered. But the last time I dared to speak of you so true thus vast, indefinite, restless, indescribable, overflowing, as softly as possible, to speak of you as honestly thus imprudently large before small I experienced an atrocious pain, as if I had tried to make immobility understand movement or hatred understand love.

I cried with shame. I promised myself I would withdraw, never again throw anything to the lions of a world that hears only the inert, slack line. I hardly ever speak of You now with words coming from my mouth. But I am afraid of silence, I speak of you silently. I say to myself: "be quiet then. And write: nobody will read you in your presence. In your life nobody will not listen to you." I do not know how to be completely silent. I cheat. I say to myself: "Write. When you write, you speak to no one." But I am not unaware: if I write to nobody, it always reaches someone, myself first of all, which does not reassure me. For I need to tell your true, but I am not capable of telling it to myself with enough precision.

I do not know how to speak of you without losing proximity. But I do not know how to not speak of you without giving up an approach. Everything I write is much weaker than you, but so much stronger than myself. Everything I write – only it is: earth revolving around the sun. My dazzled sentences revolve around your existence, I have to write to you with my eyes lowered, my body a little bent, I am writing almost blinded in your light, and I am shading myself with my own words on your hand, I am following you at a great distance, at an astronomical unit from the secret kernel of your reality, the imaginary-ideal distance that separates me from your true is equivalent to the distance between Earth and Sun, but is maintained with the same regularity. It is a long way, yet I cannot revolve around You. May I at least stay within our system, and in time give an idea of you, far away but coming from you personally.

I am a little discouraged: I shall never have the strength nor the time to write something worthy of you. Would I do better to remain silent? I know that in a certain respect it is easier to speak of God than to speak of You. And if one does not want to speak of God, it is permissible to not-speak of God with a perfect and definitive silence. For in any case, every-one has heard of God, even if most people do not even know how to count to one. God is very-famous, and everyone knows that the very being of God is to be unknowable, and everyone can think that God is the infinite whole of not-being-like-a-human-being-could-think-so by going to the extreme extremity of every thought until the point where it turns into its opposite. But I cannot speak of you with the ease that divine mathematics provides, because it is perfectly simple, because absolutely without any relation to me, which is the true benediction. With God, I never risk anything, either mistake, or an aside, or truth, and I do not make him take any risk. It is sometimes a relationship of terrifying albeit imperturbable tranquility. One can say nothing about God. And another way of speaking about God is to say God of him. And one can sum up God in his name that means everything that I do not know that it means.

Yes, one can rely on God to speak about Himself, which is a relief for say-crazy-people like me. About God, one can say everything that is on the scale of impossibility, there is all nothing to say, which is obvious, and impossible but not difficult.

This is really without relation to the torments that bring the need to speak to you absolutely non-absolutely, but absolutely faithfully. It is extremely difficult to speak of you, it is not only because there are things to say, and even more things than about almost any other human being I have ever met, save for one or two abundant creatures. But to say You, humanly infinite, inconclusive, in unforsayable changes, non-eternal, at every instant absolutely present real-virtual, relative, to say you, multi-millionly of you, that goes beyond all the possibilities, even the imaginary ones, of ever producing a successful stroke of writing. Yet I do not have the courage not to write: I write to you, I write myself to you, I fail, but at least it is to your address. I dedicate to you all my wanderings, for which I do not ask you to forgive me. I can say neither nothing nor everything about you, I am doing everything I can to say something that, while it is written in my own sphere, which revolves around myself, might have a chance, by deviating and escaping me, of approaching the edges of your mystery, at least by allusion. I am casting my words in your direction, I entrust them to your power of attraction. I am counting on your charm. My failures are not only failures. By dint of searching for the Indies one ends up by finding the unhoped for. My failures are monuments to your reality. I am unhappy at not being able to honor you better, but it is truly to You that my love devotes itself. I admit also: one day I would like to have the immodesty to have the temerity to do your portrait, face on, without turning to one side myself, completely facing you, I would like to have the humility to have the audacity, I would like one day to have the yes-love bigger than the no-love, then, if I dared, with what jubilation I would say the hundred thousand superb, subtle, surprising things I have known of you, and I would achieve, with what joyous delectation, the most beautiful of all failures.

And why should I delay this? I am still not mature enough, not strong and confident enough, not worked enough to fail well. I shall do it nonetheless, I tell myself, at the last minute a month before my silence or a day before or never. Thenceforth I shall remain silent.

Antouylia says to me: "It is not me. You are imagining me." And she is right. And all the sentences that say "she is" – "I am," "you are," are sentences that are dreaming and playing at being reality. But sad I say to her: "No, it is not you. But thinking towards you and trying to non-understand you as closely to understand you as I could, such a person

thought herself in me. It is not you but she is of you, because of you."
And gay, I find her soul overwhelming with secret understanding.

The mystery is that I do not understand the beings that I love the
most, and that even so that does not prevent me from either loving
them or understanding them: what I do not understand is their own
mystery, which not even they themselves reach. But I know their
incomprehensibility well. Do I know you? No. But I know your strangeness well: what I want to say is that your strangeness does not hurt me,
does not plunge me into darkness. Lyra is like this with regard to Nuriel:
she has never so tranquilly lain in the peaceful strangeness of a person
to whom her destiny is nonetheless bound. But Nuriel entrusts her
strangeness to her which is even more enigmatic to her than to Nuriel
herself.

But you know yourself better than I. You surprise me, you are definitely exotic to me, in twenty years time you will disorient me as always,
I am in no way of the same mystery as you, but I feel it is knowable, made
of a double unknown: the one is gentle and vigorous, with lambs and
lions sleeping in the same secret cradle, which re-astounds me every
evening for I can hear them playing and moving especially in the
evening, and I can also hear the laughter of mythical children and the
murmur of innumerable revelations, but I can also hear groaning, I can
hear the flowing of tears of your secret. I do not know what is said, but
it is said. And the other unknown is so deep and solemn like an oracu-
lar cavern, I am afraid that if I venture in I shall find out about it what I
am afraid of no longer not ignoring.

But the feared truth is perhaps that it is not only difficult to speak of
you, Antouylia, but absolutely non-possible to speak entirely simply
of you. For I can speak of you in an epic register and in a lyrical register,
and also in a Shakespearian fairytale, comedy register, but for all that
concerns your humanity, I am not allowed to, even an allusion fills me
with holy horror, I shall never sacrilege you. I have a dreamy, evasive
humanity that is too pusillanimous ever to be worthy of giving an account
of your obstinately, dangerously real humanity.

Humanity maintained and non-denied moreover always puts all words
to shame.

Here, you alone, Antouylia is the bearable witness of yourself.

(2) I pass on to the rest of my problem:

When writing, am I transgressing the law of presence that must be kept
out of the reach of absence as much as possible?

"I never know."

You say to me "There is presence. It is here. There is absence. It is not here. It is not where I am ... I always live in a presence where there is no absence. I am in my body that knows."

But me: "Presence comes and goes. It gets up, it answers the call of another presence that speaks to it at the other end of the country. Presence moves, leaps, finds." I say: "And what about absence, lapsence?" You say to me on the telephone: "love and kisses."
And I, kissed, I say: "what an instrument the telephone is! What an angel!"
And you in your body, you say: "What a demon!"

But is your voice an absence? It is very difficult for me to unravel the absences from the presences. I am not really sure where absence begins. Perhaps part of my body is only imagined? Some apparent absences seem to me to be the beginnings or the continuations of presences or pre-presences.

Am I bypassing a presence by the telephone call?

I do not think so. Moreover, it is not the telephone that interests me, I am not bothered about the line (I think; one can never swear); nor to the thing with or without a line. Lyra thinks that the relation to the telephone signifies the relation to the mother. What I like is the magic of the telephone. One doesn't need to be far away to take pleasure in it. And it is listening to the most profound voice coming, and letting it reach the most profound in the body.

Telephoning does not mean speaking from a distance; on the contrary: it is speaking to the depths of the very, very close, of one interior to another, with one's voice really disarmed, from one innocence to another, without mediation.

I like telephoning you from nearby without a telephone: closing my eyes is all I need to do. One telephones best at night, of course, when the whole world has closed its eyes. Then it is so dark that one's inner eyes are free, one can even hear the stars turning over in the sky, and one can hear voices, as they come out of the depths of interior seas, damp and naked. And things that could not be said in the distance near to the morning, striated with multicolored rags, start to be able to be said – for it is the eyes of the day that prevent intimate thoughts from being said – but the things that remain in a formless place, way below the surface of knowledge, so deeply buried underneath non-knowledge that we did not know they would ever exist, begin to find a present in the telephoning blackness. All these thoughts listened to so interiorly are sprouting, it's a springtime, and they are brilliant jade green in color, like truth in a dream recalling the pre-past.

Thus I am writing with my eyes closed, to telephone what would otherwise not come to my lips.

And I exist differently, more slowly. I forget to look or I no longer take in what I can see outside. And perhaps I am bypassing that reality? I seem to bypass from one kind of reality to another, in this passage, I can go without simple or elaborate food. I must reproach myself for this uncontrollable taste for the almost nothing I then have: I myself feel the violence there is in needing only paper and light for days on end. And I who am so easily captivated by a passion for clothes, I find myself willingly wearing any old thing: I wipe everything out, I wipe out me. To need nothing is the ultimate indulgence. It is the greatest fault, I say to myself. It cannot last, I offer to myself by way of excuse.

But I continue. Indulgent egoist, I say to myself distractedly. But when yesterday *you* yourself called me an indulgent egoist I writhed around like a fish trapped in a net. I was caught: I do not hear the same words coming from my voice and from your voice in the same ear. I put something into my voice, no doubt, a mute? So that in accusing myself, I excuse myself too.

But then, I allow myself to be caught. I do not make flight easy for myself. I run away but I catch myself again. If only I could cheat successfully, I say to myself. Fool myself. Make myself innocent!

A vain wish. When one cheats, one never fools oneself.

My soul is weary, Antouylia. I cannot wish that one should pardon me for what I cannot wish to pardon myself. But even so I cannot not wish for this. I believe: I am no more and no less guilty than the next person, but I am much more unpardonable. There is a fault. I am victim to a fatal inevitability. Whatever I say about it, however much I deny it, I can feel it and it is: excess, it is indulgence. I am suffering from indulgence. I would so much like to be pardoned for my inevitable pleasures: I am indulgent.

The idea that I could be pardoned for being so rich in pleasures makes me smile in a joy that trembles with apprehension: but then, what terror! I am well aware that I am not magnanimous enough to envisage such great grace without horror. I do not have the strength to take pleasure in the open, unshaded.

What should be thought of so many horrors? Am I condemned to condemn myself in an endless disagreement? To feel my debt increase each year?

Or else:

I am guilty of not bearing my non-innocence. I begrudge doing unpleasant things to myself. Even in the depths of misfortune I cannot bypass happiness. But there is nothing that I desire and that I forbid myself as much as peaceful happiness.

"Fortunately," I say to myself, "I have my law."

"Is there law? But is that not, precisely, my supreme indulgence? My most perverse trick? It is true that sometimes in writing to you I reach such regions of jubilation that I burst out laughing, as if you have just escaped a fatal accident. But the air in these regions is tinged with anxiety. I never reach pure jubilation. Fortunately, for the non-anxiety in these regions would cause me the worst anguish. Because I want to reach them, but not to stay there: as soon as I get there, I can only think of one thing, of calling you, of inviting you, of telling you. I cannot bear discovering all alone. I need you. What is part of the heart-rending happiness that fills me in these regions is experiencing human limits there: I am happy to feel to what point happiness in solitude is painful: to me it is intolerable. Without you being with me, me without you near to me to take pleasure in me, jubilation burns me like ice on the chest. I call out, mute with emotion: if I have grown distant from you by writing to you, it was to write you. Growing distant propels me towards you. From the furthest point in me I am crying out: I am writing towards you!"

I am cold. I am singing voicelessly: *il duol mio dir non posso, in quest'ora funeste.* This hour of felicity is deadly to me. I am writing to go beyond myself; but what anguish if I succeed. Far away from myself. I can only bear this anguish if you will please take me in your arms.

NOTES

1   See (*With*) *Ou l'art de l'innocence*, Paris: des femmes, 1981, pp. 8–9. It is noteworthy that there are two words to denote language in French: *la langue* (feminine gender) and *le langage* (masculine gender). The feminine possibilities of 'la langue' are played on throughout the text. [Ed.]

2   Jacques Derrida's work on language provides an interesting explanation of these points. See, for a discussion of this aspect of Derrida's work, Susan Sellers, *Language and Sexual Difference: Feminist Writing in France*, Basingstoke: Macmillan, and New York: St Martin's Press, 1991, pp. 20–1 and pp. 132–5. [Ed.]

Lemonade Everything Was So Infinite

Limonade tout était si infini – 'Lemonade Everything Was So Infinite' – published in 1982, takes its title from one of the phrases written by the dying Kafka. In the first of two passages translated here, the feminine subject strives to write a "love letter" that will communicate her "joy of feeling herself exist thanks to her." The word "thanks" – *merci* – becomes a figure for this endeavor. Like language generally, the meaning of *merci* has become debased, and is dependent for its value on the "soul" the writer can "breathe into it."

As in *To Live the Orange*, the question of the writer's responsibility is again posed in the context of history, presented here in terms of a war waged by the "men-men" to protect their domain from difference and "all women of the feminine gender." The letter is thus also "an antiwar letter"; love, in these "dire political circumstances," is insufficient to resist the "Great Logic of Destructions." Evoking the references to paradise in earlier texts, this is here depicted as a state human beings must continually strive for: "with what tenderness, with what fierceness we have to work every day in order to re-attach living importance to the very delicate things which we are constantly torn away from by the forces of war." Writing, with its capacity to inscribe the forbidden and forgotten, is portrayed as a powerful ally in this struggle.

The passage is from pp. 66–79 of *Limonade tout était si infini*, and is translated by Ann Liddle.

"Merci"[1] ... sighed the letter. "Merci for existing." And having started to celebrate, nearly stopped writing itself,[2] being carried away as it was by the soaring of the voice. But then it rejoiced at having been started by this word. Because it was this word that had come to alight there fluttering with self-evidence, surely coming from her. Merci she wrote, as a voice whispered it to her silently. Merci! she read aloud, enchanted. Merci was a beautiful name. Thought that it had alighted there on her lettersill to incite her, on her behalf, indicated the intonation to her: write me in the key of C.[3] How she loved this word!

Then the letter wrote itself in a flurry circling around its starting point. For everything that she had to say in the end came back to this word.

She described a large curve, saying: "I need to tell you today for the thousandth time as if for the first time: I am so happy to be a woman, bless you, you through whom I've received the news for the thousandth first time."

And humbly, but with all of her gravity, with all of her weight, calligraphed the letters of the name of joy, with a religious intensity, putting, she hoped, some spiritual breath into every stroke, her whole being humbly concentrated engraved a merci which she wanted to be finely wrought, magical, pneumatic. O, be a bird, be a smile, she ordered, be a caress in the hand of my friend, she wished with all of her might, concentrating so hard that, if magic exists, then this merci would truly be animated.

Then she wrote a bit lower, to clarify what she wanted "merci" to say. Knowing that it's a word that turns up everywhere and that there are as many thousands of species of it as there are of butterflies, and its whole value obviously depends on the soul that one breathes into it. But only needed a minimum of words, thank god, for in this case god was Elli herself, and she would know how to hear it exactly there where she'd said it, very high up, in an irridescent yellow soprano tonality. (Sometimes too when the full moon was so wonderfully perfect that one could divine everything about the origin of sculpture, she had called her[4] merci: all of a sudden, she had shot forth a full staff of notes at her from the depths of the world.)

"Merci," she said, "for being the way you are so that I can announce the essential to you."

(Because every day the mystery of living occurs with its innumerable questions. But only occurs for those who remain in the region of mysteries. A region so troubling, excessively rich, almost untenable. Because it is difficult for us to bear the riches of life. And to live the truly essential life is too great a joy to confront all alone. To live the inexhaustible vitality of the truly important life is humanly exhausting. And if you weren't there to help me enjoy it, living would be unbearable.)

"Merci for always living in the regions of origins. Because in these regions the word merci is the key for the music of births."

Tried to write an almost transparent love letter, having no other reason for writing a letter than to underscore with a fine black border love itself. Since the only news that she hadn't announced was the fact that she had just experienced for the first thousandth time the near painful joy of feeling herself exist thanks to her. Since talking together for hours every day voice to voice, they gave each other regular reports on all the events taking place abroad as well as on the domestic scene. And together wove answers, made forecasts, placed and displaced forces, each allying her own with the other's, on the map of the world.

And thus wanted to believe that the letter was necessary: the one she would write even if they were in the same city and on the same street and in the same house, because there would be one single thing which couldn't be said as well in the air as on paper: and this thing was the infinitesimal, the infinitely fragile trembling of the soul perceiving the miracle, which was infinitely profound and rapid and musical but for the moment inaudible, of feeling oneself being brought into the world moment after moment; it was the joyful awareness of being alive, of being in the process of being alive which was like the musical accompaniment of each moment of their togetherness. But in fact there were times, during a pause in the dialogue which was like a microscopic diurnal night suddenly occurring between two broad daylights, when it seemed to her that she could perceive the buzzing of this excitement. As if she could hear her own blood throbbing: "thank goodness! thank goodness!" against the walls of her veins. Then, naturally, this joy increases algebraically as you become aware of it, and then you think about it, and it intensifies, rising to the fourth power. But when you reach the fourth root of the joy, its power is so fine, it modifies your breathing, you breathe four times faster and you laugh without knowing why. Because to be living when it's multiplied by living makes you laugh. But while you're existing, because of the noise of the times and because of the speed at which one must drive nowadays to keep up with the times, it's difficult to raise the joy beyond the square root; because to do so you have to stop: you can only hear the joy growing beneath several layers of silence.

So wanted to write the little letter of four silences which she would send to her right in broad daylight, right in her presence, if by misfortune, even though they were together in the same house, they were once again beseiged and bombarded all day long. And this letter would begin with "listen . . ." It would be magical, it would play a little melody of peace right in the midst of the cacophony, she encouraged herself. "Even if there was a war going on, especially because of the war."

Encouraged herself to think with some resistance, half cautious, half fearful. For she had all sorts of mixed feelings about this question-of-war. Some of them were probably false, but given their number and the confusion that reigned among them, she was unable to form an opinion that would appear frankly clear to her. The only "clear" point about this question was that she never had a spontaneous desire to talk about it. That was the first question: And was it right to talk about it? and if so how, in what way, under what conditions could such a subject be talked about rightly? But, asked a second question, "didn't talking about it really amount to evoking it. And doesn't evoking it amount to recalling it? And when does one recall war if not when it has allowed itself to be forgotten a little? By evoking it, isn't one clumsily playing right into its hands? Isn't one in a certain way making war on oneself by giving one's own peace a warning?" Whereupon the two questions became involved in an endless palaver, everything got confused, neither one got a decisive answer; and if she gave the advantage to the first one at times it wasn't as a result of a convincing analysis, no, it was a choice whose motivations were of a moral order: in accordance with an ancient law of severity, she always took sides with whatever it was that she caught herself fleeing from. Perhaps this was a mistake. But it seemed to her that if she were mistaken, at least she couldn't reproach herself for having erred out of complacency. Having as a motto: "to be my best adversary."

Now she had often caught herself avoiding this question for long periods of time. Sometimes wasn't even aware of it. Especially in the summer. Because in the summer, this kind of war simulates tactical effacements. In order to let a false peace form again. Once she had even managed to write a whole book without thinking about it. And the result was an oriental garden, which she loved, but which was so timeless that it was rarely the right time to go there. She had no regrets. Either about having created it. Or about not having the chance to return there. Was happy to have been able just once to lose the presence of reality enough to sleep-walk as far as a premoral garden. And then, at the end of the book, she had learned a secret from it: which is that "having" paradise isn't impossible; because "being in paradise" doesn't mean having your residence there; it means knowing that you can return there. Even during a war.

Because it was only in the beginning that paradise was a garden with a precise address. But ever since, it can take place anywhere, at any moment, we have to work and struggle to let it take place. It's a state of joy which prolongs itself throughout the whole life of those people who have the strength to be wild, women for the most part.

Very near and very hard to approach in reality. Because it's not paradise that one loses; it's the desire to be there, which war succeeds in making us forget. For the state of being-in-paradise, which seems so simple when one is there, this state requires the first great intelligence, the kind that thinks and understands on the other side of forgetfulness and of things neglected by thought, before any absent-mindedness; requires the ultrasensitive intelligence of proximities; capable of discovering the treasures of life lying in store under the window, within our reach, within our embrace; requires the first, the prime intelligence, the universal, the very-fragile kind, with its very broad, feathery antennae covered with sensory cells which enable it to detect the sources of the very great joys that are quivering in the immediate invisibility. But war stuns it, deafens it, war makes its stupidity reign over the world. Power is given to the forbidden over everything capable of feeling.

And nevertheless we feel. With what tenderness, with what fierceness we have to work every day in order to reattach living importance to the very delicate things which we are constantly torn away from by the forces of war.

"Merci," she wrote. Merci was one of the words that had been reduced to mere wind in the world which was ruled by theft and ingratitude. "Merci for being," she added to be more precise. Hoping that the word "being" which was also worn out, skeleton-like, would take on some color again, in this syntax. She applied herself to the task of writing an antiwar letter, like this: thinking very hard about every word, bearing down on each word with all of her angers in order to transfuse them into it.

Thus she got to the point of thinking that she was going to give this love letter a graver emphasis than she had planned.

Since in these dire political circumstances, it was right not to be content just to love, but to arm love as well. Which stood to reason moreover. For a person well loved is a person well armed.

Because war will never stop them from living. But robs them of the rich hours of silence and immobility. With its boorish sounds blurs the refined ultrasounds of joy. Because one of the objectives of modern warfare is the development of unbelievably perfected, in other words perverse, psychological weapons: being a war of the nullification of women and similar beings, but not of liquidation; being a shameful but global, methodical war; being undeclared but public, state-sponsored, transcultural; being a hypocritical war, the first great war for the voluntary devaluation of civilizations; being a war aimed at weakening and reducing half of the world, and at enslaving nine tenths of the other half of the world,

And the modernity of this war being defined precisely

– by the dissimulation of its murderous power beneath civil, non-bellicose outward appearances

– above all, in a basely inventive way, by the utilization of means of aggression which are strictly insidious, invisible, inaudible, and which have a radical force of destruction hitherto never attained; because acting down at the deepest levels, having as targets beings with souls, being able to annihilate entire populations without ever seeming to touch them. By suppressing the zones of sensitivity. By deafening, debasing, besotting; by replacing the entire system of education with a network of tunnels, without any light full of trains that don't run but that seem to be running, with a national system of underground channels; by the total foreclosure of all evidence of libidinal, sexual, cultural difference; for nothing is more efficacious than state-perpetrated denial; because the yellow star was, in spite of everything, a recognition, for death, but was a star, was Jewish, was an affirmation, was a condemnation but was from the point of view of eternity an admission; but the New War plunges all women of the feminine gender into the night without any stars, holds their heads under darkness, until they go blind. And in the end, we may find ourselves wondering whether we've ever existed; we have to ask ourselves whether we didn't just dream ourselves up. We have to ask ourselves whether "women" aren't just imaginary. Their existence being more difficult to prove to the world than God's. Were perhaps just an idea, not even an innate one at that? Because of the blotting out of all traces in the external world. But to the would-be or so-called women is left the reserve of Psychosis, which lies between the Old and the New World.

– by its supranational, and supramilitary, supraracial extent, this war being superior to all other wars in that it has the unanimous support of all the peoples who appear to be the most violently opposed, in that it secretly reconciles colors, religions, classes, continents, the truly toxic powers, the model monsters and the mimetic states, in the ardor of a single common hostility; which is why it must be kept relatively secret: because in this war all the men-men would risk finding themselves on the same side; would be in a disastrously fraternal alliance; for would be threatened with having to abandon all of their regional microwars, or with having to limit them, thus would lose all their wars without which cannot enjoy living; for the men-men need to bite to make sure they've got teeth; need to show their teeth to their fellow men-men in order to prove that they've got 'em; need to wall themselves in, to shelter themselves in order to keep well away from each other; need to have borders; need to have wars to keep at a distance for are afraid of touching; but this war, if it were to come out in the open and spread, would reveal itself as the true new catholicism. And then might very well find themselves side by side, in a single dangerously posthistoric worldwide pack; would then see themselves as they are, with their clothes off, quite simply part of the human race, vertical beings of the male sex, at once all alike and all different, but all of them too much alike and too different, differently, unequally, indefinitely different in the same line of affiliation, would then see themselves terribly naked as one-single-man, an absolutely terrifying state of affairs because there would be billions of them. Would be billions of times more naked, more vulnerable, more solitary. For being naked was already too much for Adam, when he was the only man to be seen by one single woman. But had already ceased to be naked – before a woman by the time the second generation came along. So to avoid going mad from resemblance, would become fratricidal, would pit themselves against one another, and there would be billions of wars. Which is why this war must be waged in secret far away from the little international wars. For it's the same with the human race as with the other animal species: Everything in nature is ordered by the Great Logic of Destructions, was what she'd been forced to learn in the books. That's how it was: one species destroys a species which destroys another species which destroys another species. This is how, from destruction to destruction, life is protected. Had re-read, but something of the logic of this logic had always escaped her. Had trouble understanding how any life could come out of the chain of death. Was it still even life? Deep down inside, she had obscurely avoided understanding this lesson. Knew, incomprehensibly, that every destruction was necessary for a survival, and one always owed a life to a death, and destroying a destructive species led to the destruction of another species, and it seemed that there was really no hope of ever breaking the chain, because if you destroyed a species that was harmful to another species, you gave this species unlimited power to destroy the next species, and thus you could never save on one side without doubly destroying on the other, and once you started there was no stopping, then you were forced to go back along the chain of destructions, you would never be able to stop destroying, from the moment that you were tempted to save, an evil spell was cast over the chain, which was compelling and binding, all of the gestures divided and reversed themselves if you attempted to interfere. And could one hope to destroy the whole series of destructions, in one's own lifetime?

She had nearly been driven to despair with fatigue every time she'd attempted, merely in thought, to find the weak link in the chain. And what she saw very clearly at the end of her chain was the sum of destructions but couldn't quite see the sum of lives that came out of it. And what she couldn't seem to imagine was the beginning. Had everything begun with life or with destruction? For what she couldn't seem to make herself think about was death: could neither think that there was any death on the first day; nor that death could have had a beginning; for her the birth of death was absolutely unthinkable. And when she got to this point in her effort to think about Logic, she was nearly gasping for breath, the idea that life could give life to death and that death could give life, gave her an impression of madness, which was quite pleasant. She laughed and relaxed before going on with her steep uphill thinking, unsure of her footing, but driven on by an irresistible urge to take her chances. And perhaps her own rule was to go on existing from thought to thought, in a chain which would only make sense later on? Indeed each of her thoughts passed over another or pushed another aside while advancing.

"It will never end" she said to herself all of a sudden; and this time, this phrase which would have frightened her at another moment, filled her with pleasure. Came bursting out like a wedding announcement.

She wrote, with her eyes nearly closed to wish better. And made the wish: that this letter might be as reassuring to receive as a little bit of memory in the midst of oblivion.

In the second passage translated here from "Lemonade Everything Was So Infinite," writing's potential to inscribe the living moment is explored in an endeavor to write the "last" book. Recalling Franz Kafka's "last" writings[5] – referenced here in the simple initial "F" – this is envisioned as a book in which "action consists of the essential: living, loving. Knowing that one's going to die: all that remains is living." Echoing Cixous' delineations of a feminine writing, it will be a book in which the self is involved without pre-domination,[6] free from "habits, obligations, proprieties. Terror." Its aim is salvation, its style "unadorned" by any attempt to seduce. Unlike those works of art which are the products of ambition,[7] it will be a "work of being" in which each phrase testifies to the long and passionate "apprenticeship to be human."[8]

The passage is from pp. 260–4 of *Limonade tout était si infini*, and is translated by Ann Liddle.

Thus, it was in the suffering of measuring herself with the so-much-more-delicate, and of wanting to live as close as possible to what she would never understand with thoughts, and of wanting to say what was so-much-more-vivid than words, it was in the suffering and the discordance of *divining the god*, that she began to scribble rather than to write down in notebooks the first pantings of a kind of "diary of delicateness," partly in order to quell her anxiety, to confide to herself a little of this suffering which she didn't want to refuse. And partly too in order to preserve her shame in writing.

– "On this Saturday the first – as an exercise in humility, I admit: I would like to write the ultimate-book.

I'm a little bit sad because I would like to be able to write an ultimate-book right now. Before the end? But I believe it's impossible?

Why do I need to write the last book? Not the book of the end. Not the book of a dying woman. No but the "last" one.

I can imagine it: a book of human-phrases: phrases that can be contained in a breath. Breathed in, breathed out; no more, otherwise are phrases written for the eyes ...

I want the phrases to breathe with confidence: if addressed to the loving being, don't need to seduce, need no explanation.

Painfully the question of the degree of ultimacy of books: why not always write "last" book? I believe it's forbidden? It is forbidden – Fear?

Write an Ultimate, then, and hide It in a book?

(Perhaps this whole book to hide *the* phrase ...)

Why? Because book-of-last-day cannot lie: no time. Each phrase the truest one possible. The most immediate. Most necessary. Illusion?

All of F's works for the last phrases.

Without any drama? Without any plot. The essential drama: living.

Action consists of the essential: living, loving. Knowing that one's going to die: all that remains is living.

Not forgetting doesn't mean not forgetting oneself. Means forgetting oneself just enough. No more self.

Nostalgia for the total vocation. I am forever betraying: writing with life. Life with writing. Shame.

I am afraid to write the last book. I want to write the last book that would not be the last one. I want, and need to write this.

As a way of forgiving myself for not.

Only the last one is elegant.

Elegance of a grasshopper: elegance of F.[9] Ethereal slenderness.

Because one is in another economy. Totally free?

Last one: one is no longer concerned with false elegancies of politeness.

That day such concern for life! Telegraphical. Perpetual need to save.

De-hierarchized: at past permitted! One can be as concerned with a swallow as with a war. Even more so.

A whole book of phrases? A book always at least partly literature. Write beyond literature?

Can I? If I were sure? I wouldn't write anymore. Until the last day.

I want: the book of freed moments. (Those free of habits, obligations, proprieties. Terror. Terrible freedom.)

Bird-phrases – spring forth without any warning, without really starting; already sailing along, full speed. What falls away: articles first. Strange: names remain, at full speed.

It is a book where each phrase is a moment. Each one complete and necessary. Each one self-reliant: completes its work without leaving it up to the following phrase. As if nobody knew whether another would follow.

So each one of them at once modest, urgent, respectful, unreserved. Extremely simple, the most difficult thing: a phrase that doesn't resemble a phrase.

Getting to the essential, there are times when can't get there without going through the non-essential which hides it.

But often obstacles barring the way are fallacious: afraid simple words will displease?

So difficult to unadorn. Habit. Have to unlearn. Learn to say necessarily: mathematically, which is to say "elegant solution." God is "elegant." First nature elegance.

Ultimate-book would be unadorned, which doesn't mean ungraceful.
Each phrase full and slender: *belle demoiselle*.[10]
Will be called: *Espérance*.[11] (Elegance of words ending in ance: unexplainable? Because open sound, continues, accords: which is why the word "silence" is so disturbing ...)[12]
Free book,[13] not subject to judgement. Absolutely non-subjugated, neither insubordinate, nor provocative. Alluring as the mystery of a child's enjoyment: internal. Wild book. Initiate *of life*.
Written in a safe place. Before love.[14]
Room book, at the same time unlimited.
So would be unbound and free. Even from being a book.

NOTES

1 Here and elsewhere in the text, I have kept the French word *merci*, not only because there is no equivalent for it in English (i.e. no *one* word which can mean either "thank you" or "mercy," and which contains no address, no "you"), but also because it is indeed "a beautiful name," light as a butterfly, and rich in meaning and musicality, which Hélène Cixous exploits to the full. Thus, for example: with *mer*, we can hear *mer* ("sea") and *mère* ("mother"); with *ci*, we can hear *si*, with its multiple meanings ("so," as in the title of the text; emphatic "yes"; "if"; the musical note and key: "ti" in the "Do" system, and "B"). [Trans.]

2 "nearly stopped writing itself": in a characteristic form of wordplay, Hélène Cixous exploits the fact that in French both "the letter" (*la lettre*) and the writing subject are feminine, to create a merging between the two, an ambiguity, which is lost in English where we are obliged to choose *either* the neuter ("it," "itself") *or* the feminine ("she," "herself"). [Trans.]

3 "write me in the key of C" (*écris-moi en clé de si*): here, I have substituted 'C' for 'B' or 'ti' in order to play on "sea"/"see" and on the *ci* of *merci* (see note 1 above). [Trans.]

4 "she had called her": in French "the moon" (*la lune*) is feminine. [Trans.]

5 See Franz Kafka, "Conversation Slips," in *Letters to Friends, Family and Editors*, translated by Richard and Clare Winston, New York: Schocken Books, 1978. [Ed.]

6 The subject is often absent from the text, as is exemplified in the two passages translated here. [Ed.]

7 See p. 189 of *Limonade tout était si infini*, Paris: des femmes, 1982; also p. 192 where such works are described as "works of prey." [Ed.]

8 See ibid., p. 189. [Ed.]

9 There is a play here on the French word *élégance*, whose suffix *ance* (pronounced ãs) we can hear echoed in the name evoked by the initial *F*: *Franz* (the first name of Kafka). [Trans.]

10 I have kept the French here because of the play on the double meaning of the word *demoiselle* ("damsel," "young lady" or "noblewoman," "maiden"; and "damsel-fly"), and because of the insistence of the feminine *elle* (which here appears as a feminine suffix, but which, as a pronoun, means "she" or "her"; it is also a homophone of the feminine noun *aile*: "wing"). [Trans.]

11 Here, Hélène Cixous is playing on the fact that in Brazilian Portuguese (the language of Clarice Lispector), the same word (*esperança*) can signify either "hope," "expectation," as in French, or a tiny green winged insect. [Trans.]

12 In French the suffix of "silence" (ence) is pronounced like *ance* (ãs). [Trans.]

13 In the French the two words *livre libre* are near homophones. [Trans.]

14 "Before love": here, the French word is *devant* (preposition and adverb), which means "before" in the spatial sense only (i.e. "in front of," "in the presence of," "facing"). [Trans.]

The Book of Promethea

From the late 1970s on, Cixous' fiction moves away from a preoccupation with the difficulties of self-expression to exploration of alternative modes of relating to others in which an enabling, egalitarian and respectful love is the key motivating element.[1] In *Le Livre de Promethea – The Book of Promethea* – published in 1983, the author's endeavor to discover and communicate different forms of perception, relation and representation produce a text that fulfils many of Cixous' delineations for a feminine writing. Recalling the love letter of "Lemonade Everything Was So Infinite," *The Book of Promethea* is to be "a book of love," in which Promethea herself, rather than any narrative or intention of the author, is the source of writing. The author is not, however, the passive recipient of this source: she must work at her relationship with Promethea as she must struggle with the process of writing. Inscribing the love relation with Promethea is deemed vital since there is the possibility that through this means the love might be shared and "others can see which way to venture." This gift of the text is validated as, in a humorous reworking of the earlier figures of "inside" and "outside," the author describes her reluctance to leave the "silky womb" of the love relation and "invent the tiniest slip of golden thread to hoist outside as a sign."

Writing is both the ally of the author's endeavor and her adversary. Writing can carry the author away from the truth; it can invent, lie, wound and kill. The author must remain open to the shifts and contradictions her position entails, figured here in a splitting of the writing position between "I" and "H." The creation of this dual position circumvents any temptation to mastery, reflecting the slippages and difficulties implicit in the task of relating to an/other and the inscription of this relation through the other of writing.

The passage is from *The Book of Promethea*, translated by Betsy Wing, Lincoln: University of Nebraska Press, 1991, pp. 13–22. The French reference is pp. 20–30 of *Le Livre de Promethea*, Paris: Gallimard, 1983.

I am having trouble with this book. But this book has none with itself, and none with Promethea.

Why am I afraid? Because this is a Children's book. Capital C Children. Big Children. Of every age, type, or race.

Because it is a book of love. Sometimes I call it the Book of Rages. It is a raging book. One must leap in. Once in the fire one is bathed in sweetness.

Because it is a book about now ... to read for no reason. Without asking: "then what? what happens at the end?" Because there is no ending.

Because it is a fearless book. Besides, that is what makes it impossible for H to have written it alone. Nor could I have.

Besides it is Promethea's book. It is the book Promethea lit like a fire in H's soul.

Promethea does not understand why I let H in here, when the book was already so lush in bloom around us. I do not know how to explain. I had no choice. There are moments when I am H. I do not really want to be. I am just trying not to stop the flow of the text, even if I have almost passed out with passion.

But the one passing out the most is H.

I said this book is entirely internal. When the author that I am feels the need to build a circumferential or a scaffolding or to weave a silken tent, it is perhaps not to her credit.

Promethea is my heroine.

But the question of writing is my adversary.

Promethea is the heroine of my life, of my imagination, of my book.

I am her champion. I fight for her, to make her right – her reality, her presence, her grandeur – prevail.

I am armed with love and care. Which is not enough.

Sometimes I need to add writing as well. Promethea is so tall. Writing helps me. I climb on her.

But writing then immediately demands to be paid, and I am not exactly sure what this payment should be.

Strange things happen: I write to come close to Promethea; I seek her better, more slowly, more closely, more deeply. But then I begin to lose the surface, the simplicity and light.

That is serious.

It can go far. It can go too far.

Other strange things happen: each page I write could be the first page of the book. Each page is completely entitled to be the first page. How is this possible?

Because this is a day-by-day book, each day, the one happening now, is the most important day. For each day I need all time.

Because we are in eternity.

We. Promethea, me, the author, H, you and you, whoever wants, whoever loves us, whoever loves.

This whole book is composed of first pages.

For the author that is serious.

Sometimes, also, it is troublesome and painful. It gives me a headache: I would like Promethea to pick a page to be first, the way one picks up a shell on the beach.

The miracle: I have noticed that I can say almost nothing about Promethea in her absence. Because, in her absence, she is really absent. And what I live then is: absence-of-Promethea. I see her dimmed by absence. Nothing can make her radiant again. I am loath to make her up by applying words.

To talk about her I need her, and not her image, close by. I need to open the window and call her with my voice. I am afraid, when she is not there, that writing will carry me away, far from her, far from myself, far from writing, far from truth.

This miracle is also a nuisance. After all, I can't just write from life, can I?

Is that not what I always do? Write on what is alive? But up to now I thought of myself as writing on paper. Sometimes the paper was thick enough, in fact, for me not to feel the blood flowing under the skin, under the paper.

I open my notebook, I open the window, I call, and my heroine is there, really. I am overwhelmed.

I warn her: "I am writing on you, Promethea, run away, escape. I am afraid to write you, I am going to hurt you!"

But rather than run away, she comes at a gallop. Through the window she comes, breathing hard, and alive as can be, she flings herself into the book, and there are bursts of laughter and splashes of water everywhere, on my notebook, on the table, on my hands, on our bodies.

Which is why I said: it is a book completely in the present. It began to be written the moment the present began – long before I understood that a book was being made. I have been out of my depth ever since. Am I maybe trying now to bring it back to familiar shores? Is that why Promethea disapproves of me? She thinks it is beautiful the way it is. But I am afraid of this beauty. I am afraid to be right. I am also afraid that she is right. I am so torn that I wake up in the morning my shoulders racked.

The question driving me mad is: how can one manage to be simultaneously inside and outside?

I want to avoid tricks. I am certainly aware that I frighten Promethea when I let myself go on talking in two voices (actually only one of the two speaks audibly, the other is unheard-of). I am trying to put myself in Promethea's place. How would I feel if I thought she was two living persons? I don't know. With my extendable soul, with my person-plus-shadow, I have trouble putting myself in the place of someone who is of the magnitude of one, even if her size, the scale of her soul, her height, is that of a people in its combined forces. Promethea is a people. I am the one who is only two, one of them a shadow.

So, is H my shadow? I don't know that either. I take her to be my shadow, but certain people feel I am her shadow. So does that make me the shadow of my shadow? I can see how that might be disagreeable. When you love a person, you don't love her shadow.

But I could say H is my night person. She is more willing to be sub-merged than I. She lets herself become a little impersonal, whereas I am afraid of getting lost. I prefer being on the mare's back rather than in the cave she came from, where the earliest musics echo. But H is all set to venture into my Paleolithic, all the way into the Chamber of Mares. When it is too dark down the Shaft where H is dreaming, like now, and if, nonetheless, one wants to hear the music, one must take along the rosy stoneware lamp where little twigs of juniper burn, lighting up the Cave of the Soul to a depth of fifteen thousand years.

Thoughts build up like tears in H's breast – she is not awake, but she is not sleeping: she floats, hardly moving, not far from the edges of this text where she lies soaking – her thoughts have the same mellow salty taste as the glowing liquid that fills the nearly spherical membrane of this "story." . . .

I lay my face on H's breast. I hear tears trickling down the walls of the Chamber. It smells good: she must be dreaming of the mare's flanks. Each time the mare goes past in a dream, you can tell because of this odor that fills the night. Today just like fifteen thousand years ago. Today fifteen thousand years ago.

I hear:

H: "Now here I am . . ."

(Listen, Promethea, this is the first line of one of the first pages of the book inside. Therefore, H must be somewhere in the Hall. The inner book is laid out astonishingly like the site of Lascaux. Promethea is the one who discovered that. The same division into three principle cham-bers or chapters and galleries corresponding to the eight epochs. But in all of them one finds frescoes in the Magdalenian style characterized by its free drawing, the action-filled bodies, and the aura of eternity mark-ing all the scenes caught in their stunning, momentary immediacy. Wait:

I still have something to say about why H needs to be in this text. H comes slightly before me; she dates from my personal antiquity, she is thus both older and younger than I. From the point of view of my subjective archaeology, she is situated in the preconscious, in a rather childish state of receptivity: she is preceded by the world. Yes. The world comes first, she is plunged into it, it cradles her, lashes her, laps at her, and she perceives, perceives. A female embryo that is at the center of life, she hears all, feels all, yet has never yet seen anything. But a female embryo, already thinking and speaking: if only she could be born at will!)

I listen some more:

H: "So exceedingly hard to hoist oneself out of the silky womb of the present and tie a tiny strand of golden thread at the mouth of this cave, so others can see which way to venture,

. . . It makes me cry, I want to talk about something I am not sure I can talk about, I want to talk about the inside from inside, I do not want to leave it

I am so happy in the silky damp dark of the labyrinth and there is no thread

So exceedingly hard to invent the tiniest slip of golden thread to hoist outside as a sign: here, this way to where we can make up our minds to slip into the narrative.

(The narrative? What narrative? If only it were a narrative! But it is precisely not a narrative, it is time, burning time, beating from hour to hour, it is time beating in life's breast.)

I am painfully like a womanfish who has decided that now it is time to look the sea in its face.

All flexed and anguished, she wrings her fins and spreads them wide – to no avail, she only surfaces between two waves and still has no wings.

It makes me drool (H moans), the minute I open my mouth I dribble metaphors, "forest," "narrative," "womanfish," it is all pretend, taking advantage of my disarray, because I have no idea how to get out while staying in, I don't know how, I don't want to enough, I am so happy in the intoxicating and cosmic womb of the present! And yet I want to present this present – to whom? – to those I love, because, to my mind, it is a realm worth giving, it is an inner India, a natural palace, a country of magnificent contours – in short, all I want to say, very quickly, before the metaphors swoop straight down on my heart to steal its blood, is that I have found the entrance to a life so rich in personal events, one so stirred up, so potent and nascent, a life that never stops bursting into lives, into shouts of life, into tears of life, into laughs of life, into songs of life, into terrors of life,

the entrance, naturally, is close by, just like in stories and like in reality, it is extremely close, it is right here, here in the garden, even closer, in the house, in the breast, even closer? – even closer . . .

(moans H, body arched, scales glittering with sweat, fins spread wide, gills throbbing, trying, at the risk of bursting to make the transition from the realm of water to the realm of words)

. . . I did not even know this existed . . . this world, I did not know. I thought it existed only in one's head, and in dreams . . . And now: here I am.

H went to lie down, to rest or maybe after this exhausting foray to the outside, to immerse herself again deep in her vital innermost recesses and immediately felt herself slip into the soft, sensory interior of the present which welcomed her in again, rocked her, and made peace with her. And it was true that she was drooling over it. A trickle of blood oozed from her mouth. And she pulled away from the outside like someone leaving only a sloughed-off outer skin to mark her place on earth. But inside she went back to joy; inside; there where life, carefree, without restraint, shouted her great cries of victory; inside she regained her strength and her calm, because she could peacefully inhale the vital violence of life there without false modesty; and she could yell freely, yell her admiration and her terror . . .

For the time being I cannot do without H. I do not yet have the mental courage to be only *I*. I dread nothing as much as autobiography. Autobiography does not exist. Yet so many people believe it exists. So here I solemnly state: autobiography is only a literary genre. It is nothing living. It is a jealous, deceitful sort of thing – I detest it. When I say "I," this I is never the subject of autobiography, my I is free. Is the subject of my madness, my alarms, my vertigo.

I is the heroine of my fits of rage, my doubts, my passions. I lets itself go. I let myself go. I surrenders, gets lost, does not comprehend itself. Says nothing about me. I does not lie. I do not lie to anyone. I does not lie to anyone, I promise: that is why I has almost nothing to say about me – which raises some doubt as to the balance or harmony of the book.

In fact, there is no limit to what I can say about Promethea – other than the reader's weariness.

But about me? No. Who could speak about "me," if not myself, and since I am "the author"?

That is a burning question. Personally, I still don't have the answer.

But Promethea has one. She asks me to write that she loves me.

(I am a bit ashamed because I feel so much resistance, I disobey her, she has already asked me several times if I really did what she asked me to do. I sort of lied. I said, "I'm getting ready to. I'm going to." But it's as if she wanted me to caress myself, it makes my wrists cramp up. Yet it's not the same thing. All the same, this demands a humility I do not possess. The more she trusted, the more impossible it was to obey. Until, yesterday, when she took my papers. She read them and, luckily, I saw how sad it made her. Otherwise, shamefully, fearfully, secretly, I would have kept on being evasive. And she murmured sadly, "You never wrote that I love you?" And her eyes were like tears. And I understood how stingy and cheap and arrogant and ungracious I had been. Because it is easy to love and sing one's love. That is something I am extremely good at doing. Indeed, that is my art. But to be loved, that is true greatness. Being loved, letting oneself be loved, entering the magic and dreadful circle of generosity, receiving gifts, finding the right thank-you's, that is love's real work.

Yesterday I made Promethea the sincere promise that I would sincerely do my best to write what she wants.

It is a promise.

Which is an even newer, even greater difficulty than all the others.

Perhaps building a circumferential around a garden spoils it. Perhaps it is as bad a calculation as the invasion of Lebanon. Perhaps it is destruction under the pretext of protection. Perhaps it is precluding under the pretext of preserving. Two conceptions of the work are in confrontation: out of scepticism and distrust regarding the human race, I am for the protection of nature. Promethea trusts everything: nature, the human race, me, herself. This is a controversial problem.

But writing a book with another book growing inside is what makes a revolutionary issue of the practice of . . . I have no idea what word to use.

Obviously I am not concerned with the author's rights.

It is how serious translation is that torments me. Translating oneself is already serious – I mean putting life into words – sometimes it is almost putting it to death; sometimes dragging it out, sometimes embalming it, sometimes making it vomit or lie, sometimes bringing it to climax, but one never knows before beginning whether one's luck will be good or bad, whether this is birth or suicide. But translating someone else – that requires extraordinary arrogance or extraordinary humility. Extraordinary arrogance is something I don't have. And extraordinary humility – I don't know who has that. Except perhaps Promethea. In this book (expanding and growing richer as I sit here stewing), which is Promethea's book, a young, vigorous book is growing, one I don't know how to write.

——Because I am not Promethea, and I cannot bring myself to act as if I were, I am not a real liar, I cannot ascribe my words to her without feeling that this poisons and invents her.

So what am I to do? I can take down Promethea's words under dictation. That is a possibility. But not good enough. Because Promethea has the idea that I know better than she what she wants to say, when she speaks to me silently with her eyes, her mouth, the corners of her lips, her hands, and everything she confides in me in her other tongues. But I have my doubts, about myself and about words as well: I am not sure my written language can faithfully translate all the many living, original, cosmic, personal languages.

All I can promise is to take down faithfully the words Promethea says out loud in French. As for all the rest, I make no guarantees.

NOTE

1 In the 1977 essay "Coming to Writing," for example, it is love of the m/other that motivates the self not to give in to death (see "Coming to Writing," translated by Deborah Jenson, in *"Coming to Writing" and Other Essays*, Cambridge, Mass.: Harvard University Press, 1991, pp. 2–3. In "(With) Or the Art of Innocence," the anguish of attempting to go beyond the self is portrayed as unbearable without the succor of "you" (see (*With*) *Ou l'art de l'innocence*, Paris: des femmes, 1981, p. 271). In "Lemonade Everything Was So Infinite," life is envisaged as too difficult to confront alone (see *Limonade tout était si infini*, Paris: des femmes, 1982, p. 68). [Ed.]

Extreme Fidelity

In a landmark essay "Extreme Fidelity," published in English in 1988 but based on a lecture given in French to the Paris International College of Philosophy in 1984, Cixous gives a clear exposition of her view of sex and gender difference and outlines her concerns as a reader and teacher of literature. In the extract from "Extreme Fidelity" reprinted here, Cixous explains that she employs the terms masculine and feminine to distinguish between two different "economies" or modes of behavior. Whilst these economies are not dependent on anatomical sex, and can be found in varying degrees according to how the individual has negotiated their experience, Cixous suggests that women, because of the position women have been assigned within the socio-symbolic scheme, are potentially closer to a feminine economy than men. Cixous' insistence on the cultural interpretation of anatomical sex is important here, since her work has been branded with the charge of biological essentialism.

Cixous reads two biblical scenes as illustrations of the ways individuals may respond to prohibition. Both Eve, in the book of Genesis, and Abraham are issued with instructions they cannot comprehend, yet only Eve questions and defies these to discover the truth for herself.

Clarice Lispector is cited as the writer whose work has come closest to locating and conveying a feminine relation to others. Cixous describes Lispector's texts as books "of the right distance." Unlike the (masculine) approach which appropriates whatever he (*sic*) designates as other, Lispector's writing, Cixous argues, entails a "relentless practice of de-egoization" in which both self and other can coexist "as equals." Recalling the author's endeavor in *The Book of Promethea*, writing is again valued here as a place in which the feminine can be expressed.

The passage appears on pp. 14–19 of "Extreme Fidelity," translated by Ann Liddle and Susan Sellers, in Susan Sellers (ed.), *Writing Differences: Readings from the Seminar of Hélène Cixous*, Milton Keynes: Open University Press and New York: St Martin's Press, 1988.

In the course of our research we talk in terms of libidinal economies out of convenience. In order to try to distinguish vital functions, we distinguish two principal libidinal economies; but they do not distinguish themselves in such a decisive way in reality: in the living there are traits which obliterate themselves, which blend together. None the less at the outset one can distinguish structures – I am not saying anything new in this – which we find at work in different societies. We have worked on these economies where it seemed to me to be easiest, most amusing to work on them, approaching them where they are most visible: at the point of what I have called *libidinal education*. We have worked on a group of texts which belong to what can be called the literature of apprenticeship, the *Bildungsroman*, and all of the texts – and there are a lot of them because literature is after all their domain – which relate the development of an individual, their story, the story of their soul, the story of their discovery of the world, of its joys and its prohibitions, its joys and its laws, always on the trail of the first story of all human stories, the story of *Eve and the Apple*. World literature abounds in texts of libidinal education, because every writer, every artist, is brought at one moment or another to work on the genesis of his/her own artistic being. It is the supreme text, the one written through a turning back to the place where one plays to win or lose life. The stakes are extremely simple, it is a question of the apple: does one eat it or not? Will one enter into contact with the intimate inside of the fruit or not?

I have done a lot of work on *primitive scenes*.[1] Will the delightful Perceval of the *Quest for the Holy Grail* enjoy his marvelous meal or not? In any case, what is at stake for me in these stories is the fate of the *so-called "feminine" economy*; I say "feminine" economy in connection with Perceval too, for I do not attribute it to women as an endowment; one can find these two economies in no matter which individual. *Why "feminine"?* It is the old story; because in spite of everything, ever since the *Bible* and ever since bibles, we have been distributed as descendants of Eve and descendants of Adam. It is the Book which has written this story. The Book wrote that the person who had to deal with the question of pleasure was a woman, was woman; probably because it was indeed a woman who, in the system which has always been cultural, underwent this test, which men and women have been subjected to ever since. Every entry to life finds itself *before the Apple*. What I call "feminine" and "masculine" is the relationship to pleasure, the relationship to spending, because we are born into language, and I cannot do otherwise than to find myself before words: we cannot get rid of them, they are there. We could change them, we could put signs in their place, but they would become just as closed, just as immobile and petrifying as the words "masculine" and "feminine" and would lay down the law to us. So there is nothing to be done, except to shake them like apple trees, all the time.

"An economy said to be F," "an economy said to be M," – why distinguish between them? Why keep words which are so entirely treacherous, fearful and warmongering? This is where all the traps are set. I give myself a poet's right, otherwise I would not dare to speak. The right of poets is to say something and then to say, believe it if you want to, but believe it weeping; or else to erase it, as Genet does, by saying that all truths are false, that only false truths are true, etc.

In order to define the zones of libidinal, emotional behavior, where these structural propensities exert themselves, let us take *the scene of the apple*.[2] This scene has always struck me because all its elements, which have become illegible as they have become so familiar to us, are interesting. The first fable of our first book is a fable in which what is at stake is the relationship to the law. There are two principal elements, two main puppets: the word of the Law or the discourse of God and the Apple. It's a struggle between the Apple and the discourse of God. All this transpires in this short scene before a woman. The Book begins *Before the Apple*: at the beginning of everything there is an apple, and this apple, when it is talked about, is said to be a not-to-be-fruit. There is an apple, and straight away there is the law. It is the start of libidinal education, it is here that one begins to share in the experience of the *secret*, because the law is incomprehensible. God says, if you taste the fruit of the tree of knowledge, you will die. It is absolutely incomprehensible. What rich terrain for the theologians and the philosophers, since for Eve "you will die" does not mean anything, since she is in the paradisiac state where there is no death. She receives the most hermetic discourse there is, the absolute discourse. We will find it again in the story of Abraham who receives an order from God which might also seem incomprehensible, except that Abraham obeys without questioning, absolutely. It is the experience of the secret, the enigma of the apple, of this apple which is invested with every kind of power. And what we are told is that knowledge might begin with the mouth, with the discovery of the taste of something: knowledge and taste go together. What is at stake here is the mystery which is assailed by the law, the law which is absolute, verbal, invisible, negative, it is a symbolic *coup de force* and its force is its invisibility, its non-existence, its force of denial, its "not." And facing the law, there is the apple which is, is, is. It is the struggle between presence and absence, between an undesirable, unverifiable, indecisive absence, and a presence, a presence which is not only a presence: the apple is visible and it can be held up to the mouth, it is full, it has an *inside*. And what Eve will discover in her relationship to simple reality, is the inside of the apple, and that this inside is good. This story tells us that the genesis of woman goes through the mouth, through a certain oral pleasure, and through a non-fear of the inside.

If you take Kafka's famous fable "Before the Law"[3] the little man from the country, who is partly "feminine," does not go inside. What is more we do not know if there is an inside. In any case there is a prohibition against the inside which is absolute. In a way there is no inside, since the man who remains before the law, is in fact inside the law. Thus before and inside are the same.

In an astonishing way, our most ancient book of dreams tells us after its own fashion – though we can read it in our own way – that Eve is not afraid of the inside, neither her own, nor that of the other. I would claim that the relationship to the inside, to penetration, to touching the inside is positive. Obviously Eve is punished for it, but that is another matter, that is society's affair. Of course she is punished since she has access to pleasure, of course a positive relationship to the inside is something which threatens society and which must be controlled. That is where the series of "you-shall-not-enter" begins. It is not insignificant that in the beginning there should be a scene of pleasure which takes this form. It is a game and it is not a game. We find it throughout mythology, throughout literature.

And I find it with Perceval in the *Quest for the Holy Grail.* This is why it is interesting to read the texts which give voice to an unconscious that is completely indifferent to laws, even if the law always catches up with the wild unconscious. To begin with, Perceval is a woman's son, he does not have a father, he is a boy left to his wild state, he is on the side of plea-sure, of happiness. Then he is educated and, after a series of trials, he becomes a knight, is covered with armor, becomes phallicized, takes up a sword. One of the major, decisive scenes in the whole story of Perceval is once again the story of Eve and the apple. Perceval, a woman's son, arrives at the court of the Fisher King, a king who is deprived of the use of his legs, a king who is very hospitable and castrated. Perceval is invited to a sumptuous meal during which he takes pleasure in all the excellent foods which are served. Meanwhile there is a procession of servants carrying splendid dishes into another room. Perceval is fascinated by this merry-go-round, he is dying to ask what is going on. But only a short time before, his educator has told him: you are wild, you do not have any manners, but you must learn that in life one-does-not-ask-questions. And Perceval continues to see a lance passing by, and at the end of the lance blood dripping. And while this is happening the narrative intervenes: "Well, Perceval, are you going to ask questions? You are committing a terrible sin, and you will be punished." The agonized reader is caught between the narrative and the hero. And Perceval does not ask a single question. The meal ends, the castle disappears in a flash like a fairytale, and Perceval meets a maiden who tells him – up until then he did not have a name – "Now you are called Perceval." Perceval has committed a dreadful sin, he should have asked who was being served in this way, and since he did not ask, he is punished; he is condemned for the crime (what crime?) he has committed, the immediate consequences of which are catastrophic. He could have saved the Fisher King, the narrative tells us, he could have saved the universe, but the chance has gone. While reading this text I was seized with rage, telling myself it is not fair. I do not see why, nor does Perceval see why, he is punished because he has not done something. And we realize that we are completely in the world of the law which does not have a name or a face, which has the strange property of being entirely negative. It is as if the text were telling you that you are condemned to be inside the law, and that you cannot do otherwise. And at the same time, since the text is a poetic text, it takes into account the world of innocence and the world of pleasure. While the law weaves its web, Perceval is extremely happy, he eats extraordinary things, enjoys himself as much as he can. And suddenly he falls, no, he has fallen into the other world, the world of absolute law which does not give its reasons. By definition undefinable, that is what the law is: pure anti-pleasure. What made Perceval fall in this way is the fact that he is a mother's son, he was brought up in the forest, he is still full of woman's milk. Until he is so violently "circumcised" that henceforth he takes care of his manly parts.

The relationship to pleasure and the law, the individual's response to this strange, antagonistic relationship indicates, whether we are men or women, different paths through life. It is not anatomical sex that determines anything here. It is, on the contrary, history from which one never escapes, individual and collective history, the cultural schema and the way the individual negotiates with these schema, with these data, adapts to them and reproduces them, or else gets round them, overcomes them, goes beyond them, gets through them – there are a thousand formulae – and joins up with or never joins up with a universe which I would call "without fear or reproach." It happens that culturally, women have more of a chance of gaining access to pleasure, because of the cultural and political division of the sexes, which is based on sexual difference, on the way society has used the body and on the fact that it is much easier to inflict on men than on women the horror of the inside. After all women do all virtually or in fact have an experience of the inside, an experience of the capacity for other, an experience of non-negative change brought about by the other, of positive receptivity.

If we resign ourselves to keeping words like "feminine" and "masculine" it is because there is an anchoring point somewhere in a far distant reality. But I believe we must do our utmost to reduce this heritage. Let us try as quickly as possible to abandon these binary distinctions which never make any sense.

What can we assign as descriptive traits to these economies? Let us consider our behavior in life with others, in all the major experiences we encounter, which are the experiences of separation; the experiences, in love, of possession, of dispossession, of incorporation, and non-incorporation, the experiences of mourning, of real mourning, all the experiences which are governed by variable behaviors, economies, structures. How do we lose? How do we keep? Do we remember? Do we forget?

The greatest respect I have for any work whatsoever in the world is the respect I have for the work of Clarice Lispector. She has treated as has no one else to my knowledge all the possible positions of a subject in relation to what would be "appropriation," use and abuse of owning. And she has done this in the finest and most delicate detail. What her texts struggle against constantly and on every terrain, is the movement of appropriation: for even when it seems most innocent it is still totally destructive. Pity is destructive; badly thought out love is destructive; ill-measured understanding is annihilating. One might say that the work of Clarice Lispector is an immense *book of respect*, a *book of the right distance*. And, as she tells us all the time, one can only attain the right distance through a relentless process of de-selfing, a relentless practice of de-egoization. The enemy as far as she is concerned is the blind self. In *The Hour of the Star* she says, for example:

The action of this story will result in my transfiguration into others and in my material-ization at last into an object. Yes, and perhaps I might reach the sweet flute where I entwine myself in soft liana.[4]

We might say it is only a metaphor, but it is the dream of every author to arrive at such a transfiguration, at such a distancing as to become liana. It is a way of remembering that my self is only one of the elements of the immense mass of material, and only one of the elements haunted by the imaginary.

Another absolutely admirable moment:

How I should love to hear the pealing of bells in order to work up some enthusiasm as I decipher reality: to see angels flutter like transparent wasps around my fevered head, this head that longs to be ultimately transformed into an object-thing, because so much more simple.[5]

There is also the constant reminder of what we know in the form of a cliché: that we are dust. That we are atoms. And if we did not forget that we were atoms, we would live and we would love differently. More humbly, more expansively. Loving the "you ares" of the world, as equals. Without design.

NOTES

1 In the French this is written as *les s-cènes primitives*, with a play on the word *scène* (scene) and its homophone *cène* (from the Latin *cena* – evening meal). *La cène* is also the French expression for "The Last Supper." [Trans.]

2 The play on words is repeated in the French here as *la s-cène de la pomme* (see note 1). [Trans.]

3 The reference here is to the story which Kafka wrote in 1914 as part of *The Trial* (edition translated by Edwin and Willa Muir, New York: Schocken Books, 1977 (15th printing), pp. 213–15). The story also appears in *The Complete Stories*, New York: Schocken Books, 1971. (The story concerns a man from the country who tries to gain admittance to the law.) [Trans.]

4 Clarice Lispector, *The Hour of the Star*, translated by Giovanni Pontiero, Manchester: Carcanet, 1986, p. 20. This quotation is translated directly from the Brazilian by Sarah Cornell and Marguerite Sandré. [Trans.]

5 Ibid., p. 17. [Trans.]

The Terrible But Unfinished Story of Norodom Sihanouk King of Cambodia

In the "Conversations" that accompany "Extreme Fidelity," Cixous suggests that it is in her work for the theater that she has come closest to writing others.[1] Describing Clarice Lispector's exemplary approach to this task, Cixous writes:

I have only been able to resolve the question in an equivalent movement to Clarice's strategy which consists in making the author I am fade to the point of disappearing. I, the author, have to disappear so that you, so other, can appear. My answer has come through writing for the theater.

On the stage, I, the author, am no longer there, but there is the other.[2]

Although Cixous has been interested in the theater throughout her writing career,[3] it was in the early 1980s, during her association with Ariane Mnouchkine and the experimental Théâtre du Soleil (Sun Theater), that this interest flourished to produce two major historical plays.[4] It can be argued that the movement away from the personal other of Promethea,[5] for example, to an engagement with the others of history, represents a major shift in Cixous' work.[6]

In the first of the two history plays, performed and published in 1985, *L'Histoire terrible mais inachevée de Norodom Sihanouk Roi du Cambodge* ("The Terrible But Unfinished Story of Norodom Sihanouk King of Cambodia"), documenting Cambodia's history from the end of the Second World War to the present, the conflicting visions of Cambodia appear plausible, even beneficial, from the self-interested and therefore limited perspectives of the vying factions.[7] The dreams of the Khmer Rouge seem attractive as their leaders talk of a return to an "innocent" Cambodia;[8] and even Lon Nol's disastrous policies are initially portrayed as better than their alternative.[9]

In the first of two passages translated here, the difficulty of achieving "a god's eye view," in which things will be "in their right perspective," is dramatized in the vision through the airplane window as Sihanouk and the Princess fly to Peking. Even a moment of clear sight is obscured by clouds. The play suggests that, despite the many difficulties, only an attention to the truth and the "living earth" can prevent the self-centered, partial and destructive patterns from repeating themselves.

It is noteworthy that here it is the Princess who interrupts Sihanouk's tirade against the formerly loyal Chea San, and offers an alternative explanation for his silence. Her interruption, and insistence that Sihanouk "guard preciously the good things" and "live this moment," are characteristic of the role given to women in the play.[10]

The very different writing style required in the theater presents an interesting commentary on Cixous' delineations for a feminine writing.[11] Here, the extra-linguistic resources available to the writer are exemplified in the song that opens the scene.[12]

The following passage is Act IV scene iv of the *"Première Epoque"* ("First Epoch")[13] of *L'Histoire terrible mais inachevée de Norodom Sihanouk Roi du Cambodge*, Paris: Théâtre du Soleil, 1985, pp. 163–6, and is translated by Donald Watson.

〜ᐁ〜

In the plane over Asia, between Moscow and Peking. Enter SIHANOUK and the PRINCESS, with PENN NOUTH.

MUSICIAN: The sun has risen and I am a dead man.
             The sun has risen and the boat has sunk.
             The sun is hidden. No one on the river.

SIHANOUK: Only yesterday, with Chea San, I was talking of the battles to come! And I was winning! I would have won them! I thought I knew how to lead my country! I shall bring you back peace! But behind me there was no one. No country, no history, no way left! For me it's all over! I can see myself back there among my dead! Not only have they snatched the throne from under me, but they've tricked me, made a fool of me! That Chea San, weeks ago, I'd have made him lay his severed head in my lap.

PRINCESS: Stop, I beg you! Calm yourself! You mistake your enemy. Chea San did not betray you with his silence. He was choking with the tears he held back. Guard preciously the good things that remain.

SIHANOUK: Go on, talk to me again, lead me on with your words to the banks of a river where you can bathe my ailing soul.

PRINCESS: Well, then, now in this plane, let us live this moment. Of a day that is ours alone, up here above everything, a day with no telephone, no ministers, a whole day escaping from History!
             Let it cradle you.
             Beneath our cockleshell the sky is swimming with flowers and fish.

SIHANOUK: Yes! To live with you in a plane and have a god's eye view of the world suits my mood to perfection. It helps to get things in their right perspective! Look at that dull brown carpet which seems so lifeless. That's Mongolia. And it's when we're down below, with the banana trees no higher than our noses, that for carpets like this, more or less highly colored, we keep our thousand-year old hatreds on the boil and spend our whole lives dreaming we are slaughtering our neighbors. And it's for *my* carpet I have been despoiled and long to dissolve into a rain of tears.

PRINCESS: Oh, if only we could be quite detached from all this!

SIHANOUK: The inner pathways of our Buddha elude me now. My misfortune was to be chosen by the French to mount the throne. The day before, I assure you, I was still the happiest of boys. What frightened me most was my exams. But now, how can I forget the great dream that took me over ... I can't stop being Cambodia now. Myself, I *am* those rivers, rice-fields, mountains, and all the peasants who people me. I should like to forget myself and live another life. But for that I would have to die. Would you come with me?

PRINCESS: You ask me that?

SIHANOUK: If you like, we'll be born again together. So if we were to start again, what would you want to do or be?

PRINCESS: To be? A woman again, your lover again, yes, the same again. And I'd like to do some painting.

SIHANOUK: Had it not been for the gods and the French, I'd have been a virtuoso on the saxophone.

PRINCESS: Why not a football-player?

SIHANOUK: Why not indeed?

PRINCESS: Why not a Chinese cook?

SIHANOUK: Chinese? ... I've dropped out of our dream. I can't play games any more.

PRINCESS: Is it China you're afraid of? There's no reason. A smile from Chou En Lai will soon cure you of that.

SIHANOUK: I can't wait to see him. He's a sort of *homme fatal*, amazing! He's a Greta Garbo, a veritable Circe. The first time I ever saw him, he invites me to lunch. Off I go. I'd never seen such a handsome man. It's a good thing *I* happened to be a man! We sit down at table. From the very first dish, I was bewitched. And what if he betrayed me now too? Oh, the traitors, they make my heart bleed! Penn Nouth! Penn Nouth!? Where are we? What's the time?

PENN NOUTH: We'll be in Peking within the hour, my Lord.

SIHANOUK: Within the hour! As soon as we arrive in Peking, Penn Nouth, I shall address a powerful message to our people. I shall say:

Oh my people. Oh my children ...

Ah! But where are my people?

What lies before them?

And what lies before *me*? When shall I find them again?

These clouds are so dense, they look like a belt of ice-
bound land that cuts us off from the living earth.

> [They go out, and so do the clouds]

In the second passage translated here from "The Terrible But Unfinished
Story of Norodom Sihanouk King of Cambodia," the endeavor to discover
truth is presented as the function of theater. The difficulties involved in
attempting to discern and communicate what is true extend, here, to the
author: "When infidelity rules,/How hard it is to make a faithful chronicle."
Neither the author nor the characters can be trusted. Truth is nonetheless
offered as the antidote to "the chatter of evil tongues and the clatter of
bombardment" that create the context for the play. The only way to hear
this "voice," the play suggests, is through an attentive – and collective – listening: "For, just like lies, truth/Lives because of those who listen."

The passage is the "Prologue" to the "Deuxième Epoque" ("Second
Epoch") of *L'Histoire terrible mais inachevée de Norodom Sihanouk Roi du
Cambodge*, pp. 193–5, and is translated by Donald Watson.

Enter the CHORUS

The sequel to our story is a perilous one.

Treacherous. Earth-shattering.

The world rocks beneath one's feet. The stars have
dropped from the sky.

Up there the gods have been throwing the dice.

Gambling for Cambodia.

Some have won. Some have lost and are desolate.

The camp we live in is one of desolation.

Our hearts are lying so low, they've lost contact with our
tongues,

and it's hard to tell what our leading characters are
thinking.

It's a time of mistrust. A cold sun is rising in the North.

No more Kingdom, no memories left.

On every side destiny reigns.

Today Prince Sihanouk owes his survival, what remains
of his pride, power and honour,
And what remains of the remainder, even his board and
lodging,
To those very people to whom he never wished to be
beholden.
He is indebted to China and Vietnam,
Two scheming nations
Who gain ground like crabs, advancing sideways.
You understand?
Now the Prince is in Peking
And Cambodia is at a loss,
Not knowing where to look for itself,
In Phnom Penh or Peking,
Whether inside its frontiers or without,
Not knowing what sort of place it is,
What side it's on or how to describe itself,
As Royalist or Republican,
Or from what point in the compass blows the disorder-
ing wind,
From America or China.
Wondering in which foreign tongue,
To what gods, which masters to address itself,
Which popes or Papas now should be disobeyed.
A sharp-toothed era has torn this land to pieces.
The theater's mission is to patch them all together,
And I hope I won't forget a single shred.
When infidelity rules,
How hard it is to make a faithful chronicle.
One piece of advice: if a character you respect
Swears before witnesses that the darkest of nights
Is the brightest of days, don't trust him,
Even if it's Lord Penn Nouth (whose role I am honored
once again to interpret for you).
Oh may the voice of truth be heard again, even faintly,
Against the chatter of evil tongues and the clatter of
bombardment.
But if you love truth, attune your ears
For, just like lies, truth
Lives because of those who listen.
No truth without ears,

No theater without truth.

Aren't we all here because we want to hear it

And retrieve from a furious flood of Falsity the frail flotsam of Truth?

Shall we succeed? I don't know but I hope and think so.

My presence here now before you is an act of faith.

I believe the truth lies concealed in all of us,

Even if, short-sighted as most humans are,

I don't always manage to see it.

And, if you allow me, I dedicate this whole spectacle of ours to Truth, not discounting the errors and the blind omissions.

While I speak, a conference is being held here in Peking, of fatal import to the country of Cambodia. As you can judge for yourself!: The Prince is about to enter . . . Oh! But what's happening! I beg your pardon. What I have just announced is to be the second scene of our play: once more the author has had second thoughts!

[Exit the Chorus]

NOTES

1 See "Conversations," in Susan Sellers (ed.), *Writing Differences: Readings from the Seminar of Hélène Cixous*, Milton Keynes: Open University Press, and New York: St Martin's Press, 1988, pp. 141–54. [Ed.]

2 Ibid., p. 153. This transition is the theme of Cixous' essay "De la scène de l'Inconscient à la scène de l'Histoire: Chemin d'une écriture," in Françoise van Rossum-Guyon and Miriam Diaz-Diocaretz (eds), *Hélène Cixous, chemins d'une écriture*, Paris: Presses Universitaires de Vincennes, and Amsterdam: Rodopi, 1990, pp. 15–34. An English translation by Deborah Carpenter exists as "From the Scene of the Unconscious to the Scene of History," in *The Future of Literary History*, Ralph Cohen (ed.), New York and London: Routledge, 1989, pp. 1–18. [Ed.]

3 *La Pupille* ("The Pupil") was performed and published in 1972, *Portrait de Dora* ("Portrait of Dora") in 1976. *Le Nom d'Oedipe/Chant du corps interdit* ("Oedipus' Name/Song of the Forbidden Body"), Cixous' opera script, was performed and published in 1978. *Je me suis arrêtée à un mètre de Jerusalem et c'était le paradis* ("I Stopped a Meter from Jerusalem and This Was Paradise") was performed at Avignon in 1982. Cixous' radio play, *Amour d'une délicatesse* ("Love of a Delicacy"), was transmitted on 28 August 1982 by Radio Suisse Romande, Lausanne. *La Prise de l'école de Madhubaï* ("The Fall of the Madhubaï School") was performed in 1983 and published in 1984. Both *Portrait de Dora* and *La Prise de l'école de Madhubaï* are reprinted in *Hélène Cixous: Théâtre*, Paris: des femmes, 1986. *Celui qui ne parle pas* ("The One Who Does Not Speak") was performed in 1984, and a television play, *La Nuit miraculeuse* ("Miraculous Night"), was trans-

mitted on French television in December 1989. *On ne part pas, on ne revient pas* ("One Doesn't Leave, One Doesn't Return") was performed and published in 1991. Full details of Cixous' published plays are given in the Bibliography. [Ed.]

4 The two plays are *L'Histoire terrible mais inachevée de Norodom Sihanouk Roi du Cambodge* ("The Terrible But Unfinished Story of Norodom Sihanouk King of Cambodia"), and *L'Indiade ou l'Inde de leurs rêves* ("Indiada or the India of Their Dreams", see below). [Ed.]

5 See "The Book of Promethea," above. [Ed.]

6 Cixous details the radically different approach writing historical plays requires in "A Realm of Characters," in Susan Sellers (ed.), *Delighting the Heart: A Notebook by Women Writers*, London: The Women's Press, 1989, pp. 126–8. [Ed.]

7 The exception is the American position which, despite portrayal of William Watts' and John Gunther Dean's resignations (see *L'Histoire terrible mais inachevée de Norodom Sihanouk Roi du Cambodge*, pp. 230, 287), is depicted as pure lust for power (ibid., pp. 228–31). [Ed.]

8 Ibid., p. 61, also p. 25. [Ed.]

9 Ibid., p. 74. [Ed.]

10 In the Khmer camps, for example, it is the women who proclaim they are "against death and (. . .) for life" (ibid., p. 367; see also p. 323), while the play ends with the Queen Mother Kossomak's invocation that the spirit of Cambodia will remain alive through its language and national dances (ibid., pp. 404–11). [Ed.]

11 In "A Realm of Characters," Cixous details the very different demands writing for the theater involves (pp. 126–8). [Ed.]

12 Music was an important part of the Théâtre du Soleil's production of *Sihanouk*. [Ed.]

13 The length of the play required it to be performed in two parts. [Ed.]

The Place of Crime
The Place of Forgiveness

The second of the two historical plays Cixous wrote for the Théâtre du Soleil, *L'Indiade ou l'Inde de leurs rêves* – "Indiada or the India of Their Dreams," first performed and published in 1987, concerns the final stages of India's struggle for independence and the partition of India and Pakistan. The published play includes a series of Cixous' "Ecrits sur le Théâtre" – "Writings on the Theater," in which she outlines her view of theater and explains why it is important to her. In the text from the "Writings" presented here, "The Place of Crime, The Place of Forgiveness," Cixous repeats her insistence expressed in the "Conversations" that accompany "Extreme Fidelity,"[1] for example, that the theater has provided her with an arena in which she has been able to move away from the self-preoccupation of the fiction to engage with others "much more and altogether other than Me." Recalling the suggestion of "The Terrible But Unfinished Story of Norodom Sihanouk King of Cambodia" that "truth lies concealed in all of us"[2] and only a return to the "inner pathways" Sihanouk, for example, has lost[3] can alter the course of human tragedy, Cixous argues here that theater is precisely the place where truth may be mirrored back to us, enabling us to "see what we do." This mirroring is vital since, she stresses, history is the product of our individual struggles to perceive and act on what is true: "what causes wars, peace, massacres, heroisms – looking closely, pulling back the curtain, are tiny and powerful humans." Reiterating the implication of her earlier fiction,[4] Cixous believes theater's refusal to shy away from death – "this source of so much meaning" – is especially important in the mass-mediatized world of the present, in which human emotions and the fact of mortality are walled over.

"Le lieu du Crime, le lieu du Pardon" is on pp. 253–9 of *L'Indiade ou l'Inde de leurs rêves*, Paris: Théâtre du Soleil, 1987. This revised translation by Catherine MacGillivray was first published in *Qui Parle: A Journal of Literary Studies* 3,1: 120–5 (Spring 1989), Berkeley: University of California.

How can the poet open her universe to the destiny of a people? She who is first of all an explorer of the Self, how, in what language foreign to her ego, by what means could she write about much more and altogether other than Me?

And another question: how can I, who am of the literate species, ever give speech to an illiterate peasant woman without taking it away from her, with a stroke of my language, without burying her with one of my fine phrases? Would there never be then in my texts but people who know how to read and write, to juggle with signs? And yet I love this

Khmer peasant, I love this royal mother from a village in Rajasthan who knows so many things and doesn't know she lives in a country that I call India. For a long time I believed my texts would only live in those rare, desert places where only poems grow.

Until I arrived at the Theater. There was the stage, the earth, where the ego remains imperceptible, the land of others. There their words make themselves heard, and their silences, their cries, their song, each according to her or his own world and in her or his foreign tongue.

Once I've arrived, all begins to become clear, and first of all the nature of my need for theater.

I need a *certain* Theater, whose first name was Shakespeare or Verdi, or Schönberg or Sophocles or Rossini. I need this theater to tell me stories, and to tell them to me in the way that only it can: legendarily and yet straight in the eye.

For if this Theater is necessary that's because it allows us to live what no other "genre" does: the hell we have in being human. The Evil. What comes to pass in the theater is Passion, but passion according to Oedipus, according to Hamlet, according to you, according to Woyzeck, according to me, according to Othello, according to Cleopatra, according to Marie, according to this enigmatic, tortured, criminal, innocent human being that I am, I who is thou or you.

I believe that today more than ever we need our own theater, the theater whose stage is our heart, on which our destiny and our mystery are acted out, and whose curtain we see so rarely rise.

To tell the truth, we go to the theater as infrequently as to our heart, and it is going to the heart, ours and that of things, that we feel the lack of. We live outside of ourselves, in a world whose walls have been replaced by television screens, a world that has lost its thickness, its depths, its treasures, and we mistake newspaper columns for our thoughts. We are imprinted daily. We even lack the wall, the real wall on which divine messages are written. We are lacking earth and flesh.

We live before the paper curtain, and often even as curtains. But what is important to us, what wounds us, what makes us feel we are characters in an immense adventure, is what comes to pass behind the curtain. And behind the curtain is the *naked* stage.

We need this nakedness. We need to see the faces hidden behind the faces, the faces the Theater unveils.

And under the charm of the costumes and make-up, under the mask, what rises to the light is truth, that is to say, only the best or the worst.

And behind the curtain: words, the naked voice. What a relief when, entering this place, the lie, which is our everyday politeness, stops, and we begin to hear the dialogue of hearts! We could shout out loud from it. And we rejoice that it is not forbidden, in this marvelous land, to utter cries, to strike blows, to translate the suffering that comes from being a human inhabitant of our epoch into breath, into sweat, into song.

We are the characters of an epic we are forbidden, by the laws of mediocrity and prudence, to live. And yet it is an epic. And what is frightening and beautiful is that, no matter how majestic the epic of nations appears to be, its prime movers – what causes wars, peacetimes, massacres, heroisms – looking closely, pulling back the curtain, are tiny, powerful humans. The world is a theater. Each character who enters believes herself or himself to be the center of the world. And in a certain way, because we believe it, we are. Each one of us is the Center. And each Center is besieged by the other Centers.

The Theater has kept the secret of History as sung by Homer: History is made up of stories of husbands, lovers, fathers, daughters, mothers, sons, stories of jealousy, pride, desire. And there are faces that launch fleets of a thousand sails and destroy cities.

The human being needs to become human. Human? I mean to say: we are the scene of the war between good and evil. That there is war means there is a chance for good: a chance to distinguish oneself and to vanquish.

And we need destiny: we need to tell ourselves a story with a beginning and an end, in order to advance from one day to the next. Our destiny, which is it today? Since Shakespeare it has changed a little. I am an island. Am I still only an island? My island, even England, is rocked by the explosions, I hear bombs bursting, cannons firing. I am surrounded by wars, I am haunted by the pain of hostages. The last bomb didn't kill me, we are living under a sky of injustice, of which we are the victims or the miraculously saved. Is it not through our home that madness passes with its scythe? But yes, it is through our home, Paris, New Delhi, Beirut, Stockholm, we are walking under the same blood sun. Sometimes death approaches and strikes one street away from me, sometimes I don't hear it, one time it will strike . . . and it will be me. It is already me.

Yes, at certain moments we have this thought that I am naming here, but most often we chase it away because it would prevent us from living. But by chasing it away we lose a large part of life. This is the part the theater gives back to us: the living part of death; or else the deadly part of life.

I go to the theater because I need to understand or at least to contemplate the act of death, or at least admit it, meditate on it. And also because I need to cry.

And to laugh: but laughter is merely the sigh of relief that bursts forth at the scythe's passing: it missed us by a hair!

I admit that Theater is a form of religion: I mean to say that there we feel together, in the re-ligere, the re-linking, the reaping of emotions. I say "I admit" because this is one of the reasons I resist the call of the Theater from time to time: out of anti-religion. Out of a need for individualism.

But I declare we need these temples without dogma and without doctrine (but not without a great number of gods) where our dreads and above all our blindnesses are acted out. We are blind. We don't see what we do. We don't hear ourselves saying what we say. We don't understand ourselves. And we lie to ourselves and to each other. Because we are afraid of ourselves. We're afraid of our wickedness. We have guessed, thought, suspected, or seen that we are wicked. A little or very. But we don't really like to be wicked. And yet? Or else we are wicked without wickedness?

The enigma of wickedness, of human cruelty, that of others and my own, this is what we come and ask the Theater to reveal to us.

For the Theater is the place of Crime. Yes the place of Crime, the place of horror, also the place of Forgiveness. What does it give us to see? The primitive passions: adoration, assassination. All the excesses I throw out of my apartment: suicide, murder, the part of mourning there is in every passionately human relationship: thirst and hunger. Sacrifice, cannibalism.

Because we do not only kill what we hate. We also kill what we love. We always kill a little the beings we love.

And out of twisted love, because love is twisted, we end up killing Desdemona, Marie, our people or another people or Indira Gandhi or Olof Palme.

Why do we love so immediately, so eternally, certain works of the theater or opera? Because by showing us our crimes in the Theater, before witnesses, they accuse us and at the same time they forgive us.

We are all victims, but we are also executioners. The Beast and the Knife. What does the Theater tell us? There is death. What does the theater give us? Death. We love Carmen and Don José equally. And through the music's magic we become one and the other, we endure being murderer and murdered, murdered and murderess.

The stage gives it to us, gives it back to us, this death we are ashamed of, we are afraid of, we spurn. It gives us to live, in an instant or slowly, this source of so much meaning, death, the part of death in all life, and right up to the drunken desire to kill Marie, the young woman or the old, the mother, the father, the child, the people.

And it is then, in this moment when no longer fleeing we accept to look the victim or the murderer in the eye – like Myshkin looks at Rogozhin – that we remember we are human, that this is a misfortune, but it is a trying joy. Human *equally*: humanity passes through you and me, and through Macbeth and the king and the beggar, and we understand ourselves and each other.

There are essential things that render us equals: it is arriving by such different paths to the same door, death.

And there are moments when the monster (wicked, "*villain*," bandit, assassin) discovers his humanity. There is always the moment of hesitation, and of temptation: and if I were to kill? And if I were mistaken? And if I were a monster? And if I were blind? This moment is given to us at the Theater, it is the tragic instant when everything could be changed. No longer happen. This instant happens also in our lives. And we must be, the Theater reminds us, of an extreme vigilance so as not to miss it. For between good and evil, the step is blade thin.

The Theater doesn't give us death brutally like a blow to the back. No, it doesn't assassinate us. Because essentially, the Theater pities. It gives us one of the most rarefied times in the market of our everyday existences, the time of pity. We have become capable of no longer crying before the little Asian beggar who has lost his legs, isn't that true? Fortunately the Theater stops us and strikes us in the heart and brings us to tears.

Suddenly I hear the lament and I discover my deafness. And to recompense our refound suffering, the spectacle gives us tears, and the song's beauty reminds us that sorrow can be beautiful when there is compassion. Beautiful I mean: human, shared.

Yes pity, fear, remain the most precious emotions in the world. They are love. And they so need to be rekindled in the hearts of our epoch.

If we took pity . . .

To begin with, let's take the Theater seriously. I mean to say: it's good to go there seriously, like children. Because we can pretend to go to listen to an opera. And then nothing happens. But if we participate in *Woyzeck* or *King Lear*, with our hearts simplified, uncovered, and if by chance we shed some tears, then maybe on this earth a woman will be saved, a prisoner will be liberated – and maybe an innocent vindicated, and someone forgotten will be remembered.

NOTES

1 See above, p. 141. [Ed.]
2 See *L'Histoire terrible mais inachevée de Norodom Sihanouk Roi du Cambodge*, Paris: *Théâtre du Soleil*, 1985, p. 195. [Ed.]
3 Ibid., p. 165. [Ed.]
4 See "Lemonade Everything Was So Infinite," above. [Ed.]

Indiada or the India of Their Dreams

In a Preface to *L'Indiade ou l'Inde de leurs rêves* – "Indiada or the India of Their Dreams," Cixous ponders *why* the struggle for Indian independence – a cause which "united and carried 400 million Indians from every religion and caste towards the same goal"[1] – should have resulted in partition. Recalling the thesis of "The Place of Crime, The Place of Forgiveness,"[2] she suggests that the answer lies in the conjunction of circumstances – "the second world war, political chance, the English only too pleased to weaken the Freedom Fighters of the Indian Congress by pressurizing the Muslim League" – and the aspirations and weaknesses of individuals.

In the scene from "Indiada or the India of Their Dreams" translated here, Gandhi's vision of a healing love that would respect differences is undercut by the insistence of the head of the Muslim League in favor of partition that, given the reality, such a love would be one-way: "you're asking *us* to perform the *labor* of love, to put up with your numbers, your weight, your crass indifference." The play's persistent exploration of the need to discover a mode of living that will love others *as other* – despite our fear and self-protective desire to convert others to our view of the world – links it to the concerns of Cixous' fiction.

The following extract is taken from Act II scene ii of *L'Indiade ou l'Inde de leurs rêves*, Paris: Théâtre du Soleil, 1987, pp. 80–5, and is translated by Donald Watson.

Enter JINNAH

GANDHI: Ah! My dear brother Jinnah.

JINNAH: Mr Gandhi, delighted to see you again. How are you since yesterday?

GANDHI: Yesterday you spoke to me of nothing but separation, division and your Theory of the Two Nations. I was saddened when I left you. All night I thought about you, about what lies in wait for India. I have had the most frightful visions. I saw a body quartered, a mother disemboweled, India sliced up like a hunk of meat! A nightmare! We must wake up. Phew! That's better. Here I am with you in Bombay. In India, at home. And I'd like nothing better than to visit you again thirty years hence. You'll offer me an orange juice and we'll laugh at the reckless young men we were, when I was seventy-five and you were sixty-eight!

JINNAH: Thirty years hence we will long have turned to dust for the potter. But Pakistan and Hindustan will live for all eternity.

GANDHI: I cannot follow you there. Today, if you allow me, I shall talk to you about love. That's the remedy. Let us love one another. That's the secret. The key to the lock in the door. Do we love one another? Do Hindus and Muslims love each other?

JINNAH: No.

GANDHI: No? How can you say that? We have lived together for a thousand years, quarrelling and making up. For a thousand years we've been asking the question: does he or she love me? They don't love me any more! No, *I* don't love *them* any more. There are times, when the love is strong, that we think we have stopped loving. We are out of love.

Just now you believe you are out of love with me. But love lingers beneath the ashes. Just let me blow on them. Do Hindus and Muslims love each other? I tell you they adore one another.

JINNAH: They detest and fear one another.

GANDHI: There's no love without fear. Nor even at times without a kind of disgust, yes, of repulsion. We human beings, Hindu or Muslim, male or female, we are all so different. We are very odd. There in front of me is another creature, nothing like me! Look at the two of us! Can one imagine a greater difference? You with your fine hair, your lovely tie, your well-cut suit, your shiny shoes and with a mouth full of teeth. And me ... with none of it. Sans hair, sans suit, sans teeth. Only my toes, all busy churning up the dust on the road.

What is it about people that attracts us? Mystery. A different sex, a different religion, a different human being. There is one tree with no two leaves that are identical, yet they dance to the same breeze. The tree of humanity. Let us give it time to germinate and mature.

JINNAH: No, Mr Gandhi. The wretched story of our overlong disunity has enslaved us to one another. Now at last it is over. You don't understand me. We don't understand each other. I don't understand you!

GANDHI: That doesn't matter. You don't need to understand me. All I have to do is to stir your feelings. You don't love me. Though you loved me yesterday. You don't love me any more? Very well. We'll separate.

JINNAH: Separate? You come round at last to the idea of separation!

GANDHI: Yes, I say separation, yes. But a loving one. Two brothers may separate, yet they still remain brothers in the eyes of God and humanity. Let's assume that in my family my Muslim brothers wish to live separately. The House is large enough. We proceed fairly to share out the rooms and the kitchens. One for you, one for me, each to his own. But we stay under the same roof.

JINNAH: So you won't let go, toothless as you are! Still the same India, the same deaf ears, the same blind eyes, the same crocodile invitation to the gazelle. Love! Love! What can love mean between two nations so ill-matched in strength. Tell me! No, don't! Not another word. It's the Muslims you're asking, you're asking *us* to perform the *labor* of love, to put up with your numbers, your weight, your crass indifference. Oh, no! No, don't touch me! Keep your distance! Yes, what you're asking us is to die of love for you! We run the risks! Not you!

GANDHI: No, don't say that! It's not true! Our people love each other, in spite of us, in spite of you!

JINNAH: Enough! Enough! No more of your dreams! Men do not love one another. They never will. The India of your dreams has no existence in the real world. Open your eyes, Mr Gandhi. The leaves of your unknown deciduous tree are falling. Look, you are naked. And alone. We all of us fall . . . separately, each one of us alone.

GANDHI: I open my eyes. Falling stars. Yet the sky is still as bright. We all fall into the hands of the same God. I can see India, a vast land of numberless loving arms. I don't see Pakistan.

JINNAH: Go, Mr Gandhi, as I too shall go, each his own way towards his destiny, his party and his country. One down, the other up. We don't speak the same language. I make you deaf and you madden me. You won't hear of partition. And it's the only word I will utter. So let us say no more. Let us bravely accept what reality decrees. We are incompatible. I bid you goodbye!

[He leaves]

GANDHI: No! Don't go! If you leave me now! . . . You won't shake me off, I'll hang on to your jacket! I'll never stop ringing your doorbell!

He's gone! Oh, Lord Jesus. I have not served you well.

Enter SAROJINI

HARIDASI: Beneath the earth two men
              Are searching for the moon,
              Who, laughing, says with a sigh,
              Don't look there for my house,
              It's up here in the sky
              And I'm sitting on a mouse.

SAROJINI: Oh, you're still here, Bapu! I saw Jinnah storming out! As
              if he was about to leap off the planet, slamming the door
              of the Universe behind him!

Enter KASTOURBAÏ, who has come through "the other entrance"

KASTOURBAÏ: Say no more! I feel ashamed! Instead of loving you more,
              he loves you even less. Do you hear me?

GANDHI: Of course I do, as my own heart speaks in you. He wants
              to rob me of my Muslim child, but I won't let him go. I
              shall mold myself round him like a glove. You'll have to
              cut right through me to reach him. I shall be hard as
              iron. If you bite me, I'll crack your teeth. If you scratch
              me, you'll break your nails on my leathery skin. This is
              war? Yes, a war I'm waging on hatred and on war. God
              himself could not help declaring this war of mine. If not
              Jesus, at least Lord Krishna would.

SAROJINI: Inexorable Jinnah! Always there, outfacing us. That is his
              destiny. Bapu, I'm afraid we can only despair.

GANDHI: Why despair? Love is not defeated. It's just that Gandhi
              displeases Mr Jinnah. If I can't, someone else will win him
              round.

NOTES

1 See *L'Indiade ou l'Inde de leurs rêves*, Paris: Théâtre du Soleil, 1987, p. 12. [Ed.]
2 See "The Place of Crime, The Place of Forgiveness," above. [Ed.]

Manna to the Mandelstams to the Mandelas

In her most recent writing, Cixous has again returned to fiction.[1] In *Manne aux Mandelstams aux Mandelas* – "Manna to the Mandelstams to the Mandelas," published in 1988, Cixous combines her theatrical concern with historical others – here Osip and Nadezhda Mandelstam and Nelson and Winnie (also called Zami) Mandela – with the attempted delineation, made possible through the poetic resources of writing, of an alternative mode of living and relating.

In the first of two passages from "Manna to the Mandelstams to the Mandelas" translated here, the dangers of oblivion are graphically figured in the fate of Alfios Sibisi, murdered and then disappeared by the white South African authorities. The problems inherent in the author's relation to her subject – a relation that is, for the most part, hidden in Cixous' work for the theater[2] – are explored as the author describes the difficulties she faces in trying to imagine the consequences of apartheid. The "book is an attempt at compassion. Only an attempt, for (. . .) I will never manage to feel in my feet the nails Sergeant Visser drove into the feet of old Willie Smit." The endeavor is nevertheless heralded as important if repression and negation are to be overturned: "here where all is silenced and stopped, the impossible song must be invented."

This passage is on pp. 25–32 of *Manne aux Mandelstams aux Mandelas*, Paris: des femmes Antoinette Fouque, 1988, and is translated by Catherine MacGillivray. A forthcoming translation by Catherine MacGillivray, *Manna to the Mandelstams to the Mandelas*, will be published by the University of Minnesota Press, Minneapolis.

This book is an attempt at compassion. Only an attempt, for I am capable of going to the foot of the olive trees, but I will never manage to feel in my feet the nails Sergeant Visser drove into the feet of old Willie Smit, in spite of the supplications and tears. Only the supplications pass through my heart. I hear and do not feel, I weep and do not bleed. The next day my tears come no more. I have spent all I had.

Without a witness how to die our death how to suffer our suffering? I need you to give me my suffering and my death. I need you to give me my pleasure. May my sufferings be mine, and my pleasures also!

I am not great enough to suffer even my own suffering alone. Whenever suffering has happened to me I have suffered the most possible, as well, as terribly as possible, and sometimes with the help of hollering, but this was never enough. One day I lost my father. The whole world caught fire. Curled up, I could not take my eyes away.

Between my father and myself, fire. Alone, I watched, I cried out. I suffered so much from not suffering enough. I had a puny and fake voice. I was suffering, suffering, and all the suffering remained above me, inaccessible, majestic and indestructible, like a suspended ocean that did not drown me, that I could not drown. Until I stopped shouting and resigned myself to suffering softly.

But at least I know a little how to suffer from suffering and how not to suffer.

And I also know things one knows from having been a tiny child living in front of the too great universe. Even without knowing we know them, we know them, these unknown and future sorrows. Whoever lives knows the worst even without ever meeting it. For having seen several times in my dreams my whole family die in a concentration camp, I know to what depths the sword can hollow out the heart in a single secular minute. Absolutely suffer absolutely one minute I know how. But then I wake up and I know no longer.

I also know that everything that occurs in dreams can occur in reality. Because we only dream true. I know unknown sorrows because my heart is fruit of the human tree. I am fruit of unknown good and evil. A same blood burns in each human heart.

But all I am speaking of here are sorrows of the heart. I know nothing of the sorrows of solitary flesh. Ah bodies are terribly separated from each other when it is a question of suffering in the body's dough and unto the hidden meat. The worst part of crucifixion is to be so infinitely alone in one's body. Because no one can understand, not even God, not even the mother.

The road that leads to dying is deserted, my brother.

God-the-Grief grounds and silences me.

If only I could take you in my arms, my child, my crucified one, if only I could hold your passion in my arms, this would be a consolation to me, suffers the mother without arms, without succor. Double is the dolor.

The mother who watches the crucifixion and lowers her eyes, the mother who cannot console herself for not being able even to console, I cannot look her in the face.

I watch her secretly. I cast a furtive glance and forthwith retrieve it, mute, struck with a shameful reverence. I do not accompany she who cannot accompany. And all here is solitude and silence. The rivers swallow their floods.

– All is you, silenced. And yet You is alone.

The sobs remain chastely in the chest. The words remain in the throat.

In the region where the Double Dolor burns, ash is immediately word.

And it is exactly here that the poem is needed. Here where all is silenced and stopped, the impossible song must be invented.

To watch the fire devour the world, stroll in the swamps of infernal Hell All we cannot do, must be done.

To make the stones speak, on which there is nothing more inscribed, this must be done. Otherwise it is true that none of the dead that have been lost shall ever survive.

The only chance remaining to the dead whose death we have stolen is the rock on which one day we may stumble.

If we have no ear for what the rock, become naked, smooth, mute, tells us, then all that has been silenced and assassinated is going to die again.

The ones who have died alone on the frozen boulder will die again for eternity, thus there will have never been a Prometheus, if we do not lay our hand on the stone, so as to blindly read the tale of solitary death.

All rocks recount Prometheus, and our forgetting of Prometheus.

Stones, ashes, high walls, fields of mud, bits of paper, barbed wire, here are our books, everything is written, everything silently shouts. May the reader come forth, may the ear, the hand come forth to hear so much silence.

When Alfios Sibisi was tortured on 1 March 1962, in the Dundee countryside near Natal[3] (But I shouldn't recount this here, so as not to cause too much anguish) . . .

It is not the pain that hurt him, it is seeing wickedness face to face, and having the devil for a witness.

As for Alfios Sibisi, I know nothing of him save this name and the date of his death. Neither his age nor his face. I know the list of tortures, in order, I know the club, the nails, the ladder, the chains. I know he did not cry out. All night he wept, he was heard weeping.

And the price of the axe he did not steal was: £1.5s.9d. Through his nostrils, his ears, his throat, through his esophagus, his entrails, his anus, he gave the axe back, in tears in blood in flesh, and in vomit.

But this, no one can understand.

– Your suffering is beyond my strength

Your solitary face is beyond my gaze. And meanwhile crouched, my runny nose between my knees, rolled up under the rock of Dolor, I try to hoist up my insufficient soul toward You,

You innocent initiate of atrocious mysteries, you living inhabitant of insane hells.

You meat hung alive on night's hooks.

I glance toward you, wretched ordinary man hoisted up to the divine by the all-powerfulness of misfortune. I throw just one frightened glance toward A. Sibisi, who entered skinless into the region of mysteries, because I cannot look him in the face.

"Where I am nailed, no nor any ordinary man has ever gone, from the high frozen exile where I am attached no one has ever come down again. An interminable abandon holds me separated from the earth. You who do not follow me, you cannot see what I can see,

"Countless deserted, lifeless, endless, mountains encircling my two human eyes, and there is no echo.

"And there in front of me, sole movement in the immobility, comes and goes sole presence in the abandonment, the sore with the iron teeth.

"Where I am planted, only agony stirs.

"And up there is not one more word."

Mute the angel of God. No appeal. The knife falls on the young man. God did not follow A. Sibisi.

It is not the pain that hurts, it is seeing absence face to face, and not crying out. So as not to hear the silence.

Up there, in a foreign land, where no one has ever gone, I am – I follow. Null, nude, and annulled. Strange and foreign clouds, cover my skinned body.

The path leading to absolute solitude needs to be traveled. Someone up there is crying. I have the impression it was me. But I cannot find the path

Till early morning, no one has found, no one has come. Quartered on his ladder, only witness to the end of the world, he said: oh my cherished mother, today I go away.

And finally a wild and savage solitude carried him off, with his mother in his breast. Then A. Sibisi himself finally abandoned A. Sibisi. He let him fall.

And all was finished and forgotten.

The ladder was found. The axe not. Sibisi could just as well have dispensed with being born. Being born not to be, that is what happens in this country.

Stories like Sibisi's I do not know how to recount. I stay at the bottom of the ladder leading to the heavens of echoless sand. I can only feel them while they are slipping away, weep for them while losing my tears, and then, so as to live, forget them.

So it goes; not only do we have to kill in order to live, kill the echo, we also have to silence ourselves and die, all this to stay, across earth, across blood, alive.

In the second passage from "Manna to the Mandelstams to the Mandelas" translated here, the political exile that links the Mandelstams and Mandelas is depicted in an account of Nelson Mandela's prison life. The capacity of love and new invention to transform the repressive order of self/other relations so graphically figured by apartheid is portrayed, here, in the glass screen through which Nelson Mandela and his wife must conduct their prison meetings. Writing, symbolized by the letters Winnie Mandela writes to her husband, plays a crucial role in this transformation. Significantly, writing is shown to depend for its effect not only on the writer – whose struggles to find the "tongue of rock" that will convey Mandela's prison experience are explored here – but also on the reader: "everything depends on you who read." The reader's role is dramatized in the passage in the uses the prisoners make of the sudden appearance of a whale.

The passage is on pp. 307–25 of *Manne aux Mandelstams aux Mandelas*, and is translated by Catherine MacGillivray.

A Life of letters

It is a life with death. World almost without earth. Here and there after three oceans every six months a letter to light on, a letter to rest on, to sleep at last, regain a bit of flesh, a bit of me, a bit of consciousness. In order to live with so little life and so much death one must know how to change bodies, be first a dove then a dream then pure means of transport, soul stiff across the abyss, fleshless feet walking on pebbles of air, six months not looking, not feeling the serrate ridges of six month days, not breathing, endless swimming under time without olive tree, and without stopping, holding back from dying, from expiring, not stopping to split the Nothingness, to not be (born),[4] to go, not being, to fly over, searching with one's eyes on the thick surface of the waters for a sign, a branch, a leaf of paper.

It is a life with five hundred words per letter, five hundred breaths per month, and the rest is silence and asphyxiation, and night.

For one birth, ten deaths.

And sometimes in the darkness stretched out between two letters, one no longer knows if it is non-being or being born[5] that is being barely written in the dark. Between two letters such inanition.

My wings closed once more, here I am standing in the pit, on the lowest step in the world, the sky is so far off, it is only barely that, throwing back my head, I manage to make it out. I am waiting, for the single flake of manna to fall from the invisible on high, I have been waiting for six months, I have been waiting for a thousand years. I am writing you the letter that will not leave, the letter I will not write, I am singing you the letter from the one who is buried alive.

Here time is killing us, breaking our heads with shovel blows, crushing our brains, setting our thousand nerves on fire, spitting us into the mud, sweeping us up in the courtyard, grinding our bones between two rocks, but powder, debris, dust, delirium, we never stop suffering and clinging to the date, so distant, of the next far-off mail.

I will not write to you the interletter[6] and the mysteriosities of time, yes, its audacities, its monsters, its terrifying masks.

Here below, fifteen days last two years, one has to lift an earth to be born, but in a day two years go by, no, two years have just gone by, and in these two years I have done nothing but go to bed and get up, I took two years to go from one wall to another wall, I will not write to you the grimaces that for us make up time.

And I too have for a face the torment of a grimace. With only the wall for a mirror, my face is a wall, a hardened crust that is waiting for a lava to lacerate it. Or the letter.

Buried under the impalpable tons of emptiness, to smile I move the muscles of my mask, and I cleave the crust from the corner of my lips.

The worst torment: this phantom burying, this being mad without madness, this drowning without water, with eyes open this blindness that can see itself. I am a blind man who can see the world's extinction.

This is why I do not write to you: what I see does not exist. Is an inverse version of life. A corpse's nightmare but the dreamer isn't dead. He has only fallen into the interletter, and for six months he comes to know what living on this earth he never knew.

The letter falls. Burying flees. Death was but a six-month dream. Here is notification of life. So light and strong. And the letter more true than time. So brief and so powerful.

In five hundred words, to rebuild the temple, glue back together the boat pieces, render night unto day and North unto South, restore the soul to human time, for some time, for some weeks, a letter! I get up immediately, I throw off the coat of stone, it is I who live and death that dies, my love, I was a skeleton, I did indeed receive the five hundred words of your letter, immediately slipping my parched voice into the humid heart of your words, I put your flesh on my bones

Five hundred words, a fleet, I put my body on and I set sail

Manna, sails, wings, tanks and planes on the paper, the curtains of stone fall at the horizon, Africa too leaves its sepulcher, I am in a hurry,

I am impatient, I am infinitely patient, I am capable of waiting five hundred deaths more if necessary. *Amandla! Nwagethu!*[7]

I would never have believed that a letter could be my mother and my boat! Look walls, look bars, I know how to pass through your teeth and your irons. And you, hysterical century, in vain you shout that I am dead forgotten and erased. Look, I know how to survive you. See my wings open. It is I who will wake up in the future, it is you who will not see it.

A letter, I open, the twenty-first century enters.

I received a letter of five hundred doors. By five hundred pathways it leads to tomorrow. It is a "Ticket to the Universe."

What's in a letter? There is what there is and what there isn't too. There is everything and almost everything and everything that isn't there is there too, is omitted and promised there. Everything depends on you who read it. The Universe in each letter, if you are child enough to receive it. In each letter all the music of all the spheres, if you are musician enough.

Little infinity, to be deciphered from all sides, by the white and by the black, by the leaves of paper and by the secret roots.

The first letter from Zami arrived on 12 January 1965, not a letter, a transfusion of the entire being in two pages of paper, a sea and in each word a pearl, an interlacing of all the legs and all the nights, and in between all the words a world, time, her skin, her hand, bread, it isn't a letter, and it is a letter just the same, not the world and the world just the same in two populated, planted, constructed, irrigated pages,

It was a plant. It was a leaf of paper. It was a closed door on which Zami could feel some keys. It was the mirage of a wall and I cannot find the words that will make it tremble.

But the tension of desires around the leaf of paper delivers it from its servile fetters.

The leaf of paper under Nelson's fingers is now the cooing of turtledoves that wakes the lovers. It was a forest, it still stirs from winds and storms. Messenger, kin to the pigeon, the plane, the boat, anciently and always plant and soul bearer.

One can read it. And also not read it. Take it. Barely on board, start it up and cross the city. At dusk a sort of peace rises in Johannesburg. At night peace climbs back up through the net's mesh. Before us in all its sparkling breadth flows the city bordered by pillars of steel. From one building to the other, the sky is stretching orange-colored tulle. The moon is in the hammock as though there were no danger. And it looks like the announcement of tomorrow. While I write to you, day twists in today's claws, but I can see it tomorrow, rolling out its great sparkling boulevards before you, contemporary at last.

To not read it, to follow its footpaths without haste, and sink step by step into its enigmatic breast like the Jew into the Torah. In the middle of the text, is the secret. In the middle of your life, there is the key.

And each letter is Bible, promised revelation, problem and deception. Who can say where the middle is, where before ends, where after starts?

Do you know there was a word missing in your letter of 1 May?

I carefully counted and recounted, there is one less word, I wonder which one it is.

Or else it isn't missing. This is the word that makes for dreaming and hoping. The last word of this story. The first word of the other century.

O there are so many letters in the letter, and yet so few, and yet there is an extra letter in the letter, always an extra letter in each letter, and once all the letters hidden in the letter have been discovered, reading is a limitless journey, in the letter is all the air in the world and almost all the earth,

– But writing was such a torment, my love, this I will not write to you. How this letter fled from and provoked me, and how it rose up before me like a wicked army, with its five hundred words mocking me, I do not write this.

Counting the words on my page a hundred times, there are too many and not enough, from day to day anxiety mounts, in five hundred which words for saying everything I'd like to tell you, and may each word be the right one, full and juicy, each word true and not lying, I have not succeeded, I struggle for weeks surrounded by ten thousand words, my tongue becomes strange and foreign to me, this is not exactly what I wanted to tell you.

And how, saying these words, to sing, and how, with all these words, to write the depth of my silences, and how, counting the words, to kiss your mouth and nose? My head is full of bookkeeping. Neither one more nor one less.

My love I send you five hundred words but I do not tell you from out of what a mass of words I have taken them, and that I am beaten and bewildered. May you manage to read behind the hurdle all I wanted to write you, in only three words, life, victory, future, and these three words in only one: we.

My love, I am sending you the cinders. I ask you to read the fire.

Happily there is paper, happily there are the hands of paper on my cheeks, on my brow on my chest on my belly, I read your letter with my whole skin and without words, with my whole skin I drank your paper caresses, I rubbed my whole body with your letter of 12 January, eyes closed I sipped and sniffed it and it was really your perfume I was reading, line by line.

Or else it is "the senseless and blessed word" that Osip talked about, the word he was going to say, the word he would have said, and will no one ever know what it is?

What is it, this marvelous word Nadezhda has been dreaming about for twenty-six years? For only in dreams can she still hope.

Which is it, what will be the first word to reach his liberated lips when the coffin is taken out? I do not know it. But I know who will receive it.

Without hands, without nose, without tongue, without music, without stars, without sex. But not without letter. And for a moon the bulb of feeble filaments.

The rest is silence. Silence must be learned. It is such a difficult language. It isn't spoken. It speaks itself in a low voice, so very low . . .

And for the eyes? A life of panes.

The landscape of the prison visit is the dark and icy well, six months deep. In order to depict it as harsh as it is, I need the famous rude hoarse raspy tongue of rock, tongue of tusks, of rack and rock, tongue dirtied with dung and daub, of flaking rhymes, this tongue that Dante lacks in the treacherous region number thirty-two, for even his mouth, skilled at making so many different accents resound high and low, dry or soft like butter, pale and strong in color, even his mouth, capable of Tartar, of Greek, of woodpecker, of worst, and of horrible bursts, would not have withstood the usage of a tongue so cruelly strange and foreign to all human modulation. Without the juice of vowels, of pounding diphthongs, I need a guttur and affricate tongue, with striking dentals and cacophonous orchestra. And up above a thick bed of ice.

For none can live in this heartless circus without having first frozen his nerves of compassion and of shame.

I mean to say no voluntary inhabitant, no guard. Here in the dark depths of the Universe dwell freely only those who have abandoned all sensation. Prison means refrigeration of the soul's faculties. A guard does not live, he is conserved. For if he were alive he would die of pity. Here is the horror: the condemned man, he, wants to suffer. And it is with all his strengths that he fights to not allow the ice to take his heart and mortally appease it.

Only torture and separation happen here. Separation is scattered everywhere. Nothing escapes it, neither thought, nor body, nor phrase, all that is separable is struck with separation. All is cut out, sectioned off, broken up, dismissed, dispersed, denied.

When, after having crawled for six months between ranges of rocky teeth, Zami arrives within sight of her goal, she is finally going to see him with her eyes of flesh, a day of twenty minutes, after six months of shadows, finally the source, a single sip of blessed water for forty deserts, he is going to come, he is coming, he enters, no, he only enters recaptured, refused, in vain the eyes in vain the lips hope for the sip of light.

Through a pane of glass – O why don't I have the tongue of rack and rock so as to try to scratch it – this isn't a window but rather the Cocytus[8] raised up before her before him, a sheer lake a double lake of ice and mud, as if the bottom of the entire Universe were standing straight up like a door, so as to separate them more.

Through a wall of ice – a sliver of Nelson. Like half a fish caught in an ice of tears. Almond tree cut through the middle. A trunk. Twenty years go by. Springtime after springtime recaptured by the ice, half a Zami can see no more than half of Nelson.

Who invented the glass torture? In vain the eyes fold themselves and twist the eyelids, nothing can bite the worst of walls, the most perverse, the one that effaces the hope it has aroused.

Never did the Danube in Austria, or the Neva under the January sky, or the Volga under the boundless bridge, cover its body with such an opaque crust. It is zero degrees between the gazes. And the glass is voracious of each expression. The voice too is devoured. The timbres shatter on rocks of glass. And like frogs that keep their faces above the infernal water, slivers of livid life visible to the waist, and for the rest vanished, thus separated from in front and through the middle, and under the sway of glass metamorphosed into half-batrachians, Nelson and Zami exchange snatches of conversation crushed and splintered by the ice. Trying to see, through the glaucoma that masks them, the unalterable truth. "How beautiful you are, my love, how handsome you are!" They croak. And make of the menacing pane of glass a bizarre bond of ice. All that separates them clandestinely unites them.

Twenty years go croaking by. But I remember Mozart of the well-nourished birds, of the rapid arpeggios of satisfaction, I have, deep down in my ear, a little transparent but clear, the roundish roulades of your voice, that is why I do not surrender to the pane's argument. Twenty years without milky sounds have not succeeded in killing the music sown in my memory. It is dozing alive under the beds of ice. And even if twenty years have passed since my last words rang out in the African air, snow is good for the rosebush, I am not afraid of winter. Today in the middle of summer we are cold like Russians. Today like the damned enraged by jealousy, the pale century plants its fangs in my throat and keeps me from moving, I look like half a frog, I know it, but I haven't changed a bit, my voice hasn't lost a B. And tomorrow, as soon as the pane melts away, you will recognize me at the gong of the first word.

I am not of the vitreous species, I am not of the glacial epoch, I will not die by a foreign hand, but under our own stars, by a hand with familiar skin.

And it is in 1981, after seventeen years of panes, that Zami found out what Nelson would eat at least this year, 1981.

This year, 1982, I saw your body down to your hips.

And I saw your left foot in its entirety through the pane in the year 1983.

This is how he comes back to her, through slow and cruel and fantastic evolution, unpredictably, as though reconstituted out of order by a chance naturalist.

Pains riches.

Isis is paralyzed, birds bring Osiris back to her in fragments, without any vision of the whole. Now she has a foot, the right one is missing, the chest is breathing but not the belly.

Waiting for the whole she adores the part. And everything that Zami did not know when she was little, when the beauty of the hills, the far-off, blue breasts of the earth, let her believe her mother the world belonged to her in her entirety, and when the tunic of barbed wire had not yet been placed upon her body,

all the strange ruses our species tirelessly invents for surmounting infernal separation and reclaiming the mother, the air, the blueness, the milk, the honey, the marrowy, and all the goods privation kills in us, all the secrets of survival below zero,

she has discovered through exile and through separation.

How can so many anguishes added to so many angers and so many regrets and so much fatigue and so much despair added together produce in the end such an exaltation, the heart's marvelous response to the knife!

And as the child makes child's play out of taking the air by playing with the rubber ball, Zami takes the air by going out with her superb hat. And for bread and wine? For visiting the bottom of the well she has chosen the long earrings that hang down all along her neck and rest upon her breasts. All one has to do is follow them.

The earrings pulverize the pane's ambition, and lift the mountains of time, for no matter how deprived of palms and fingers the lovers are, just as it is said that Persian poems are sweet enough to attract the appetite of bees, so the earrings arouse on the forsaken skin the living memory of past caresses. I think I feel, I feel caresses caressing me and I do not know how my soul finds this agile and magnetic body capable of passing through the wall and coming to nestle on your chest. Yes, these are the mysteries that occur in the places where desire outwits the laws of matter.

And from the whale of 20 January, 1973, Nelson received the sea he had lost, nine years ago, for the second time.

. . . It was a day like the thirty thousand days before, so much the same so gray of sky and sea, and for thirty thousand years nothing new under the sun of Robben Island,

On the island all equally white with dust and all equal in non-hope. No one uses the future tense anymore, and from the word "future" even dreams turn away. One no longer dreamed except in the past tense.

Drop by drop of blood the years are lost and one desires shamefully for the exsanguine hour to finally come.

One feels kinship with the dust. My mother the dust, my sister the pick-axe, my dog my ankles' chains. And for cathedral without walls and without rose-window a colossal boredom.

And to think that alive I saw complexly planned cities branching out in all directions, just like my brain and my thoughts used to do. What is left of the universe: the unreadable ocean, a senseless sum of vaguely wavy waves.

If only from the rock we could still see the mountain and its tables furrowed with signs, there would be something to read. But here for books we have this infinite chiffon, forgetful of everything at every moment. On Robben Island we hated the sea.

But suddenly, between the coffin and the horizon, over there, in the far-off middle of the desert, see how a fountain bursts forth. Like a dying sailor crying: land! land! like the lost cameleer moaning at the mirage, Walter cried out: a whale! And they all saw the gush the first time, and like a second trumpet blow the second time and at the third burst it was like their gushing tears, shooting forth from the bosom of the earth, up into the closed sky.

A whale! A free whale! a giant dove! someone! a big black mammalian angel.

No one saw the body of the whale from here with his own eyes but they all felt it, and the sea, deserted and the same, which for nine years had never brought them any consolation, as though around Robben island the sea itself ceased being sea, suddenly the sea was pregnant and good and its belly was full of mystery and freedom and also of play. The whale engendered all kinds of legends. She became a submarine train that whistles three times, she became the mother of all the Xhosa and Tembu ancestors, but for the Indians she was an avatar of Ganga,[9] for all of them she became the black egg out of which the first ocean came out of which came the earth, and for Nelson, the powerful and vulnerable giant to whom he is devoted. No one really saw the whale but none doubted having seen the promise, all the sea's doors having opened before their so ancient, so discouraged desire.

And for one day and one night each believed according to his belief, according to his hope and according to his taste.

And none felt the irons the walls the bars.

They were all at sea, swimming and riding, and winning the war. And exultant childhood memories were coming back from all parts. They had all come out of their coffins like children in pajamas. And there were boastings and delicacies. The whale, the fairy, the woman, the ring that circulates from hand to hand, the queen one only asks for the first kiss. Each one knowing anew how to find the strength to vanquish monsters with a simple nod of the mother's head.

Unfortunately Rohlilahla missed the second whale, the one in 1981, detained as he was on that day by an Australian journalist. Having been deprived of the whale caused him a pain he would not avow. But fortunately there is always Walter to play the ostrich part. At night, under the thirty-watt moon, Walter said to the air: "Don't regret the whale, my son. In two months you will have a visit from your own whale."

Courage is finding the courage when there is no more courage. And where to look for it? When he feels abandoned by hope, aged, with the child dying inside of him, Nelson gets up and goes to clean the prisoner Daniels' hygienic bucket. And in the bottom of the bucket he finds the courage.

But this infernal torment of bodies, this torture of the pane, Zami and Nelson cannot want it to stop, all they can want is to submit to it again and again for it is all that is left them to enjoy, yes, it is pain cut out of desire, always alive, its bite is the ultimate benediction.

Grant that I may not be disembodied by separation. Grant that the ice not seize my soul. Grant that I may be devoured again in my chest and in my belly by the same intolerable hunger, may I go through the veldt my arms full of flames, flayed by the roses of separation, grant that I believe I am dying one more time at each visit, before the hour after the hour and at each minute of the hour, in twenty years, in thirty years and when my hair is white,

Grant that I may try in vain to extinguish the fire, grant that I may dream in vain of closing the abyss again,

Grant that the harsh tears of mourning roast my eyes,

Grant that I may feel absence uproot my organs, so that lack tears my soul from me like a tooth, may I feel my widowed body turned all tiny and naked like a dwarfed heart detached from the world's chest that beats crying,

Grant that separation not stop attacking, and may I never begin to bear the unbearable,

keep us forever from all appeasement, give us to taste the bitterness of consolations

that come to us under the innocent guise of our grandchildren

may each tender morsel of baby that comes in delicate pity to our lips may each kiss turn straightaway to glowing embers on our tongues,

if the aurora sky transports our heart in a chariot of red colors, may joy itself dash us to the bottom of pain, once we arrive at the peak of exaltation,

Fill us with happinesses that burn like nettles,

Sharpen our senses, suffocate our throats with beauties, may each magnificent hour be our agony

And when day sets in a concert of crickets and the charivari of birds, may our souls deplore yet another murder, yet another life with its womb full of children and of the little birds they have assassinated in us, yet another mother yet another child,

Haunt our fleshes with the blind eroticism of the newborn, that seeks, as if its entire life were but a mouth, the absolute breast, and from the strong depths of our bodies may our shouts of fury rise up like irrepressible sap

And may the day of crucifixion be every day. Amen.

For I say to you I want to enjoy the fruits of this martyrdom. At dawn my pain rises with red cheeks and covers my body with a wild and opulent absence of flowers. Everything is lily, lilac, arias of freesias for me, inaudible hymn of iris and trumpet of amaryllis, I have everything I do not have, lack celebrates in me the inexpressible ecstasies of satisfaction, I have your invisible and heavy hands upon my breasts, I am an almond tree that burns without rest, like two damned people closely bound for thousands of years, I inhale eternity through my roots with clutching fingers, up above I disappear in smoke, under the earth I am born I suck I cling immortally, I am firmly planted with all my fibers I who am doubled by you, in the uterus of the future.

Martyrdom is my placenta. The atrocious bread.

In the bitter kernel the milk seed. The almond is there, in the bitterness. It is the secret Mandela: the manna. The manna come from the heaven hidden under the earth. It has a taste of necessity. *Amandla!*

In the lack of hope, hope. One must despair alongside abrupt and rending time, the vertical desert, face against the wall, chest lacerated on the rock's fingernails, eyes wounded by the sand, from step to step, until hope.

NOTES

1 The exception is *On ne part pas, on ne revient pas*, performed and published in 1991, Paris: des femmes Antoinette Fouque. [Ed.]

2 See, however, *L'Histoire terrible mais inachevée de Norodom Sihanouk Roi du Cambodge*, Paris: Théâtre du Soleil, 1985, pp. 194–5. [Ed.]

3 A province of South Africa, on the Indian Ocean. [Trans.]

4 The French has *nêtre*, a play on the French for "to be born" (*naître*) and the negation of the verb "to be" (*n'être (pas)*). [Trans.]

5 The French has *nêtre ou naître*; see note 4 above [Trans.]

6 The French has *l'entrelettre*. [Trans.]

7 *Amandla* means power, which is what Nelson Mandela cried to the crowd at his trial. They answered him *Nwagethu!*, which means "to the people." It is the last of the rivers of Hell in Dante's *Inferno*. [Trans.]

8 In Greek mythology, the river of wailing, a tributary of the Acheron in Hades. [Trans.]

9 Ganga is one of the manifestations of the Hindu Great Goddess. [Trans.]

FirstDays of the Year

In *Jours de l'an* – "FirstDays of the Year," published in 1990, writing is itself the subject of the fiction. The text opens with a description evoking Cixous' delineation of a feminine writing, in which a writing of the other, committed to expressing the truth and deriving from and received by the body, is vividly portrayed.[1] In the passage translated here, the paradoxical predicament of language is dramatized as the author endeavors to find an alternative means of expressing her love. Echoing the problematic of "Inside,"[2] where the "I" must accept constraint if she is to exist and so influence "outside," the author wants not to use yet cannot avoid the word "love." The negative constructions language carries are exemplified in an exploration of the ways "Death" has been symbolically invested. This enmeshment is contrasted with an earlier, pre-Oedipal relation to the world in which "we went without counting (. . .) each feeling a benediction." The recreation of this paradise is the writer's task. Words, our "antique and enemy inventions," must be purged, opening a new space for writing: "the universe to rewrite." This new cultivation will transform our relations to the world, others and ourselves.

The passage is on pp. 250–9 of "Une Histoire idéale" – "An Ideal Story," in *Jours de l'an*, Paris: des femmes Antoinette Fouque, 1990, and is translated by the editor. A translation by Catherine MacGillivray of *Jours de l'an* is currently in preparation for the University of Minnesota Press, Minneapolis.

Clarice: Another word than the word "love," my love: it concerns this labor at the extreme and ultimate limit of thought. It means piercing old opaqued thinking. And for this rid ourselves of the words that cling to our feet, to our knees, to our eyelids by their thousand tiny frightened fingers, begging us not to advance. Not any further. And which hold us back and tell us the worst, the lifeless and soiled and chilly terrestrial version of the human condition. Get rid of the words that separate us from the world, and that cry out their fear, and that are made to dissuade us from reaching and leaving, and from touching and going beyond and tasting everything promised us in the world, and that make us believe all is not good, this is not good, that is good, mystifying and petrifying us, and separating us from the world which is entirely good. It means becoming resplendent again. Once we suckled roots entwined in Nature. Sucked sweet bitterness. We knew how to grasp life's taste in extreme suffering. We have been free and powerful, we no longer even know where or when. Everything that happened to us: thanks. When were we generous? When were we not the dupes of fear? When did we make a minute the occasion for the grandest and finest, the time for a journey with a wedding, feast, construction of a palace and great oranged light? We could. When did we play all the instruments? Between language and ourselves there was neither obedience nor disobedience, only exact conjugation of feeling and music. Saying did not crush. When did we still draw from the paste of words the hoped for, unique, necessary accents?

When did we naturally live very high up, and very profoundly, and now we look at the high from below, and we call it impossible and superhuman, so as to protect our acquired baseness, our laziness, our leanness of imagination?

We have not always been thus subhumanly human, so seated, so miserly, so reduced in soul and so large of stomach, and grabbing, soul for stomach, and everyday frightened of being hungry.

We were evidently happy in another time and effortlessly, we have forgotten but the nights remember, we did not compare "much" with "a little," "how much" did not exist, we went without counting, we knew how to take pleasure in the heavy as in the light, losing was a find, each feeling a benediction, each moment a master, each hunger celebration of bread, when we supernaturally lived naturally. And no complaint, only a marvelous curiosity.

I had the power. The women who saw me pass admired the promise of my back. I too felt my broadness glisten. I can carry the world. Worries grow on the sea's shores. Opposite is my country, my unknown, my future, my book. How to gain entry, coming from this side without a passport, and without papers? And without a costume to go in the sea. I am before words. I have the unknown power of myself, which is nakedness. I dive. The leap is so strong it carries me for a long time over the waters' surface without ever weakening and without breaking it, for a long time I skim the waters like a giant swallow. In truth I am flying. Tirelessly without wings. My back, my body are my wings, and in my body the endless desire and destiny. I will do it, I will. I let nothing stop me, neither illusion of ocean nor illusion of words. Let us go the edge of the world, and be able.

When did we fall into the old net of poisoner words, and farewell our gaiety our genius, our powers in a single blow!

And up to the memory of our fall. And we believe we were foetus in the net, born to mesh and impediment. We get up without eternity, and one hour later we have withdrawn from great adventures. We exist with our eyes on the eye of clocks. We will not follow the Beauty that passes, we will not jump this river, we will flee the abyss, we will be completely blind, completely deaf, completely worn out, our dreamless backs thoroughly docile. The book of the world? a dictionary, everything is in the dictionary, loving is in the dictionary, everything is ordered, described, dictionaried, known, my body is in the dictionary,

oh my love, we are in the monster's mouth and it has thirty-five thousand teeth

I have just looked up the word "love" in the dictionary, and I confirm this to you it is not with "love" that I love you, with love as well, but not only with known "love" and known synonyms,

no my love is not this love. This very much is not a very much. I look up "scale" and I do not find my scale, the one that grows according to my spring, for each spring a new branch.

If we no longer have the grace of the native heights, let us plant the vegetable ladder and climb back up again. I collect myself, I lift my foot and already it is the other world. We are always much stronger than we think.

I hear my own cry of joy rise up in the space growing again round my heart. I do not know what I am writing you. I follow the movement. I am the scale. I am sure. I have gone on to life. I advance: this is happiness. I do not look around me nor at the clock's eye: happiness. I do not think, I respond. I am called to living and I respond.

Who says this happiness is not happiness? Who reckons my eternity in hours? Who judges my copy, who notes my infinity, who claims to take my measurement? I do not answer to your University. At the desk I am nothing.

Who frowns? Who summons me to the butcher and with lowered head I make my way there, my briefcase under my arm, without knowing the matter?

It is: "Death" with all its synonyms, derivatives and representatives, its paper soldiers, and its allies, our unimaginable lack of imagination and the tyranny of our lack of imagination. It is Death and its untrue scythes.

"Death," what a story! And to say that we invented it, invented it so well that we no longer even know we are the authors of its stories. We who have drawn it painted and crowned from our weakness, ensuring our weakness with weak days. Then we arm it with all the words that diminish us. The miracle is we have invented "God" and feel so much better for it. The anti-miracle is that we have invented "Death."

And the mystery is that we confuse invent and believe. We invent this word Death and the word becomes our master, and do we not disinvent? One word, and here we are crippled, cold, off course, and for years. Its strength is in its weakness. The enemy is almost invisible: mistrust a word? And here it is biting in a thousandth of a second our myriads of neurons and one second later, poisonous messages course through our veins, and one minute later we are tainted and mortalized down to the smallest state of feeling.

And then what an ugly word: "Death." Die for a word? At least let it be magical, and ring at God's door, like the word "Absinth," or the word "Mystical." At least a quicksilver horse, or the star with the singing horses. This life for the white pebble that has our new names engraved, though nothing less. Or the word "missed" recto verso: I missed you, I didn't miss you, a word that doesn't miss any sparkle: this tear, suspended from my lashes that ripens, your name murmured by my eyes.

Today I am attacking the words that bite, our antique and enemy inventions. It is Friday, day of thorough cleaning, I will give language a fine combing. And cleanse and scrape the ground and walls and ceiling of my brain, it is exhausting work, you have to turn against yourself, you have to be on the watch for yourself, surprise yourself, foil yourself. And careful because words come back at the slightest distraction. I will make a mistake. But I know it. I will suspect myself of deceipt. As long as is necessary. I will never disarm. To begin with I make no mistake: I have decided to cut with "Death." It is a very simple war. There is a battlefield.

What a vast cosmic pretence! There we are in our hundreds and thousands presenting ourselves for the exams. In waves of generations. And they give us ration tickets for life. But I am not born on this slip of paper. In 1789, I already said in the streets we are born free to be millenarians. Against us the weariness that wants "the cessation of life" (I found that in the dictionary). But already no longer against. For we immediately leave the battlefield. This is our way of waging war: we leave. My river has changed beds. Death? We no longer believe it: we cut its livings. Thinking this is enough. Everything is the work of beliefs. We make death from a belief. We open time's portal in belief: there we are, each minute is granted to our desire.

You, wretched Death, whom I attack, I don't bear you any ill will, creature of our anguishes, vast illusion we have sculpted in nightmare lining, to then revere you with hatred, monster child of our entrails, in whom we swear we see our assassin, powerless thing transported on the blazing throne, fruit of our pallors, poor divinity we make in the image of our terrors and our sicknesses, condemned innocent, you whom we beg to help us live basely, to live slowly and pinched in little shoes, and to whom we dedicate piles of smoking lies, how will I forget you, obedient fierceness we make a show of obeying.

No, Death, you are not this, this dragon denture. You can go in peace, you can disperse. Go, I don't need to run against you to live and revive.

I went out. Before me the field of time: everything to cultivate. I must announce this. Even so it is a change of nature. The universe to rewrite. I do not yet know how, in freedom, on high, going down. Trumpets!

Clarice's voice to Isaac's voice: – I have just effected a break with Death.[1] It is not a game. It means purifying the word. Are you listening to me?

Isaac's voice: – I am listening to you, I am obeying you.

Clarice's voice: – These shivers – these nights during the day, these fallings of stars and organs we call "death": only the flesh seeks. Life herself calls for help. So if we call this hunger, this momentary empty belly, "you," we will suffer in joy. I feel a great joy blowing, coming to me from the world: it is the absence of fear that inspires the inner landscape. The world and I are laughing.

Should I be frightened of losing you? I am the sole author of the threat: I have to fear my own betrayals, my absences of spirit, my de-centerings. Yesterday when you phoned me, I was not at the right height. I was underground, half buried in my own silence, far from our territory, in deliberation, looking for the root of a feeling, when you called me. And lacking strength and speed I did not manage to climb to your height. I saw you very clearly, up to my neck in darkness. I spoke with my mouth and throat, the rest of my body in silence. A dumb animal's suffering: you hold your hand out to me. And my hand does not obey me. It is a dumb animal. I need five minutes to awaken it. When it finally returns I hold it out, your hand has been withdrawn. Living us requires my utmost strength. I am challenged. I am the challenge. I am scared of not succeeding our minutes. Living is my affair. But dying? That will come to us, I will tell you. I already know that I will have to fight like never before to be up to this high high moment. I want to be there. I will be there.

NOTES

1 See *Jours de l'an*, Paris: des femmes Antoinette Fouque, 1990, p. 5. [Ed.]
2 See "Inside," above. [Ed.]

Deluge

In "Extreme Fidelity," Cixous cites loss as a key factor in the subject's formation.[1] In this next extract from *Déluge* – "Deluge," published in 1992, the experience of personal loss at the end of a love relationship joins to the loss – of the m/other, death – at the heart of the human condition in a rewriting of the biblical flood. In a graphic depiction of death, the passage describes the "compulsory murder" of the self's own needs and desires losing entails, and highlights the "poison" of illusion. The work mourning involves is dramatized through the character of Ascension, as she struggles to discover and invent solutions to the problems that confront her. This never-ending struggle is nonetheless presented as vital, since it is *in* the work that we live.

The extract appears on pp. 168–77 of "On perd toujours l'enfant" – "One Always Loses the Child" – in *Déluge*, Paris: des femmes Antoinette Fouque, 1992, and is translated by the editor.

Portraits of afflictions

By night, as well as by day, the murdered dead send their red corpses back by the hole in time and have their dripping wet clothes taken before the room where we think in their direction, we think in vain, our thoughts cannot unmurder them, and we too feel wet.

It does not dry,

Everyone is so tired.

Different dead outlive us, and all kinds of afflictions haunt our bodies,

They are people without a face

Visions without pictures

Flights without steps

We lean forward we would like there to be something to see. We scrutinize without eyes, we brush the dark night with our lashes, we would so much like stars. Shovelfuls of silence are heaped on the bedded form.

Inside the body has become confined. The dead cannot believe they are dead. They hurt everywhere. I feel how the dead suffer during decomposition.

Suffering on the one hand, and remembering on the other. Their powerlessness. They cannot. They cannot believe it as long as they still have some marrow not-to-feel-can-not.

And self-murder, not suicide, the compulsory murder of oneself, what is that called which comes after love, this unnamable which is love cut with its own teeth, wasted love, rotten suffocated love, strangling of love, huge hardened tongue, full hardened pain, and which is not hate, which does not reach that state of well-being, which is love's unburied never buried corpse, the fear and desire that there is still something living in the corpse, the great and shameful fear, in the corpse, a muscle, a hand, an old smile, and the necessity of killing the rest, everything must die, everything must be denied, we cannot bury half and leave the rest, a prey to regret, mute decay,

it is necessary to release this body and strike half this heart with the other half, and if there's courage keep quiet and kill ourselves,

And we bury ourselves inside ourselves, this is the hardest,

And then sometimes, like an enchantment, the illusion rises up. The illusion, as heart-rending as a dead person's dream. When a dead person dreams they are alive, ah! what transparent force, throughout the dream they no longer know they are dead, the dream is so vast, the illusion stretches beyond memory, the dead one lives as far as the dream carries them – and suddenly, what decomposition. It's then that we truly feel the infinite horror of being dead.

Ah the gentle poison of illusion! How it tells us we are not dead. How it returns precisely what we have lost! How it extinguishes the flames which ate our heart, and how it launches us on its extraordinary boat: it's a boat of such vast dimensions that we cannot see its sides, we don't see that we are on its boat.

How it distances memory. And how it makes us drunk on oblivion. And oblivion is so powerful. And so in the illusion a dead one leant over her living lover. She listened as she contemplated the beloved face with joy. The lover was saying that the worst was never having any time to resolve his difficulties. She (the dead one) held him in her arms and understood. She told him he would finish by finding time, that she would help him, she sympathized, she was saying the word "time" and, suddenly, there was the explosion. She remembered. What was she saying? It was *she* who no longer had any time at all, she had forgotten that she was no longer living, for a moment, one of these profound slender seconds of illusion, she had been inside the old relation, entirely, and suddenly the flame had just been blown out. Outside! She felt she was going to cry dreadfully but she didn't even have time. It was dark. And nothing else. But *there remained* the hellish pain of remembering the brief happiness without memory and of feeling that it had not been real. Only the work of a very powerful deception. The illusion does not dissipate without trace. It makes us pay, after the event, when we have again lost everything we only believed we possessed. This life will have been so short, a minute, and we have not tasted it. But the mourning which overtakes us, the second mourning is as great as the first. Everything has to be begun again. It breathes over our decayed body a double regret. There is no worse pain than these cinders of desires the dead haunted by a posthumous memory suffer. We must extinguish ourselves. We see skeletons scratching the dust from their breast in the attempt to bury a remnant of their heart there. The pain of these remains is unimaginable.

To leave death behind you, you have to run very fast straight ahead with the lightness of a deer, be yourself the swiftness and lightness. This is what Ascension had learnt to do. As soon as she felt her teeth quiver, she leapt. Counting on her own body which was slender and strong and knew not death, she could cross threatening places, she ran down the rows during masses, along the great corridors of the universities, her fine forceful flight attracted the stares of people sitting in rooms around the world, she skirted assemblies, at eight o'clock at night it was almost the end of the day, of the world, of performance, people gently shook themselves, she sped like an arrow, on her own, ready to triumph, almost gay almost happy in the joy of being able to count on her own speed, and at the limit of the dull country at the end of the dark, there will be the other continent, life obtained.

Sometimes she encountered obstacles, she had been suddenly stopped, but then she had found solutions, where there were none, she had invented them. One day of great threat – she relates – which seemed incredible to her, as if pronounced by Hitler, she tells, I set off running at top speed, I had split the crowd which already encircled me, was about to recognize me, hand me over, there I was in my Renault 5, I drove over this foreign ground which would have happily killed me, I knew the feeling of violent exile where I was, for where I was in this land I was rejected and disgraced, where I put my foot hostility arose, it was the earth itself which no longer loved me and attacked me – I feared it, I looked at its roads and hills and it would have been war if we had been able to kill each other, it would have happened. I escaped. Here I am on the outskirts of the town. I chose the more wooded route. But ahead of me everything is closed. Rubble blocks the road, trees are across it. I get out, I look, the road has been broken up, and raised vertical. In truth it has been raised against me. No, this is not an obstacle that will surrender, the road itself has become wild and animate. Can I get through by the side? There is forest to the left and to the right. What can I do? A man appears, a woodcutter. A very small round and gentle man, who is neither from one country nor the other. One might call him an inspiration. I showed him my difficulty. I needed to take this road. Yes but as from today and from now on it is blocked, he told me. You must go round the town, and take the road on the other side towards Czechoslovakia. Ah no! I wholeheartedly refused. I would lose too much time, perhaps years, generations, I would never find my road again, whereas from here it was straight ahead. No detour, no regression, I said. I must go. I pleaded with this man. Would he not agree to help me? My car is not heavy. Together we could carry it through the forest and pick up the road on the other side of the raised section. It was a matter of a few metres. Life two metres away, I cannot give that up. Already I smell the odor of the earth called life on the other side. If this woodcutter had not existed I would have invented him. I got ready to lift the car with him. The impossibility of going back fired me to such an extent that I could not not find a solution. We bent forward. Lifting it was really not very hard. Won over by my own inner conviction the woodcutter even put it under his arm. And now we were advancing sometimes on the broken edge, sometimes by the edge of the forest. Carried in this way my car looked like a large toy. This was how an insurmountable obstacle was overcome.

After several months of a flight begun over almost daily, crossing one lost country or another, and leaving time behind her from town to town, she could no longer be far from a future land – she felt – a virgin blameless land where no one would remember, and she would remember no one. Already when she went out early the sky was clear and harmless. The street in front of the house did not attack her as she opened the door. Things resumed their studious nature of just things. An ordering took place. She was no longer the cherished object of head hunters. She could roam the districts like a free woman, proud, unnoticed, bound to herself, shops no longer wavered in her sight, squares no longer produced bitter plants, the voices of the dead no longer floated her dead name in the cafés.

The weather: dry, cold, current. She went towards her joy, she sensed it because of a slight drunkeness: something at the extremity of loss, which was a purity. An empty purity, slightly dazzling: the quivering nothingness that precedes the first time. Emotion of purification. Everything calmed down, fell back, she stopped feeling noticed. She came close to sweet impersonality. End of the tragedy. She did not say "I am happy" out of modesty. But she said "I am" with a small secret joy. Herself. And so unknown! Everything to do, everything to accustom. The heart beats, we're going to "start again."

One evening in April, at the corner of a street, all of a sudden, mourning overcame her with the violence of a storm. This is how it is. The wheel turned. Once again mourning broke loose. Mourning weeps.

Mourning wept without her being able to do anything about it. Without measure, without proportion. You never saw so many tears. They meet with no resistance. It is not up to us. They gush. Ourselves, we do not want to weep, but mourning listens only to its own, so powerful, so ancient, desires. An endless affliction carries our tragedy in its unfolding. A hundred mournings flow into this mourning.

No it is not you we cry for, it is not us who cry for you, mourning weeps the best of ourselves within us. I mourn eternity, I mourn the person in whom I had invested eternity, I mourn speech, I have lost the imagined, predicted, dreamt human being, I mourn innocence and all the innocents.

Where does mourning overtake us?

It is at the summit, on the cliffs which hold dominion over the beach from their walls, that Ascension will soon lose her life. Without any warning. On the contrary. We are in time as if we were in immortality. We do not see its end. To such an extent that I did not think of it, Ascension recounts. I was in the middle of discussing the mysteries of sexual difference. An interlocuter was asking me questions about women's sex, about that of C. L. and I. B. I explained: I am woman, I said. I pointed to the sky. It was clear. It was a beautiful day, with a clear view. Suddenly a wave rose up from the depths. A vast green wave that not only reached our high height but continued, overtook us, rose green and limitless, rose up to the platform and beyond. Immediately I was seized with an anguish that stretched out to the horizon. This wave rising like a green night is the tip of a tidal wave. You can no longer see the shore. And the children? My adored child who was playing down there? I began running towards the left of what was the earth. Meanwhile the wave slowly unrolls above us its vast fateful banner. Up there beneath the deadly flag everyone suddenly rendered miniscule was running. People cry out. Ask for news from people who have been down in the zone of the tidal wave. I met Ingeborg who was also running for her daughter playing over there. The children, the children! I shouted. Rumor cried that they had found two bodies there, no one knew if they were dead little ones or alive. I rushed over there in a wink and ran amongst the cliffs, unfortunately I ran on the ground, that is at the foot of the walls, for above on the crest rode the wave, but below you could not go in a straight line, I ran, I burrowed, I made detours, just now I went astray, then I drew nearer the path to the place where they might have found two bodies, I wept as I ran, I sobbed from love and terror, my child, my love, I pushed back the earth, Ingeborg followed behind me, though she was not writhing in pain. She slowed down, she grew weary, she said "Let us go. It was a baby.

I will have another." Ah! this was perhaps wise. But not for me. No. My child my love I would not have again. I would find him, I could not console myself, it was him I wanted. Moreover to have a child, I hurled at Ingeborg who wanted to stop, you need a man. Do you have one? I said. Not really, she replied. But the race seemed to her pointless. She no longer followed me. I began running again, I wept, obstinate, oh universe, through hope and despair, I will force the earth, such a race must vanquish destiny, this is no prayer, this is loyalty, an order, an oblig-ation, I went right to the end of the labyrinth, under the roar of the tidal wave, I ran beneath the sea, I ran on the earth, I went right to the end of misfortune, above the racing tide rattled to the wind, below I forced my way, I went right to the limit which I pushed back, alive I abruptly entered behind the time after hope, as long as we advance we prevent the story from ending, I ran, everlasting the love-mourning in me the child-suffering created a flow of tears matching the tidal wave above, bearing love death life farther, no I would not let myself be comforted and dried out, I would run on until dream or reality gave me back my love, to the end, I run

because after all I could always dream

Mourning unfurls its storm over the whole country, ourselves in torrents we weep joining our afflictions to the world's afflictions, deluge is our condition, but it is not our end, while it pours off our plumage, inside the dream lights a candle.

NOTE

1 See "Extreme Fidelity," above. [Ed.]

Three Steps
on the Ladder of Writing

Three Steps on the Ladder of Writing, published in 1993, is Cixous' revised presentation of three lectures given in English at the University of California, Irvine, in May 1990, as part of their Wellek Library Lectures on Critical Theory. In the first of three extracts reprinted here, Cixous explains her frustration with the debate on sexual difference as this is currently conceived. Evoking her insistence in "Extreme Fidelity" that masculine and feminine modes of behavior are not tied to anatomy but derive from our response to life, she argues here for the complexity of gender. Only writing, Cixous suggests, can at present convey the truth about identity.

The passage is taken from pp. 50–2 of "The School of the Dead," the first of the three lectures in the series, in *Three Steps on the Ladder of Writing*, New York: Columbia University Press, 1993. The text of *Three Steps on the Ladder of Writing* is edited by Sarah Cornell and Susan Sellers from an English transcript with French additions, and is substantially revised by Hélène Cixous.

It's only at the end – all of Ingeborg Bachmann's books are books about the end – she writes each time in agony – that everything we weren't able to say will be said. Not only is there a war between people, but this war is produced by sexual difference. And not just by sexual difference. By the wiles, paradoxes, and surprises that sexual difference reserves for us. This is why the man–woman conflict is insufficient for me, in my time, in my place. It *is* a question of sexual difference, only sexual difference isn't what we think it is. It's both tortuous and complicated. There is sexual difference, and there is what it becomes in its appearances and distributions in each one of us. We already knew it with Shakespeare: ourselves we do not owe and we do not know whom we love. Before the final hour we will not be able to say that such and such a woman was a man. Why can't we say it? Because it would be saying what the world is not yet ready to hear. Besides, it's dangerous, since we are on the way toward what could be retaken and distorted by misogyny. Let's imagine we love a woman who is a man inside. This means we love not a man exactly, but a woman who is a man, which is not quite the same thing: it's a woman who is also a man, another species. These complexities are not yet audible. Although this is true, strangely enough we are still today at a clear-cut difference, we continue to say man and woman even though it doesn't work. We are not made to reveal to what extent we are complex. We are not strong enough, not agile enough; only writing is able to do this. Sometimes we are married to a man because he is a woman, even though we believed we had married a man. Whom have we married? Our grandmother perhaps. A woman who was the replica of a woman-eating man passed off in the world as a woman par excellence. In this guise she slaughtered women wholesale, while being extolled by men for her maternal charm. This is a true tale. We should write "The Fables of Sexual Difference." They should be the tales of our times; they would be staggering. The Greeks did it. In the Greek tragedies Aeschylus tells us right away that Clytemnestra is of virile strength. But then who kills Agamemnon? I'd like to know. Is it a man or a woman who kills Agamemnon? Does it mean that a woman who kills a man is a man, etc.? In other words, that only a man kills a man. But then why accuse Clytemnestra of being a woman? There's no end to it . . .

We could think over these mysteries but we don't. We are unable to inscribe or write them since we don't know who we are, something we never consider since we always take ourselves for ourselves; and from this point on we no longer know anything. I'll tell you frankly that I haven't the faintest idea who I am, but at least I know I don't know. I am not the other able to perceive me. I know some things about myself. I know who I'm not, I believe.

As for you, the other, I am where I think you are not who you believe yourself to be, who you seem to be, who the world believes you to be – I am using the second person to avoid the difficulty of speaking either in the masculine or the feminine – on the other hand, given that the definition of me or you is the most vulnerable thing in us, this prevents me from thinking what I think. When we say to a woman that she is a man or to a man that he is a woman, it's a terrible insult. This is why we cut one another's throats.

We have extremely strong identifications, which found our house. An identity card doesn't allow for confusion, torment, or bewilderment. It asserts the simplified and clear-cut images of conjugality. If the truth about loving or hateful choices were revealed it would break open the earth's crust. Which is why we live in legalized and general delusion. Fiction takes the place of reality. This is why simply naming one of these turns of the unconscious that are part of our strange human adventure engenders such upsets (which are at once intimate, individual, and political); why consciously or unconsciously we constantly try to save ourselves from this naming. The one whom a woman calls "husband," is he the father, the son, or the he-mother? The one who governs the country, is he father or son? The war that divides the world in two halves is a war between father and son, or else a war between the archaic father, i.e., a type of mother and the jealous son. And what about women?

In our impassioned times on all political fronts, where it is largely a question of an open and covert struggle with the mysteries of sexual difference, as women we are at the *obligatory* mercy of simplifications. In order to defend women we are obliged to speak in the feminist terms of "man" and "woman." If we start to say that such and such a woman is perhaps not entirely a woman or not a woman at all, that this "father" is not a father, we can no longer fight since we no longer know who is in front of us. It's so destructive, so destabilizing that those of us who are conscious of what is at stake are often pushed toward a form of interdict. Only when we are posthumous can we place the earth in question; make the earth tremble.

In the second passage from *Three Steps on the Ladder of Writing* reprinted here, Cixous stresses the importance of dreams as a source for writing.[1] Citing Kafka's insistence that "a book must be the axe for the frozen sea inside us,"[2] Cixous suggests that dreams have the capacity to shatter the "eggshell" constructions we create about our lives.[3] The passage also exemplifies the rich textual layering characteristic of Cixous' critical style, as she refers to works by Kafka, Lispector, the brothers Grimm, Mandelstam, Dante, Hofmannsthal and Rimbaud.

The passage is taken from pp. 63–5 of "The School of Dreams," the second lecture in the Wellek series, in *Three Steps on the Ladder of Writing*. The text is edited by Sarah Cornell and Susan Sellers from an English transcript with French additions, and is substantially revised by Hélène Cixous.

Staring at length at the face of God

What we hope for at the School of Dreams is the strength both to deal and to receive the axe's blow, to look straight at the face of God, *which is none other than my own face*, but seen naked, the face of my soul. The face of "God" is the unveiling, the staggering vision of the construction we are, the tiny and great lies, the small non-truths we must have incessantly woven to be able to prepare our brothers' dinner and cook for our children. An unveiling that only happens by surprise, by accident, and with a brutality that shatters: under the blow of the truth, the eggshell we are breaks. Right in the middle of life's path: the apocalypse; we lose a life.

To my sincere surprise, which is only the product of a form of blindness, I realized in time that the writers I love above all are of the dyingclairvoyants kind. What also reunites these authors is that they wrote, as I like to say, *by the light of the axe*: they all dared to write the worst, dared to "shatter the frozen sea," as Kafka puts it, break eggshells, the hulls of boats; they all dared to crack skulls, their own skulls, and return to the forest. All these things are discharged through violent separation, loss, and sudden good luck – without which we would indeed be limited; we are able to do this at the School of Dreams. Where is it situated?

The School of the Dead is behind the wall.

The School of Dreams is located under the bed

I have a faint recollection from an apparently naïve *Grimm's Tale* of a king whose daughters were ruining him. He kept them carefully locked in, as is proper, and didn't know why each day they needed to change their shoes. The daughters mysteriously wore out their shoes. Until the day the king planted a spy to throw light on this matter. At nightfall the daughters pulled the bed aside, lifted up the trap door, climbed down the ladder beneath the palace, and went out into the forest and danced all night. Perhaps my version is not completely accurate, but that is of no import- ance, since it's the perfect metaphor for the School of Dreams, bringing together all the elements, including jouissance. It's about doing what is forbidden: sexual pleasure. There is also the wearing out of the shoes, which gave me particular pleasure when I was little without my knowing why. Now I know much better why and I dedicate this tale to Mandelstam.

Mandelstam asks very seriously in his "Conversation about Dante": how many pairs of shoes Dante must have worn out in order to write *The Divine Comedy*, because, he tells us, that could only have been written on foot, walking without stopping, which is also how Mandelstam wrote.[4] Mandelstam's whole body was in action, taking part, searching. Walking, dancing, pleasure: these accompany the poetic act. I wonder what kind of poet doesn't wear our their shoes, writes with their head. The true poet is a traveler. Poetry is about traveling on foot and all its substitutes, all forms of transportation.

Mandelstam wore out hundreds of pairs of shoes. You cannot write such intense, dense poetry without the kind of dance that dances you round the world. Mandelstam himself could not write without walking round and round. When he was prevented from walking he died.

So perhaps dreaming and writing do have to do with traversing the forest, journeying through the world, using all the available means of transport, using your own body as a form of transport. *The Wanderer*, a beautiful text by Hofmannsthal, tells the story of a journey through Greek and Turkish lands in which the narrator meets a strange traveler.[5] This man has apparently been walking for centuries, he is never named, but when you have lived in the country of poets, you immediately recognize who he is: he is Rimbaud. To meet Rimbaud we have to walk to Austria, to the Greece that is hidden within Austria; we have to travel to the heart of the country of the unconscious, where we may again find those countries we have lost, including Algeria and the Jardin d'Essais. But for this we have to walk, to use our whole body to enable the world to become flesh, exactly as this happens in our dreams. In dreams and writing our body is alive: we either use the whole of it or, depending on the dream, a part. We must embark on a body-to-body journey in order to discover the body.

(...)

In order to go to the School of Dreams, something must be displaced, starting with the bed. One has to get going. This is what writing is, starting off. It has to do with activity and passivity. This does not mean one will get there. Writing is not arriving; most of the time it's *not arriving*. One must go on foot, with the body. One has to go away, leave the self. How far must one not arrive in order to write, how far must one wander and wear out and have pleasure? One must walk as far as the night. One's own night. Walking through the self toward the dark.

In the third extract from *Three Steps on the Ladder of Writing* reprinted here, Cixous cites Clarice Lispector's *The Passion According to G.H.* to argue that what is spurned by the Bible as "unclean" – *immonde*, literally "out of the world," "imund" – is the "root" of writing.[6] Cixous suggests writing derives precisely from this place which precedes prohibition, and so has the potential to return us to "paradise."

The passage is on pp. 118–19 of "The School of Roots," the final lecture in the Wellek series, in *Three Steps on the Ladder of Writing*. The text is edited by Sarah Cornell and Susan Sellers from an English transcript with French additions, and is substantially revised by Hélène Cixous.

Writing (. . .) does not come from outside. On the contrary, it comes from deep inside. It comes from what Genet calls the "nether realms," the inferior realms (*domaines inférieurs*).[7] We'll try to go there for a time, since this is where the treasure of writing lies, where it is formed, where it has stayed since the beginning of creation: down below. The name of the place changes according to our writers. Some call it hell: it is of course a good, a desirable hell. This is what Clarice calls it: *inferno.* She does not always use the word hell but all kinds of parallel denominations ("*the other side*" cited in *The Stream of Life* is Tsvetaeva's abyss).[8] It is deep in my body, further down, behind thought. Thought comes in front of it and it closes like a door. This does not mean that it does not think, but it thinks differently from our thinking and speech. Somewhere in the depths of my heart, which is deeper than I think. Somewhere in my stomach, my womb, and if you have not got a womb – then it is somewhere "else." You must climb down in order to go in the direction of that place. But as I said yesterday, this sort of descent is much more difficult to achieve, much more tiring, much more physically exacting (*physically* because the soul is body), than climbing up. It is a climb, but it requires the whole strength of everything that is you – which I don't want to call "body," since it is more complex than the body – to go through the various doors, obstacles, walls, and distances we have forged to make a life. I know besides that what also prevents us in our society from going there is not our inability – because *all of us* are able – but our cowardice, our fear. Our fear, since we know perfectly well that we will reach the dangerous point where those who are excluded live – and we hate exclusion. This is our emotional, our personal, and political problem, the fact that we can't bear exclusion. We are afraid of it, we hate to be separated, that is why we are apt to commit all kinds of small crimes, self-denials, and treachery.

But one has to choose between losing what is mund and losing the best part of ourselves that is called imund. Since we are shaped by years and years of all kinds of experiences and education, we must travel through all sorts of places that are not necessarily pleasant to get there: our own marshes, our own mud. And yet it pays to do so. The trouble is we are not taught that it pays, that it is beneficial. We are not taught the pain nor that in pain is hidden joy. We don't know that we can fight against ourselves, against the accumulation of mental, emotional, and biographical clichés. The general trend in writing is a huge concatenation of clichés. It is a fight one must lead against subtle enemies. Our personal enemies in this fight are those Kafka denounced in preventing our return to paradise. Kafka insists paradise is not lost, it is there. But we are lazy and impatient. If we were neither lazy nor impatient we would be back in paradise. But we have to deal with this laziness and impatience. And of course with all the representatives of "Those Bible."[9]

NOTES

1 See also "The Double World of Writing," in Susan Sellers (ed.), *Delighting the Heart: A Notebook by Women Writers*, London: The Women's Press, 1989, p. 18. [Ed.]

2 See Franz Kafka, *Letters to Friends, Family and Editors*, translated by Richard and Clara Winston, New York: Schocken Books, 1978, p. 16. [Ed.]

3 The reference is to a short story by Clarice Lispector entitled "Love," in which a woman, carrying a basket of eggs, has a sudden vision that momentarily changes her perception of her life ("Love," in *Family Ties*, translated by Giovanni Pontiero, Austin: University of Texas Press, 1972). See *Three Steps on the Ladder of Writing*, pp. 62–3. [Ed.]

4 See "Conversation about Dante," in *Mandelstam: The Complete Critical Prose and Letters*, translated by Jane Garry Harris and Constance Link, Ardis: Ann Arbor, 1979, p. 7. [Trans.]

5 See "The Wanderer," in *Hugo Von Hofmannsthal: Selected Prose*, translated by Mary Hottinger and Tania and James Stern, New York: Pantheon, 1963. [Trans.]

6 See *The Passion According to G.H.*, translated by Ronald W. Sousa, Minneapolis: University of Minnesota Press, 1988, pp. 64–5. See also *Three Steps on the Ladder of Writing*, p. 117: "that is my theme for today: to be 'imund,' to be unclean with joy. *Immonde*, that is, out of the *mundus* (the *world*). The monde, the world, that is so-called clean. The world that is on the good side of the law, that is 'proper,' the world of order. The moment you cross the line the law has drawn by wording, verb(aliz)ing, you are supposed to be out of the world. You no longer belong to the world." [Ed.]

7 See *The Thief's Journal*, translated by Bernard Frechtman, New York: Grove, 1964, p. 45. [Trans.]

8 See Clarice Lispector, *The Stream of Life*, translated by Elizabeth Lowe and Earl Fitz, Minneapolis: University of Minnesota Press, 1989, p. 13. [Trans.]

9 The reference is to Clarice Lispector's *The Passion According to G.H.*, p. 64. See, for Cixous' detailed discussion, *Three Steps on the Ladder of Writing*, pp. 114–15. [Ed.]

AFTERWORD

Hélène Cixous' Book of Hours, Book of Fortune[1]

Mireille Calle-Gruber

A woman immortal gathers you, one by one your flowers, plus one of every kind, an anemone, besides your tulips, your hands with velvety stems, a knee, a leg, two loins round and pale like eyelids, tries your name in all tongues her tongue moves, your body parts in her hands an iris, and one by one the parts of a phrase that she tries to compose, adjusting your gladioli your great smooth bones, your lotus, groping with discerning senses, and in the many genitals one from another, unforseeing, your ever more lovely bouquet, unknowing which All-other you will mould yourself into with which new names to touch you then, to make you speak?

(Hélène Cixous, *La*,[2] pp. 137–8)

To make one's way: Le Livre d'Heurs (the Book of Fortune)

We set off. We are already there: advancing. At the junction of the paths and the languages which branch.

For never has the composition of a book of essays – chosen (*logos*) flowers (*anthos*) placed side by side, differing, dialoguing, dissembling – done less violence to the whole, better signaled the movement of the work towards which it carries. Towards which it fashions so elegantly a stepping-stone. In fact, this dance around the emptiness which the preceding anthology of the texts organizes, gives, feature by feature, the portrait of Hélène Cixous' writing: multiplicity, differentiality, happenstance. By which the work is: *straightaway*. Awandering. Always already on the way: "A way that presented itself, took hold of me, carried me away" (*Angst*, p. 17); and right in the middle: "It is always so when one sets out to begin a book. We are in the middle (. . .) Thus we have begun to exist, thus we write: begun, and by the middle" (*L'Ange au secret*, p. 11). And to write is: to make: that *it happens* – surprises, discoveries, following the lines of language which writes itself, blurs over, opens up: "questions have come, bitten me right down to the marrow (. . .) Answer! They questioned me *right down to the meaning*. Stricken" (*Angst*, p. 16; emphasis added).

This book of essays, with its fragments and their attendant absence-to-be-read which shapes them, is a Book of Fortune: Hélène Cixous' *Book of Fortune*.

Inscribing the joys of writing, as they say – florilegium = the most beautiful, the most successful, the most – but also, as is less often said, the fortune of writing – by which writing becomes an augury, of that towards which it tends: lends an ear, captures resonances and rhythms, this Book of Fortune is symptomatic of making (one's way towards) the work. It presents a *moment* (as the term is used in physics) of the driving forces that constitute the Cixousian text. Moreover: it does not simply give texts to read. It *gives the gift* of the texts: the thrust of language, the happening of meaning.

When I set out to write, friends ask me "about what?" What is the subject? I, of course, never know . . . It is a mystery: there where it grabs, where it bursts forth, where it gathers like rain.

(from a recent interview with Hélène Cixous)

It is the gift of the heuristic, of writing as heuristic, where words speak and make marvels.

This gift of telescopy which, at every moment, makes the pen a telegraph-flash, lightning, a stroke of writing – disrupts, as we know, the structure of space-time in this fiction. The result is a narrative without *reason*; a temporality without chronology: "from one minute to the next no bridge" (*Angst*, p. 14). And the question, emblematic, from *Beethoven à jamais*, remains: "How they got from coffee to eternity, one will never know."

In other words, the only time which *holds* (which exists, and ties the scenes together) is that of narration, of writing and of reading themselves: their going, their passing makes Time. Marks the Hours.

This anthology, itself made from gaps, syncopation, from the collisions of eras, also arranges itself as Hélène Cixous' *Book of Hours*. Designating at the same time diachrony (by the fan of the fragments which it deploys, outlining the skeleton of the work) and synchrony (by the illustrative bouquet it assembles in one volume), it carries no other temporality than that of the trajectories of reading and writing.

There is more. If, in being read, they scan the unfolding of time, Hélène Cixous' narratives, through the symbolic tenor of the scenes they arouse, also propose a poetical-philosophical understanding of our daily life, of our gestures, of everything we do not know that we know. The Book of Hours thus constitutes the place of the quest that summons the writer: quest of the secret; of the mystery of the Real. And so, working on the letters' body, it is into the heart of things that the writer strives to carry the reading.

From inside to outside, from the Angst outside the secret to the Angel within it, from the Letter to the Being, from the portrait to the boundary of (her) unknown, what is coming into play is the *displacement*: incalculable, unequal; brief hours or time downcast. Sometimes by leaps and bounds, sometimes by cardiac arrest, the style signals the dial of the imaginary. And as on the clock face, returning is not repetition but *always* another passing; twelve is double, one two, day and night on balance. Every minute in the book is firstday(s) of the year: anniversary of the birth where meaning is born; where the being makes its way: "every morning, I am a little girl" (*Dedans*, p. 77).

It was 5 June 1937. Someone was being called. "Well?" The tongue grumbled. "It'll soon be time," said the mother. So it was not a dream. Imagination had started working (. . .) If you were being called, it must then be because one had some ground on which to place oneself. It was time! (. . .) The mother was preparing the first nappy, she was folding it in a triangle, she was announcing me. So I was about to be born! Myself my mother, my child. Bashful. First I had heard of it.

(*Angst*, pp. 24–5)

Scenes of the human

It is the scene of laughter and tears: good times, bad times blended. Hélène Cixous takes us along to the theater of the everyday, to our theater, comedy and tragedy together. That is to say: dream, contemplation of reality, revealing existence. There, unremittingly, under the signature of Shakespeare (but also Verdi, Schönberg, Sophocles, Rossini), of this theater which knows how to tell stories "legendarily and yet straight in the eye" ("Le lieu du Crime, le lieu du Pardon," *L'Indiade ou l'Inde de leurs rêves*), she attempts to seize, painting with strokes and lively scenes, our tensions, our paradoxes, our contradictions. To give to the human a form entirely of contrast.

Let us make no mistake: it is not a question, with Hélène Cixous, of psychologism or of moralism. At the pole of categorization and the simplistic recourse to models, the writer applies herself to dis-concealing complexity and singularity, to describing the irrepressible conflict of which we are the ground. Dwarf-giants, noble-and-poor, scene, accordingly, of Great Suffering, Flood(s), Apocalypse just as much as of Joy, we never know very well "in which costume we are dressed, nor into which handkerchief we blow. If it is a kleenex or if we go look for fine cloth" (recent interview). Riveted on our images, untiring spectators of ourselves, to "the very edge of the grave, we live, we blow our noses, a mirror looks at us" (ibid.).

In short, it is she herself (the author), it is we ourselves (we who "are made from a star on a piece of stick," *L'Ange au secret*, p. 70), it is the dis-astra of the human condition that the writing passes through the crucible of the text: giving the analysis of an existential dynamic to be read.

The human which Hélène Cixous explores has nothing to do with "humanism" nor with any anthropocentrism. What she places on the scene are the perspectives of a "human better" (recent interview) by which all frontiers are crossed, the being human enters in floods and expands from its others, vegetal, mineral, animal: knows itself to be dust, convolvulus (*Dedans*), butter (ibid.), air (*L'Ange*), body-fruit (*Vivre l'orange*); recognizes its arch-vegetal kinship (*La*), its wound of terrible meat (*Déluge*), and that it is necessary to have brushes to clean shoes. The souls too (*Beethoven à jamais*).

So it is, doubtless, that the reader has the feeling of emerging strengthened by the crossing of these texts: we are strengthened by our weaknesses, by our dichotomies, by our censures. By our lacerations. Hélène Cixous gives us these. Let us make no mistake: she does not reconcile us. She gives us the gift of the irreconcilable. Gives us "*unversöhnt*."

The gift of languages

The principle of duality, the calling into question of labels and categories of thoughts, the naming un-naming that is at work, constitute the foundation of the Cixousian approach. It is a systematic game-playing capable of dynamiting (and of dynamizing) the conventions, the clichés, the expressions that suit the ready-to-think.

It is a kind of explosion machine by which the writer "tries [the] names in all the tongues her tongue moves" (*La*, p. 137).

Her task, in other words, consists in restoring to language its fabulous disposition, and all its vocal cords; carefully handling the echo chamber, the sound boxes, the metaphorical journeys; burrowing between words, between-letters, between-strokes in order to deconstruct our dead language habits.

The envoy of *Vivre l'orange* is in this respect exemplary: giving voice and flight (from the "window," the last word in the book), it makes us hear through Clarice Lispector's name, the other in language, the language of the other, the other languages which pass – near, far, aslant.

If one takes her name in delicate hands and if one unfolds it and unpeels it following attentively the directions of the shells, in accordance to its intimate nature, there are dozens of small glittering crystals, which reflect each other in all the tongues where women pass. Claricelispector. Clar. Ricelis. Celis. Lisp. Clasp. Clarisp. Clarilisp. – Clar – Spec – Tor – Lis – Icelis – Isp – Larice – Ricepector – clarispector – claror – listor – rire - clarire – respect – rispect – clarispect – Ice – Clarici - O Clarice you are yourself the voices of the light, the iris, the regard, the flash [éclair] the orange flashing [éclairs orange] around our window.

(Vive l'orange, p. 113)

By the metaphors of fructification, a whole poetic announces itself: where the text is crystallization; celebration and cerebration. On the tracks of the lexicon, a whole poetic shows itself at work: where, truly, it makes meaning. The idioms weave and blend; foreign bodies decouple my tongue, forming veins, opening seams.

As for the stakes, the priorities are reversed: it is the mage voice which forms the image. One can "call forth clarily" the meaning (*Vivre l'orange*, p. 105), or according to the word "Celante" (Paul Celan) (*Jours de l'an*, p. 14), or following Kafka: *Limonade es war alles so grenzenlos* ("Lemonade Everything Was So Infinite").

The eternal making surges from the breath of the letters. The writing is even in language.

Floribunda writing

The writing of Hélène Cixous abounds in flowers: those of the art of tropes – above all, of the metaphor. "A woman immortal" (*La*) becomes immediately flower, immediately bouquet, arranging itself, like the parts of a text.

But metaphor alone would not suffice for the arts' élan: for it is on the back of phrases that it rides. It is a matter then of *touching* the things *by name*; and the true touch is touching (within) language. Therefore, no effervescent figure without a literal and a syntactical deflagration. In other words, without these varied geometrical phrases of which Hélène Cixous holds the secret.

Limonade tout était si infini [emphasis added]:
– I would like to write in French *because of the word swallow* [hirondelle].
(. . .)
I will write a free phrase. All the questions going from it [*iront d'elle*] to their answers, without detours.

(pp. 304–5)

By playing on words (clashes of signifiers and signified), the analogy, making syntax leave its bonds, sets up another principle of cause(s) and effect(s). There is no allegorical figure of liberty here except through the cracks: where un-connecting connects. And a swallow heralds the spring (contrary to the saying). But it is not just a stroke of writing (nor a stroke of the wing). Or rather, the Cixousian stroke is always *portentous*: through configuration (textual rhizome), it shows the metatextual process. The flowers of these books are not embellishments but essences. They bear fruit: beauty and *intelligence* (of the text). It is this that Joyce calls: epiphanies.

The specter of the work

The efflorescence, however, must not hide the bereavement. Writing weaves itself from loss; the book written from that which has not been written: "on the edges of each new born chapter lie the pages which have passed away" (*Jours de l'an*, p. 155).

Death nourishes art as it nourishes life. And it is necessary pain. For only the incompletion encourages pursuit. To write, to paint is: never to see the end; attempt after attempt, to begin again, to begin *oneself* again. By which the work is infinite desire. The desire to work.

Writing, for Hélène Cixous, also tells mourning through the traces left by others – books, writers, whose reading has excited an emotional and scriptural journeying. Writing is making (the journey) *with*. In honor of. In memory. Clarice Lispector, Rembrandt, Tsvetaeva, Franz Kafka, Paul Celan, Ingeborg Bachmann, Thomas Bernhard. "All these people in me have lived their lives. They have written. They die. They continue, never ceasing to live, never ceasing to die, never ceasing to write" (*Jours de l'an*, p. 162).

The book writes itself at the confluence of two lines of perspective. On the horizon, the writing-to-come sketches, behind the leaf (of paper), a forest. It designs the roots of the work. Bereavement takes on debt.

The keystone: Ankh

The keystone in Hélène Cixous' work is the key to Life: Ankh. The Egyptian cross marks out the crossing: convergence-rupture, but also encirclement: infinite rebeginning. It is the sign that there is breath passing out from the teeth. And breath between the letters, that give themselves voice, take on body and come to life with all the *"animots d'une langue"* (*La*, p. 93).[3] For if we follow Hélène Cixous to the letter, until we are short of breath, "we no longer have *reason* to live, we are wrong" (*Angst*, p. 20; emphasis added) – "Live for nothing (. . .) If an answer occurs to you, save yourself, save your life" (ibid.) – there is nothing but *rhyme*. And rhyme is what constitutes "*Lettre-Là*" (*La*, p. 21), the "Letter-There," the "Being-there," which carries along a game of forms and of metamorphoses. Which gives life for what life is: passage – *form(s) of the movement*.

The key of the Being-there – which is also key to the lies (*mensonges*), key to the dreams (*songes*), the key to her I (*son je*) – finds itself between the hands of Isis, goddess of the same and of the other, sister lover, with the name that rings. She watches over the rites of passage through the gates, from Death to Life, from the Book of the Dead (*mort(e)s*) to the Book of Words (*mots*). For it is she who reunites the pieces of Osiris' dismemberment, re-forms the body from all parts, and from each part draws, shapes, invents an entire body.

She is the goddess of recollection, of difference, of multiplication. It is the principle of the Osiriac text (she says "osirisk"): "Her art of arriving from all parts" (*La*, p. 92). From all lives. From "Allanguage" (ibid., p. 82).

Redemption, for Hélène-Isis, comes down to evoking the germinating image recognizable/unrecognizable. "It is to speak [to eat] languages [dandelions] by the roots" (ibid., p. 86).[4] "In a language, one cannot die" (*Jours de l'an*, p. 120).

Giving the feminine, giving the music

One must guard against obliterating this germination which ferments the writer's text under the cover of "feminism."

Cixousian writing does not name a he without a she: never *un il* without "*une île*" (a he-she), nor without "*un el*" (a she-he) (*La*, p. 185; *Déluge*, p. 196). In other words, this writing is informed by the differential of sexual difference, the strange truths that it conveys.

Hélène Cixous' books give precisely the feminine, the music (*donne le la*): other entries to meaning; the between at work which escapes classification; a between-two, which makes three and more; a between-time which exceeds time. They multiply the differences (for example: "son who is a daughter," *La*, p. 132; "the man who is your mother," *Angst*, p. 72), even the smallest: *Jours de l'an*; *Promethea*; an ant transposed, in French, from the feminine to the masculine (*un fourmi*). They inscribe the overturning, differentiating activity: especially the mute "e" (used to designate the feminine) which at the same time changes and mutates the meanings. There is the she-child (*enfante*), the female falcon (*fauconne*), the sky as feminine or sky as feminine blue (*cielle* or *ciel bleue*); there is a she-brother (la *frère*), there is, in silk (*soie*), for herself-inner-self (*en soi*), and this masculinized ant which is the linguistic *happening* par excellence;

that which happens. That which passes. Vector. Mark of an accident, cause of trouble, in the circulation of meaning.

This trouble is beneficial: it awakens, it softens the hard of hearing – makes them receptive. Opens the eyes, awakens the heart.

Giving the feminine, giving the music, is giving the fertile separation (she says: "sacred"), the "separation with great desirable arms in which we make our beds and our fusions" (*Beethoven à jamais*, p. 211).

She. It is the other which is called with the feminine pronoun: the title of Hélène Cixous' book, *La*, plays on the definite and on the infinite. On every possible designation: all is *terra incognita*. Designating the gesture of designation.

There is more. When *La* takes an accent, it takes on the accent of the beyond (beyond, over there), and co-responding to the *It* (*Ça*), crosses the limit: gives to the body "the desire to run through overflowing regions, the desire to invent transports, carriages to draw oneself within reach of the Unknown, the art of going Là" (*La*, p. 83).

Reach of the unknown

Art creates a conduit from the inside to the outside, leads abroad, to the unknown. It is always there that I know nothing about *it*. Hélène Cixous writes "abroad," "to the stranger," in the same way Rembrandt painted "*hinaus in die Fremde der Heimat*, leaving by the painting's door" (*Jours de l'an*, p. 129). There gestures are needed for an address with no addressee. Or rather, whose addressee is: Nothing. No One. An address whose nature is that of a promise. Of the star being followed.

Art is the arch thrown over the void, carried by its own momentum, its advance on the abyss. There one needs courage, confidence. Faith. And humility. The humility of the laborer's technique: there one must grasp with both hands – to tomorrow returned with both hands (*demain à deux mains*). "In the hand, invisible dice, invisible tomorrows" (*Beethoven à jamais*).

Art is door and loss. Window ("An unknown woman at the window of infinity," *La*, p. 55). Opening from all sides. Art clears the way for an inside-outside. It puts within reach that which is unknown to me. Unknown in me. A You(Shelter) (*Un Toi(t)*), some Me's(Time) (*des Moi(s)*). The constitutive strangeness "which vertigos my life" (*La*, p. 58): not to know knowing, not to think thinking.

There fear is necessary, instability: setting foot right in the text's earth, so as to be able to let oneself go there, blindly. Doing the splits. *Le Livre de*

Promethea: "I am a little afraid for this book (. . .) It would be better to throw oneself in." (p. 20)

The reach of the unknown (woman) is incommensurable. She gives (to) me. Discovery that we are much more than ourselves. She stretches us, lays us down. Somewhere, she *becomes* (she *makes us*) earth (*elle (nous) fait terre*):

> She sees herself stretched out upon the earth as if it were the familiar pose (. . .) in relation to the earth which bears her, which does not disturb her, which receives her and stretches her out, she sees herself in all *her/its* length.
>
> (*La*, p. 156)

(Emphasis added to the amphibiological possessive where "she" and "earth" melt together: Her length and/is the earth's length.)

A subject at risk

The Cixousian subject presents itself in practice. In the present: from the theater of writing. It is the application point of existential phenomena and, as such, may fall to pieces. A being of intermittencies, not ceasing to disconnect: lives a thousand lives, lives a thousand deaths. Does not recognize itself there. Does not recognize its defunct faces. "We carry within us the speechless dead. My mummies" (*La*, p. 20).

> (. . .) time our painter is slow. It needs twenty years to assemble a portrait that is our result (. . .) Time pursues its work, taking note of and retaining our elements in transformation, until the person we have ended up being comes to our consciousness, and everything has changed. And everything will change again.
>
> (*Jours de l'an*, p. 45)

This is what the books strive to tell: a subject that *does not have time*, is atomized. And how time smashes it to pieces, holds it, in suffering, on the point of: "between already and not yet" (ibid., p. 47); "Between nothing-more and nothing-yet" (*Beethoven à jamais*, p. 33). At every instant, they (the book and the subject) risk a short-circuit – breakdown or bursting into flames.

It is a subject at risk. Tied to the instant, it can only be *instance* ("Isay") – of enunciation, of fabulation: "The yesterday is traveled. Between Ihadto [*jedus*] and Isay [*jedis*]" (*La*, p. 20) – and not proprietor of the proper name. Nor of identity. Nor of an entity. It lives on (narrative) credit and wears borrowed skins.

The subject must be risked. That is even what the subject is: by definition: risk. "At the risk of losing oneself. The risk is necessary" (*Jours de l'an*, p. 53). That is why the Cixousian subject does not stop running: it races against itself and against its narratives. Its truth is in this race: since the only safeguard for this subject so *subject to*, so much of a *taken* course, is to multiply the points of view, the points. The blind spots.

It is thus a singularly subjective subject which is at work: summoned, assigned, affected. Affected with common scaling (*commun*). *Comme-un*, like David/one david, Clarice/one clarice, Ascension/one ascension, stone (*pierre*)/Peter, Thomas Bernhard/mention T.B.,[5] the almond (*Mandel*) in Mandela and Mandelstam, and so many other de-nominations, other running, ordinary subjects (like an ordinary, common title, rendered banal) swarm in the text, constituting semantic force fields, sectors of magnetization. Where *meaning is magnet*.

For the subjective subject has a tendency to lose its head: it thus becomes "Ubject" (*Neutral*), thinks with the heart, reads "with its head cut off" (*L'Ange au secret*, p. 91), becomes capable of apprehending the sentences' cardiac truth. Of the subject, it is above all je(c)t: pro-ject, tra-je(c)tory, variable of a geometry which creates narrative economy. In the unflagging combat the subject wages with the angel, the heart stands up to the head and the soul takes on the body.

The subject at risk is the unparalleled *subject of writing*, in the double sense of the genitive, passive-active: writing matter, producer of the text. There, it makes a scene, scenes are made for it. As in these lines: "We guess that we are guessed, we are crafty, *we are crafted* [*on est rusé*], we slip" (*La*, p. 21; emphasis added), where, through the mechanism of the double tracks in the first proposition, the third – "we are crafted" – crosses the boundaries of grammaticality and becomes laden with a passive (mis)interpretation: to be crafty = to deceive; to be crafted = to be deceived. While the slippage names straight away what the text has just done.

On the scene of writing, the subject thus exhibits itself as palimpsest, memory, parchment, receives inked impressions, can lose "too much sense" ("I had lost too much sense. I saw things dimly," *Angst*, p. 35), can sign and bleed letters, can be faulty, can give itself over to madness. And to the splitting of the narrative instance, which is never one without the other: The Author-she and I-Me ("The author that I am can say: I am not me," *L'Ange au secret*, p. 29) instance which most often makes neither one nor two and proliferates, refining proximities. It is thus that appears, between "the makers" H and Promethea, an "I of the author": "It is a thin character" whose purpose is to "slip as closely as possible to the being of the two real makers, so as to be able to meld the contour of their souls with mine, without, however, causing confusion" (*Le Livre de Promethea*, p. 12).

The subject? They are the voices-ways of the text. It is the book. The book of hours is the book of instants, delivers instants.

The oxymoric narrative

"From what is it our lives are hanging? Our lives are hanging by their narrative" (*Beethoven à jamais*, p. 19). And in order that this narrative *holds* in its turn, it must be like "all that which lives [which] is oxymoric" (ibid., p. 172). Such is the principle of equational drift which organizes the texts: it shows that there is no tautology and that *nothing is equal*. Each inscription counts.

The oxymoron permits antipodes to be brought together, allows the gap to be rendered infinitely sensitive. It is the principle of the minuscule abyss, which fissures significations and risks extraordinary footbridges – principle all the more effective in that it plays on points, to within a comma. In a breath.

"The Secret – we do not have it. For us it is. Faith" (ibid., p. 18). The semantic commotion arises here from the punctuation. The expected "For us it is faith" would make the text smooth. The cesura, unexpected, drives the reading upstream where all the attention (the tension) is brought to bear on the verb "to have." Thus confronted, to have and to be establish a non-symmetrical symmetry: "we do not have it" calls up "it has us," but leads to "for us it *is*." The reading falters, halted before a difficulty in thinking (aporia, unthought-of) then, rebounding downstream, echoes the parallel deciphering to be/to have onto "faith" (to have, to be held by faith).

The broken line of this trajectory offers an exemplary process of Cixousian writing where it is a matter of giving greater importance to the rhyme a–not-a (as opposed to the rhyme a–a). This figure of thought informs all the works and confers on the narrative a parabolic function. Mixing literary genres and discursive genres, the oxymoric mechanism allows it to be said: "the trial for us to be human. The Pain" (*L'Indiade ou l'Inde de leurs rêves*, p. 253). The difficulty in hearing: the Suffering of Joy, the Truth of Error, the relation Reason/non-reason/Madness ("Madness! I lost my non-reason," *Angst*, p. 21) which are some of the narrative's major articulations.

An unusual writing is thus elaborated: a tale with two bloods, with opposite directions and doubly without:[6] Story without plot; event without character – in other words *with* (No) One. The heterogeneity which shapes this unbridled narrative, completely dislocated in appearance, reveals itself as everything but anything: in fact, a dynamic of compensation organizes the equilibria of the de-construction at work. That is what the song says, in such a beautiful manner, at the centre of *Beethoven à jamais* (pp. 112–13).

– O that we are not of the same blood (. . .)
– But then we would lose (. . .) these flights by which we struggle to
prevent the cleft from broadening (. . .)
It is because we are not of the same blood
That I have such breathless love
Between us no tie, no knot
Only the musicality –
O that we are not of the same blood (. . .)

(Each time *one tone higher*)

From coffee to eternity: the philter of the text

Strength does not come from preservation (of the same) but from the irruption of alterity. My life comes to me from the other, love is the mainspring
of writing: such is the axiom at the heart of the workings of Hélène Cixous'
narrative, the secret of her art's vitality. A magnetic sense – attraction and
difference – organizes what the writer calls "separateunion" and which is:
the work of passion.

From this point onward, there is no worthy literature but that which
strives towards the writing of passion: under the regime of lightning, fire,
blaze, oxymoron, of the dative (To You (*Te*): "Between coming and going
only the time of To . . . You [*Te*]," *Beethoven à jamais*, p. 56). Of All-
Nothing, coffee-eternity.

It is, in fact, the parabola of creation which Hélène Cixous' narratives tell;
of the magical force which trans-figures but whose passing happens word
by word, drop by drop, through the filter of the text – which purifies,
balances. With the "fear of writing at too low a flame" (ibid., p. 42), that
language neither sees nor hears far enough, that the coffee-filter is not fine
enough, the interstices not sufficiently small. Nietzsche, exemplar, gives a
lesson of mad love by homophony: where naming is burning.

> Die Liebe ist's die mich mitgehen heißt
> Die heiß ersehnte!
Heiß et heißt, same letter same fire, the call burns me, the fire calls me. All the names
of love pass through me.

(*La*, p. 67)

The text must be like a good, strong coffee, as they say – that it may
become magical philter. That the gaps in meaning gap, the fire ashes where
meaning is reborn, the scorched earth of the text sends forth narrative
shoots. Like *Le Livre de Promethea* which, at the end, stops at these words:

– Oh I forgot! Promethea falls in love.
– Falls?
– Is.

(p. 248)

The fall – or the tip – of the sentence, of the book, makes earth; the text rebounds to the point where it finishes, thanks to the oxymoric force of this ultimate device: which, by explosion of the cliché, reinscribes everyday banality at the center of what is vitally at stake: Death, Life, Resurrection. For "Fall" (*Tombe*) also names "the tomb" [*la tombe*], summons the opposition under/on the earth, makes an ascent of this fall of the fire thief. Promethea liable to fall and taking flight is, like the writer, Phoenix – bird of fire.

Or the existence of God[7]

From book to book, Hélène Cixous has constructed for herself an entire collection of registers and keys. An entire scale: to play, to climb and to descend. Scale of what is possible, musical scale. Do re mi fa sol la ti. It is a Jacob's ladder, a ladder of vocal chords, always resumed ever higher, which leads to the ascension to heaven. Degree by degree.

do – madness, abyss; it is the note *do* in Schumann's ear (*On ne part pas, On ne revient pas*)
re – recollection from loss, the awakening
mi – by the middle, always already begun
fa – nymphs' voices, the new year, the new sap: "the nymphs speak in fa, the dead are forgiven and forgive us, writing arises"
sol – there where the soul makes earth in language; "the sol/Of the soul which is language"
(*Beethoven à jamais*, p. 160)
la – gift, difference
ti – the infinite; "each mouthful was *too*, was *ti*, and what she was in the process of understanding then, was the infinite"
(*Limonade tout était si infini*, p. 300)

It is in this way that the rigorous economy of the text has brought order to the upward and gravitational laws of force; and succeeded in making (the) work: in other words, in creating an expanding universe. Held out towards. Between Madness and Infinity. Madness and Faith ("I see it the word Faith in the word Madness,"[8] *Beethoven à jamais*, p. 48). Eternity at the moment.

This is probably why, in the work of Hélène Cixous, the greatest risk is not without the greatest serenity. At the end, on the edge of the abyss, of the emptiness of the blank page and the earth, *Limonade* inscribes, exemplary acceptance where "living the moment" is finding force in precariousness ("for the moment"), this portent of a writing infinitely begun anew:

- When I will have payed. Afterwards.
But *for the moment, there are enough flowers.*
(*Limonade*, p. 306, emphasis added)

Enough flowers to breathe, to write.

NOTES

1 Translated by Agnes Conacher and Catherine McGann.

2 All quotations are translated directly from the original French texts. [Trans.]

3 *et s'animent de tous les "animots d'une langue"*: literally "and animate themselves with all the *animots* (neologism in which it is possible to read 'animated words'/ 'animals') of a language/tongue." [Ed.]

4 I am including the words of the saying in order to see the displacement at work in Cixous' text. [Calle-Gruber]

5 "Mention T.B." is *mention très bien* (very good). [Trans.]

6 The French text plays on the signifiers *sangs*, *sens*, and *sans*. [Trans.]

7 Subtitle of *Beethoven à jamais*, at the time of printing the most recent of Hélène Cixous' books. [Calle-Gruber]

8 In French there is an anagrammatical relationship between the words *foi* and *folie*. [Trans.]

SELECT BIBLIOGRAPHY

The following bibliography gives details of Cixous' French book publications and translations of her work in English (interviews in English are also listed). Details of publications on Cixous in English are included.

French book publications

(The place of publication is Paris unless otherwise indicated.)

(1967) *Le Prénom de Dieu*, Grasset.

(1969) *Dedans*, Grasset.

  L'Exil de James Joyce ou l'art du remplacement, Grasset.

(1970) *Les Commencements*, Grasset.

  Le Troisième Corps, Grasset.

(1971) *Un Vrai Jardin*, L'Herne.

(1972) *Neutre*, Grasset.

  La Pupille, Cahiers Renaud-Barrault, Gallimard.

(1973) *Tombe*, Seuil.

(1974) *Portrait du soleil*, Denoël.

  Prénoms de personne, Seuil.

(1975) *La Jeune Née*, in collaboration with Catherine Clément, 10/18.

  Un K. incompréhensible: Pierre Goldman, Bourgois.

  Révolutions pour plus d'un Faust, Seuil.

  Souffles, des femmes.

(1976) *La*, Gallimard; des femmes (1979).

  Partie, des femmes.

  Portrait de Dora, des femmes.

(1977) *Angst*, des femmes.

  Le Venue à l'écriture, with Madeleine Gagnon and Annie Leclerc, Union Générale d'Editions. (The title essay of this collection, by Hélène Cixous, is reprinted in *Entre l'écriture*, des femmes, 1986, pp. 9–69.)

(1978) *Chant du corps interdit/Le Nom d'Oedipe*, des femmes.

  Préparatifs de noces au delà de l'abîme, des femmes.

(1979) *Anankè*, des femmes.

  Vivre l'orange/To Live the Orange, des femmes.

(1980) *Illa*, des femmes.

(1981) *(With) Ou l'art de l'innocence*, des femmes.

(1982) *Limonade tout était si infini*, des femmes.

(1983) *Le Livre de Promethea*, Gallimard.

(1984) *La Prise de l'école de Madhubaï*, Avant-scène.

(1985) *L'Histoire terrible mais inachevée de Norodom Sihanouk Roi du Cambodge*, Théâtre du Soleil.

(1986) *La Bataille d'Arcachon*, Collection Topaze, Trois, Quebec.

Entre l'écriture, des femmes.

Hélène Cixous: Théâtre, des femmes.

(1987) *L'Indiade ou l'Inde de leurs rêves*, Théâtre du Soleil.

(1988) *Manne aux Mandelstams aux Mandelas*, des femmes Antoinette Fouque.

(1989) *L'Heure de Clarice Lispector*, des femmes Antoinette Fouque.

(1990) *Jours de l'an*, des femmes Antoinette Fouque.

(1991) *L'Ange au secret*, des femmes Antoinette Fouque.

On ne part pas, on ne revient pas, des femmes Antoinette Fouque.

(1992) *Déluge*, des femmes Antoinette Fouque.

(1993) *Beethoven à jamais ou l'existence de Dieu*, des femmes Antoinette Fouque.

English translations

(1972) *The Exile of James Joyce*, translated by Sally Purcell, New York: David Lewis, and London: John Calder, 1976; New York: Riverrun, 1980.

(1974) "The Character of 'Character'," translated by Keith Cohen, *New Literary History* 5, 2 (Winter): pp. 383–402.

—— "Political Ignominy: Ivy Day," in William M. Chace (ed.), *Joyce: A Collection of Critical Essays*, Englewood, N.J.: Prentice Hall.

(1975) "At Circe's or the Self Opener," translated by Carol Bové, *Boundary 2*: 397.

(1976) "Fiction and its Fantoms: A Reading of Freud's 'Das Unheimliche' ("The Uncanny")," translated by R. Denommé, *New Literary History* 7, 3 (Spring): 525–48.

—— "The Fruits of Femininity," the *Guardian*, 16 May.

—— "The Laugh of the Medusa," translated by Keith and Paula Cohen, *Signs* 1–4 (Summer): 875–93. This translation is reprinted in Isabelle de Courtivron and Elaine Marks (eds), *New French Feminisms*, Minneapolis: University of Massachusetts Press, and Brighton: Harvester, 1981.

(1977) "*La Jeune Née*: an Excerpt," translated by Meg Bortin, *Diacritics* 7, 2 (Summer): 64–9.

—— "Boxes," translated by Rosette C. Lamont, *Centerpoint* (Fall), New York: 30–1.

—— "Partie: an Extract," translated by Keith Cohen, *Triquarterly* 38 (Winter): 95–100.

(1979) *Portrait of Dora*, translated by Anita Barrows, London: John Calder.

(1980) "Come the Following Chapter," *Enclitic* 4, 2 (Fall): 45–58.

—— "The Laugh of the Medusa," translated by Keith and Paula Cohen, in Isabelle de Courtivron and Elaine Marks (eds), *New French Feminisms*, Minneapolis: University of Massachusetts Press; Brighton: Harvester, 1981.

—— "Poetry is/and (the) Political," translated by Ann Liddle, *Bread and Roses* 2, 1: 16–18.

—— "Sorties: Where Is She . . .," translated by Ann Liddle, in Isabelle de Courtivron and Elaine Marks (eds), *New French Feminisms*, Minneapolis: University of Massachusetts Press; and Brighton, Harvester, 1981.

(1981) "Castration or Decapitation?," translated by Annette Kuhn, *Signs* 7, 1 (Autumn): 41–55. Reprinted in Robert Davies and Ronald Schleifer (eds), *Contemporary Literary Criticism: Literary and Cultural Studies*, New York: Longman's, 1989.

(1982) "Introduction to Lewis Carroll's *Through the Looking Glass* and *The Hunting of the Snark*," translated by Marie Maclean, *New Literary History* 13, 2 (Winter): 231–51.

—— "The Step," translated by Jill McDonald and Carole Darring Paul, *The French American Review* 6, 1: 33–41.

(1984) "Going to the Seashore," *Modern Drama* 27, 4 (December): 546–8.

—— "August 12, 1980," translated by Betsy Wing, *Boundary 2*: 8–39.

—— "Joyce, the (R)use of Writing," translated by Judith Still, *Post Structuralist Joyce*, Cambridge: Cambridge University Press.

—— "Reading Clarice Lispector's 'Sunday Before Going to Sleep'," translated by Betsy Wing, *Boundary 2*: 41–8.

(1985) *Angst*, translated by Jo Levy, London: John Calder.

(1986) *Inside*, translated by Carol Barko, New York: Schocken Books.

—— *The Newly Born Woman*, translated by Betsy Wing, Minneapolis: Minnesota University Press.

—— "The Last Word," translated by Ann Liddle and Susan Sellers, *The Women's Review* 6 (April): 22–4.

—— "The Conquest of the School at Madhubai," translated by Deborah Carpenter, *Women and Performance* 3: 59–95.

—— "The Language of Reality," in Harold Bloom (ed.), *Twentieth Century British Literature 3: James Joyce: Ulysses*, New York: Chelsea House.

(1987) "Her Presence Through Writing," translated by Deborah Carpenter, *Literary Review* 30 (Spring): 445–53.

—— "Life Without Him Was Life Without Him," *New York Times Book Review*, 1 November, pp. 2–35.

—— "The Book of Promethea," translated by Deborah Carpenter, *Frank* 6, 7: 42–4.

—— "Foreword," translated by Verena Andermatt Conley, in Clarice Lispector, *The*

Stream of Life, Minneapolis: Minnesota University Press.

—— "The Parting of the Cake," translated by Franklin Philips, *For Nelson Mandela*, in Jacques Derrida and Mustapha Tlili (eds), New York: Seaver Books.

(1988) "Extreme Fidelity, " translated by Ann Liddle and Susan Sellers, in Susan Sellers (ed.), *Writing Differences: Readings from the Seminar of Hélène Cixous*, Milton Keynes: Open University Press, and New York: St. Martin's Press.

—— "Tancrede Continues," translated by Ann Liddle and Susan Sellers, in Susan Sellers (ed.), *Writing Differences: Readings from the Seminar of Hélène Cixous*, Milton Keynes: Open University Press and New York: St. Martin's Press.

(1989) "From the Scene of the Unconscious to the Scene of History," translated by Deborah Carpenter, in Ralph Cohen (ed.), *The Future of Literary History*, New York and London, Routledge.

—— "Writings on the Theatre: Dedication to the Ostrich," translated by Catherine Franks, *Qui Parle* (Spring), Berkeley, California: 120–52.

(1990) *Reading With Clarice Lispector*, edited and translated by Verena Andermatt Conley, Minneapolis: Minnesota University Press and Hemel Hempstead: Harvester Wheatsheaf.

—— "Difficult Joys," in Helen Wilcox, Keith McWatters, Ann Thompson and Linda R. Williams (eds.), *The Body and the Text: Hélène Cixous, Reading and Teaching*, Hemel Hempstead: Harvester Wheatsheaf.

(1991) *The Book of Promethea*, translated by Betsy Wing, Lincoln: University of Nebraska Press.

—— *"Coming to Writing" and Other Essays*, translated by Sarah Cornell, Deborah Jenson, Ann Liddle and Susan Sellers, Cambridge, Mass.: Harvard University Press.

(1993) *Three Steps on the Ladder of Writing*, translated by Sarah Cornell and Susan Sellers, New York: Columbia University Press.

(Forthcoming)
Manna to the Mandelstams to the Mandelas, translated by Catherine MacGillivray, Minneapolis: University of Minnesota Press.

Interviews in English

(1976) "Hélène Cixous: Interview with Christiane Makward," translated by Beatrice Cameron and Ann Liddle, *Sub-Stance* 13: 19–37

(1979) "Rethinking Differences," translated by Isabelle de Courtivron, in Elaine Marks and Georges Stambolian (eds), *Homosexualities and French Literature*, New York: Cornell University Press.

(1982) "Comment on Women's Studies in France," *Signs* (Spring): 721–2.

(1984) "An Exchange with Hélène Cixous," with Verena Andermatt Conley, *Hélène*

Cixous: Writing the Feminine, Lincoln: University of Nebraska Press.

—— "Voice 1," with Verena Andermatt Conley, *Boundary* 2: 51–67.

(1985) "Hélène Cixous," with Susan Sellers, *The Women's Review* (7 May): 22–3.

(1988) "Conversations," with Susan Sellers, in Susan Sellers (ed.), *Writing Differences: Readings from the Seminar of Hélène Cixous*, Milton Keynes: Open University Press and New York: St Martin's Press.

(1989) "The Double World of Writing," in Susan Sellers (ed.), *Delighting the Heart: A Notebook by Women Writers*, London: The Women's Press.

—— "Listening to the Heart," in Susan Sellers (ed.), *Delighting the Heart: A Notebook by Women Writers*, London: The Women's Press.

—— "A Realm of Characters," in Susan Sellers (ed.), *Delighting the Heart: A Notebook by Women Writers*, London: The Women's Press.

—— "Writing as a Second Heart," in Susan Sellers (ed.), *Delighting the Heart: A Notebook by Women Writers*, London: The Women's Press.

—— "Exploding the Issue 'French' 'Women' 'Writers' and the 'Canon'," with Alice Jardine and Anne M. Menke, *Yale French Studies* 75: 235–8.

(1989) "Hélène Cixous," with Catherine Franke, *Qui Parle* (Spring), Berkeley, California: 152–79.

Books and articles on Cixous in English

Allen, Jeffner (1988) "Poetic Politics: How the Amazons Took the Acropolis," *Hypatia* 3 (Summer): 107–22.

Cameron, Beatrice (1977) "Letter to Hélène Cixous," *Sub-stance* 17: 159–65.

Carpenter, Deborah (1986) "Hélène Cixous and North African Origin: Writing 'L'Orange'," *Celfan Review* 6,1 (November): 1–4.

—— (1987) "Translator's Introduction to 'Her Presence Through Writing' by Hélène Cixous," *Literary Review* 30, 3 (Spring): 441–53.

Conley, Verena Andermatt (1977) "Missexual Mystery," *Diacritics* 7, 2 (Summer): 70–82.

—— (1978) "Writing the Letter: The Lower-Case of Hélène Cixous," *Visible Language* 12, 3 (Summer): 305–18.

—— (1979) "Hélène Cixous and the Uncovery of a Feminine Language," *Women and Literature* 7, 1 (Winter): 38–48.

—— (1984) *Writing the Feminine: Hélène Cixous*, Lincoln: University of Nebraska Press.

—— (1984) "Voices," *Boundary 2 Symposium on Feminine Writing*: 12, 2 (Winter): pp. 51–67.

—— (1992) *Hélène Cixous*, Hemel Hempstead: Harvester Wheatsheaf.

Cornell Sarah (1988) "Hélène Cixous' *Le Livre de Promethea*: Paradise Refound," in Susan Sellers (ed.), *Writing Differences: Readings from the Seminary of Hélène Cixous*, Milton Keynes: Open University Press, and New York: St Martin's Press.

—— (1990) "Hélène Cixous and 'les Etudes Féminines'," in Helen Wilcox, Keith Mcwatters, Ann Thompson and Linda R. Williams (eds), *The Body and the Text: Hélène Cixous, Reading and Teaching*, Hemel Hempstead: Harvester Wheatsheaf.

Corredor, Eva (1982) "The Fantastic and the Problem of Re-Presentation in Hélène Cixous' Feminist Fiction," *Papers in Romance* 43, 2 (Autumn): 173–9.

Crowder, Diane (1983) "Amazons and Mothers? Monique Wittig, Hélène Cixous and Theories of Women's Writing," *Contemporary Literature* 24, 2 (Summer): 117–44.

Davis, Robert (1988) "Woman as Oppositional Reader: Cixous on Discourse," *Papers on Language and Literature* 24, 3 (Summer): 265–82.

Defromont, Françoise (1990) "Metaphorical Thinking and Poetic Writing in Virginia Woolf and Hélène Cixous," in Helen Wilcox, Keith Mcwatters, Ann Thompson and Linda R. Williams (eds), *The Body and the Text: Hélène Cixous, Reading and Teaching*, Hemel Hempstead: Harvester Wheatsheaf.

Duren, Brian (1982) "Cixous' Exorbitant Texts," *Sub-Stance* 32: 39–51.

Evans, Martha Noel (1982) *Portrait of Dora*: Freud's Case History as Reviewed by Hélène Cixous," *Sub-Stance* 36: 64–71.

Faris, W. (1981) "Desyoizacion: Joyce, Cixous, Fuentes and the Multi-Vocal Text," *Latin American Literary Review* 9, 19: 31–9.

Feral, Josette (1980) "The Powers of Difference," in Hester Eisenstein and Alice Jardine (eds), *The Future of Difference*, Boston: G.K. Hall.

—— (1984) "Writing and Displacement: Women in Theater," *Modern Drama* 27, 4 (December): 549–63.

Fitz, E. (1990) "Hélène Cixous' Debt to Clarice Lispector: The Case of 'Vivre l'Orange' and L'Ecriture Féminine," *Revue de Littérature comparée* 64, 1 (January–March): 235–49.

Freeman, B. (1988) "Plus-Corps-Donc-Plus-Ecriture: Hélène Cixous and the Mind–Body Problem," *Paragraph* 11, 1: 58–70.

Gallop, Jane (1982) "Keys to Dora," in *The Daughter's Seduction: Feminism and Psychoanalysis*, New York: Cornell University Press.

Gibbs, Anna (1979) "Hélène Cixous and Gertrude Stein: New Directions in Feminist Criticism," *Meanjin Quarterly* 38, 3 (September): 281–93.

Gilbert, Sandra (1986) "Introduction: A Tarantella of Theory," *The Newly Born Woman*, Minneapolis: University of Minnesota Press.

Jones, Ann (1981) "Writing the Body: Toward an Understanding of 'l'Ecriture Féminine'," *Feminist Studies* 7, 2 (Summer): 247–63. Reprinted in Gayle Greene and Coppelia Kahn (eds), *Making a Difference: Feminist Literary Criticism*, London: Methuen, 1985; in Elaine Showalter (ed.), *The New Feminist Criticism: Essays on Women, Literature and Theory*, New York: Pantheon, 1985; and in Mary Eagleton (ed.), *Feminist Literary Theory: A Reader*, Oxford: Basil Blackwell, 1986.

Jouve, Nicole Ward (1990) "Hélène Cixous: From Inner Theatre to World Theatre," in Helen Wilcox, Keith Mcwatters, Ann Thompson and Linda R. Williams (eds), *The*

Body and the Text: Hélène Cixous, Reading and Teaching, Hemel Hempstead: Harvester Wheatsheaf. Reprinted in Nicole Ward Jouve, *White Woman Speaks with Forked Tongue: Criticism as Autobiography*, London: Routledge, 1991.

—— (1991) "The Faces of Power: Hélène Cixous," in *Our Voices, Ourselves: Women Writing for the French Theatre*, New York: Peter Lang.

Juncker, C. (1988) "Writing (with) Cixous," *College English* 50, 4: 424–36.

Kiernander, A. (1985) "The King of Cambodia," *Plays and Players* 386 (November): 17–18.

Kogan, Vivian (1985) "I Want Vulva? Hélène Cixous and the Poetics of the Body," *L'Esprit créateur* 25, 2 (Summer): 73–85.

Lamar, Celita (1987) "Norodom Sihanouk, A Hero of Our Times, Character Development in Hélène Cixous' Cambodian Epic," in Karelis Hartigan (ed.), *From the Bard to Broadway*, Lanham: University Presses of America.

Lamont, R. (1989) "The Reverse Side of a Portrait: The Dora of Freud and Cixous," in Enoch Brater (ed.), *Feminine Focus: The New Woman Playwrights*, Oxford: Oxford University Press.

Lindsay, Cecile (1986) "Body Language: French Feminist Utopias," *The French Review* 60, 1 (October): 46–55.

Miller, Judith (1985) "Jean Cocteau and Hélène Cixous: Oedipus," in James Redmond (ed.), *Drama, Sex and Politics*, Cambridge: Cambridge University Press.

Miner, Madonne (1986) "Lizzie Borden Took an Ax: Enacting Blood Relations," *Literature in Performance* 6, 2 (April): 10–21.

Moi, Toril (1985) "Hélène Cixous: An Imaginary Utopia," *Sexual Textual Politics: Feminist Literary Theory*, London: Methuen.

Pavlides, Merope (1986) "Restructuring the Traditional: An Examination of Hélène Cixous, *Le Nom d'Oedipe*," in Karelisa Hartigan (ed.), *Within the Dramatic Spectrum*, Lanham: University Presses of America.

Picard, A. (1989) "L'Indiade: Ariane and Hélène Conjugate Dreams," *Modern Drama* 32, 1 (March): 24–38.

Rabine, Leslie (1987–8) "Ecriture Féminine as Metaphor," *Cultural Critique* 8 (Winter): 19–44.

Richman, Michèle (1980) "Sex and Signs: The Language of French Feminist Criticism," *Language and Style* 13, 4 (Fall): 62–80.

Running-Johnson, C. (1989) "The Medusa's Tale: Feminine Writing and 'La Genet'," *Romantic Review* 80 (May): 4383–495.

Salesne, Pierre (1988) "Hélène Cixous' *Ou l'art de l'innocence*: The Path to You," in Susan Sellers (ed.), *Writing Differences: Readings from the Seminar of Hélène Cixous*, Milton Keynes: Open University Press and New York: St Martin's Press.

Sankovitch, Tilde (1988) "Hélène Cixous: The Pervasive Myth," in *French Women Writers and the Book: Myths of Access and Desire*, Syracuse: Syracuse University Press.

Savona, Jeannette L. (1984) "French Feminism and Theatre: An Introduction," *Modern Drama* 27, 4 (December): 540–5.

—— (1989) "In Search of Feminist Theater: Portrait of Dora," in Enoch Brater (ed.), *Feminine Focus: The New Women Playwrights*, Oxford: Oxford University Press.

Sellers, Susan (1986) "Writing Woman: Hélène Cixous' Political 'Sexts'," *Women's Studies International Forum* 9, 4: 443–7.

—— (1989) "Biting the Teacher's Apple: Opening Doors for Women in Higher Education," in Ann Thompson and Helen Wilcox (eds), *Teaching Women: Feminism and English Studies*, Manchester: Manchester University Press.

—— (1990) "Learning to Read the Feminine," in Helen Wilcox, Keith Mcwatters, Ann Thompson and Linda R. Williams (eds), *The Body and the Text: Hélène Cixous, Reading and Teaching*, Hemel Hempstead: Harvester Wheatsheaf.

—— (1991) "Woman's Abasement," "Blowing Up the Law," "The M/other's Voice," "Masculine and Feminine," "Writing the Other," "Writing Other Worlds," in *Language and Sexual Difference: Feminist Writing in France*, Basingstoke: Macmillan, and New York: St Martin's Press.

—— (Forthcoming) *Hélène Cixous*, Key Contemporary Thinkers, Cambridge: Polity Press.

Shiach, Morag (1989) "Their 'Symbolic' Exists, it Holds Power – We, the Sowers of Disorder, Know it Only Too Well," in Teresa Brennan (ed.), *Feminism and Psychoanalysis*, London: Routledge.

—— (1991) *Hélène Cixous: A Politics of Writing,* London: Routledge.

Singer, Linda (1989) "True Confessions: Cixous and Foucault on Sexuality and Power," in *The Thinking Muse: Feminism and Modern French Philosophy*, Bloomington: Indiana University Press.

Spivak, Gayatri (1987) "French Feminism in an International Frame," in *In Other Worlds: Essays in Cultural Politics*, New York: Methuen.

Still, Judith (1990) "A Feminine Economy: Some Preliminary Thoughts," in Helen Wilcox, Keith Mcwatters, Ann Thompson and Linda R. Williams (eds), *The Body and the Text: Hélène Cixous, Reading and Teaching*, Hemel Hempstead: Harvester Wheatsheaf.

Suleiman, Susan Rubin (1991) "Writing Past the Wall or the Passion According to H.C.," in Hélène Cixous, *"Coming to Writing" and Other Essays*, translated by Sarah Cornell, Deborah Jenson, Ann Liddle and Susan Sellers, Cambridge, Mass.: Harvard University Press.

Willis, Sharon (1985) "Portrait de Dora: The Unseen and the Un-scene," *Theatre Journal* 37, 3 (October): 287–301.

—— (1986) "Mis-Translation: *Vivre l'orange*," *Studies in the Novel* 18, 4 (Winter): 76–83. Reprinted in *Sub-Stance* 52: 76–83.

Wilson, A. (1989) "History and Hysteria, Writing the Body in 'Portrait of Dora' and 'Signs of Life'," *Modern Drama* 32, 1 (March): 73–88.

Wiseman, Susan (1990) " 'Femininity' and the Intellectual in Sontag and Cixous," in Helen Wilcox, Keith Mcwatters, Ann Thompson and Linda R. Williams (eds), *The*

Body and the Text: Hélène Cixous, Reading and Teaching, Hemel Hempstead: Harvester Wheatsheaf.

Yaeger, Patricia (1988) "Honey-Mad Women," in *Honey-Mad Women: Emancipatory Strategies in Women's Writing*, New York: Columbia University Press.

INDEX